SURVIVING
THE FOURTH CYCLE

By

NATHAN DANIELS

PART ONE

The Bottom of the Barrel

PART TWO

Treading Water

PART THREE

Getting My Life Back

PART ONE
THE BOTTOM OF THE BARREL

1.

JOURNAL ENTRY
(I Want To Die)

08 / 01 / 11

I want to fucking die!

I tried going to work today, but it proved to be impossible. Finally, I have to face what I've been hiding from for the last four months. It's happening again, and I'm so fucking scared! Every time I go through one of these... Cycles, I come closer to death.

I'm such a fucking disaster!

I can think of three separate times in my life when I've been this lost, alone, and confused. I can't believe it's happening to me again! I'll refer to this as "The Fourth Cycle."

It started creeping up on me a few months ago when work-related stress had me feeling withdrawn and alone. At the same time, ghosts from my past began to haunt me with increasing, and relentless intensity.

I feel like I'm doomed!

It culminated over the summer when my irrational and delusional thought process caused me to abandon my family. I really thought I was protecting them, but it's all so hazy in my mind. I still can't believe I moved out of my home.

3

I still can't believe Hailey allowed me back in.

I'm not convinced it's for the best. Now, my loved ones are subject to the sight of me tearing myself apart with insanity and guilt. It seems to get worse all the time, and today everything changed... again.

It's getting worse!

I felt like shit the second my alarm went off at 4:45 this morning. I lay in bed crying as quietly as I could into my pillow, searching for the will to get out of bed and start my day. This went on for well over an hour before I finally found the strength to rise up on my shaky legs.

I put my pants on slowly, and then cried for twenty more minutes. I struggled to figure out how to put my shirt on as if it were a fucking Rubik's Cube, then I cried some more. I put my socks and shoes on in a daze, wiped at the drying streams on my cheeks, and tried to leave.

Just approaching my front door made my heart rate quicken, and I reached for the knob as if I expected it to be scolding hot. My legs felt weak, my vision went blurry, and my hearing became muffled. I opened the door and saw the world rush in at me... attacking me!

I could feel the impact and nearly fell.

Dizzy, I stepped outside and my knees buckled. I knelt down on my front step, and felt like I was going to throw up, but since I hardly eat anymore, I dry-heaved instead. I was sweating and could feel my heartbeat banging against the inside of my chest and skull. I crawled back into my house... a failure.

I lay on my floor crying again... shaking. Searching for inner strength and coming up empty. My eyes burned and my mouth was dry as I sucked on air that seemed to keep getting thicker and harder to breathe. I tried to leave again, but ended up leaning my forehead against the door, feeling defeated and wishing the Grim Reaper would come for me in all his silky, black glory.

No cloaked figure came to me, but my first rational thought since I woke up this morning did. If I made it outside, and by some miracle into my car, there was no way I would be capable of driving myself to work without risking innocent lives.

Somewhere deep inside my mind, I already knew I would be going to the hospital, not work. I could no longer function, but it was so fucking hard to admit that to myself. I've been stubbornly ignoring the obvious signs for months, with the false hope that my problems would just go away. They never do.

It's hard to acknowledge that I've reached a point where I can no longer take care of myself, and if I don't seek help, I'm going to die. I can feel myself dying this very moment! The walls are closing in quickly... but back to this morning.

I had to wake Hailey, who is impossibly accepting of all my issues, and told her about my struggle, and my realization that I needed to go to the hospital. I asked her if she would drive me to work, so I could talk to my boss about my situation in person. I didn't want to do this over the phone. I wanted him to see what she was seeing... a quivering, fucking mess!

We dragged our four-year-old son out of bed and headed toward Providence, as I stared out the passenger side window, wishing I were a better man for my family.

When we arrived, Hailey went inside to get my boss. There was no way I was getting out of that fucking van! The world was waiting for me out there... with its teeth bared!

When he approached me in the parking lot, I told him how screwed up I was with a trembling voice, through my cracked window. I told him I'd be going to the hospital and had no idea how long I would be in there, or what would result. He was worried, but assured me that my job would be safe. Wishing me health and luck, he disappeared back into the building with a distraught look in his eyes.

It was a quiet ride home, as I focused on breathing and keeping my eyes squeezed shut. I counted to twelve-hundred, sixty-two.

So, here I am now, sitting in my spider-infested basement, whining silently into these pages about my pathetic life. I have a small desk in the corner, surrounded by paint-chipped concrete. I can hear the rusty pipes dripping behind me, and the pungent smell of mildew and stagnant smoke envelopes me. It floods from time to time and there's a musty dampness in the air. This is my comfort zone.

Things scurry about on the floor, descend from the overhead beams, and buzz about the room. I have a single candle burning on the edge of my desk, making slithering shadows dance around me, with its flickering flame. I can hear every creak and stretch of the house in the night, and my tired mind is playing tricks on me. I do my best to ignore the things that aren't real and just keep writing... but it's hard.

I decided to put the hospital off until tomorrow. I might be in there for a while, and I wanted to spend some time with Hailey and the kids before I have myself committed to a mental institution for the second time.

It's the middle of the night and sleep is just a fantasy to me. I'm driving myself crazy pondering the intense mysteries of my mind. What happened to me? Where did it all go wrong? Can anybody else hear that sound? Are the shadows in my peripheral vision really moving toward me like that?

I'm nervous and it's difficult to write with my hands shaking so violently, but I don't want to stop. Picking up a pen and desperately trying to organize my thoughts was the only thing I could think of to do. It has been helpful to me in the past, when my mental illness has decided to stick its chest out and show me who's boss. I should've embraced this familiar, but neglected passion sooner. Writing is one of the only things that has the potential to keep me somewhat anchored to the planet.

That... and taking a razor to my flesh.

I'm tired of feeling like a stranger in my own skin and struggling, daily, to find the strength to go on. I'm scared to go to the hospital tomorrow. I'm afraid to talk to people about just how fucked up I really am, and how badly I need help. I'm scared of that fucking whispering I hear, and those goddamned shadows... one is touching me now.

I want to go crawl into bed with Hailey and feel the comfort of her arms around me, but I feel like I'm a disgusting thing that belongs in the basement... hidden away. I don't want to disturb her rest with my pathetic weakness, and irrational frame of mind. It wouldn't be fair... I should suffer alone.

I'm afraid of everything, and I don't want to be alive anymore. The self-loathing is intolerable and I know my family deserves so much more than I'm capable of giving them. I can't even look in the mirror anymore, because I don't recognize the reflection. I feel... far away.

Where did I go?

Who the fuck am I?

2.

ALLOW ME TO INTRODUCE MYSELF

My name is Nathan Daniels.

I'm a thirty-six year old man struggling through, what I consider to be tough times. I'm a middle class, blue-collar guy who wears jeans and t-shirts. I have dirty blonde hair, shaved in a military style, green eyes, and a few tattoos. I'm five feet, ten inches tall and weigh one hundred sixty pounds. I hate shaving, so I usually look rather scruffy, and I would consider myself an average looking man.

I'm quite sure I'm dying. I've lost sixty pounds in the last four months, and I've cut myself over a hundred times. I want to save my life, but it's not going to be easy considering I'm also the one trying to end it.

I'm fucked up in many different ways and on many different levels. At times like this, I tend to define myself by my problems, and have to make a great effort to remind myself that I'm also many different things, to many different people. I need to explore everything if I'm to find the truth behind what's been happening to me for more than half my life.

I'm in the hospital right now, searching for help. I have a substantial list of disorders that have plagued me in various combinations, and various degrees throughout the majority of my existence. Four times now, I've had my life interrupted and threatened by these ailments. Twice now, I've been here... in a room that locks from the outside, staring out a window that's sealed shut.

I'm depressed.

I hate saying, "I suffer from depression." It sounds so whiny and pathetic, but there's no way around it. I'm fucking depressed! I'm currently slithering through my life trying to avoid visual and audio hallucinations, severe panic attacks, and blackouts.

I cut myself frequently to keep from totally slipping into the black abyss of my mind. This terrible coping skill developed in my youth, and has grown in both frequency and severity throughout my adult life. I think it used to give me a certain sense of control, and helped anchor me to the real world.

Lately, however, there's been a new development in this old ritual. I've been blacking out and doing it. This is a new and terrifying experience for me. All of a sudden, I'm holding a bloody razor blade and have twenty fresh wounds on my leg. There's a certain creepy awareness of having done it, but not actual recollection.

I feel like I'm falling apart and it just keeps getting worse instead of better. I can see the toll my struggle is having on my family. It makes me feel guilty, exhausted, and hopeless. More and more, death appears to be the only way out, and I know my sub-conscious is steering me violently in that direction.

I'm suicidal.

Intellectually, I understand the reality of my potential suicide. I would be murdering my son's daddy, and abandoning the love of my life and her children. How could I ever do such a terrible thing to the people I love? I have to admit though, I think about it more than ever, and have become an expert at telling myself dangerous and convincing lies...

"They'd all be better off without me!"
"I'm just making everyone's life worse!"

It's fucking scary how I can warp reality sometimes and make suicide seem like the right thing to do. When I'm at my lowest, I try to keep myself as sedated as possible with my substance of choice.

I'm a drug addict.

I love marijuana and have been using it for more than half my life. I also hate it, and believe that my usage has become out of control. I'm currently a miserable person to be around if I don't smoke several times a day. I don't get mean or anything, just very sullen and impossible to please. It's reached a point where I don't even get that high anymore. I can smoke bowl after bowl and not be completely satisfied.

I have Post Traumatic Stress Disorder from many lingering memories.

My sister molested me when I was six years old. This went on for almost a year before my mother walked in on us one day. I also grew up with a constant threat of violence from my father, and the never-ending verbal emasculation he administered... pussy, faggot, and mama's boy were just some of his favorite nicknames for me.

He died when I was seventeen, so did my grandfather, and my mother too. This parade of death took place in a three-month period. It's clear to me today that I've never fully recovered from that horrible storm, and I don't know if I ever will.

Later, during my twenties, I had a ten-year dysfunctional relationship with a virtual ghost of a woman. This was a severely depressed personality, who was a master manipulator of every negative emotion. I made her my wife during my Second *Cycle*, and allowed her to chip away at my sole for the better part of a decade. I know we never truly loved each other.

Every woman I've ever been in a serious relationship with has cheated on me, sometimes more than once. Even my beloved Hailey repeatedly betrayed my love and trust in the beginning of our relationship, opening the flood gates for even greater lunacy and emotional despair.

Every one of these situations has injured my heart and mind. All of these events and relationships still cause me great pain through flashbacks, nightmares, and in some cases, daily reminders. When the pain lies dormant, I lie to myself that I've worked through it and achieved closure, but it always comes back with a vengeance. I haven't worked through shit and I'm crazier than ever!

I have Obsessive Compulsive Disorder.

This can be extremely frustrating at times. I count... a lot. The steps I take when I walk, how many times I chew my food, how many commercials in each break during a television show. I time everything as well... how long it takes to smoke a cigarette, take a shower, or drive to the gas station and back. Sometimes I get lost amidst the relentless numbers marching through my head. Half the time I don't even realize I'm doing it, then all of a sudden I can hear... *sixty-seven, sixty-eight, sixty-nine,* in the back of my mind.

I have Agoraphobia and severe Social Anxiety Disorder.

When I'm outside of my comfort zone bad things tend to happen inside my mind. This limits me to my house, my therapist's office, and a few places where I do my shopping, banking, and other routine errands. Driving has become all but impossible, so when I do go out it's always in the passenger seat.

Having a family, and being in a relationship with a woman that I love and care about, I try to push the boundaries of my Agoraphobia almost every day. It's difficult to describe the symptoms that attack me accurately, and get people to understand that the things I see and hear are as real to me as this paper.

I become Hyper-Vigilant, and normal sights and sounds overwhelm me. My very own senses turn against me and knock my world upside down. It's a mutiny from within.

At a grocery store, my vision rebels against me. The lights are far too bright all of a sudden. The isles seem impossibly long and are twisting and warping before me. The people become horrible reflections in a funhouse mirror. I'm dizzy and disoriented, sweaty and shaking. I'm reacting physically to my irrational terror. I want to vomit. My heart is beating way to fast... way to hard. I think I can actually see it kicking against my chest! Paralyzed, I want to run, but I can't.

I see lines of every size, shape, and color scratching at my eyes everywhere I look. Lines linked together in intricate and familiar ways. They horrify me, because I know that they're letters, and they form words that I should be able to read, but I can't because I've become a deer in the headlights and I feel like I'm going to start crying.

I'm wondering where they keep the razor blades... I think its isle seven.

"Clean up in isle seven." My mom's voice, impossibly, says over the intercom. I have a vision of my pale dead body lying in a pool of blood on the shiny white tiles. Customers shop around me, because I don't matter. My wrists are open like crying mouths, and there's a backwards seven reflected in the growing red mirror I made on the floor. The image swallows me up, and I can't find the real world for a moment.

Meanwhile, the kids are running around out of control. Part of me knows I should be parenting and dealing with them, but it's taking all of my strength and will not to freak out next to Cap'n Crunch and Count Chocula! I glimpse a frustrated Hailey. She's trying to get the best deal on cereal for us, restrain a screaming four year old, and plead with the older ones to act their age.

There's worry on her beautiful face too. Worry that her psycho boyfriend is about to go "rain man" in the grocery store. As I'm absorbing all of this, I have a moment where I truly wish I were dead.

My illusions gradually subside after we leave, and I'm in the sanctity of our minivan. Emotionally drained, I cry the entire ride home.

"Deep breaths" Hailey always tells me. It works, and I never implode as I think I will. She is truly something special, and I must never lose sight of the effect it would have on her if I were gone. I suppose there are many relationships in my life that I need to think about, both past and present, in my quest to find myself again.

I'm somebody's son... of course, or at least I used to be. My mom was the best friend I ever had, and I still miss her immensely. I'll dream of her sometimes and wake up with a tear-soaked pillow. It hurts me beyond description, that Chris will never know his grandma. They would have loved each other.

Then there's my dad...

In some ways, after all the time that has passed since his death, I'm still trying to get to know the stranger that was my father. This mostly takes place in my imagination, or my heart, if you want to be sentimental about it. I'm not sure if my dad would have been any better at being a grandpa than he was at being a father. I'd like to think so, but unfortunately I'd never know for sure.

I'm somebody's brother, but I have no relationship with my sister whatsoever. In fact, we've spent most of my life completely estranged from each other. My sister moved out of our house a few years after "the incident."

I did crash at her place from time to time when I was homeless, but this was short lived. I get physically ill when I'm in her presence, and I don't know if that will ever change. Three decades after the fact, I'm still battling demons that were born in my sister's bedroom.

I'm an athlete, at heart anyway. I've spent half my life developing my body, and the other half trying to destroy it. I've been passionate about bodybuilding since I was a child, but you would never know that looking at me now. I used to be able to leg press a thousand pounds in the gym, now my legs can barely handle descending a flight of stairs without vibrating uncontrollably.

I'm an employee, who has always done well climbing that metaphorical ladder in any company where I've worked. Then I go through one of these *Cycles,* and lose everything I've achieved. I'm currently a Production Manager, and responsible for more than thirty line workers, but I'm not capable of handling that kind of responsibility right now. I fear I'm going to lose it all again.

I'm a father... and a stepfather. My son's name is Christopher, and in his short life, he has already done so many powerful things for his daddy without even knowing it. He vanquished all regret I may have had before he was born, as all the roads I've travelled lead me to him. He has given me the gift of the truest, purest form of love a human being can ever experience... that of a parent and their child. He has also saved my life on more than one occasion, when thoughts of him were the only thing preventing me from throwing in the towel.

I love my son. I love him with all my heart and soul. I'll do my very best to make his life as beautiful as possible, and shield him from the misery that haunts me. I will always strive to be a better father for him. Just being there could be the most important thing I do with my life. I'm so proud to be

Christopher's daddy, and when I look into his deep blue eyes, I know we will love each other forever.

As a stepfather, I've come up a little short these days. I've stumbled and fallen as a male role model. Hailey's twelve-year-old son David, and eleven-year-old daughter Amy, deserve more than I'm giving them right now. I know that I hurt them both deeply when I hurt their mother. I can see the reflection of the mistake I made in their young eyes.

How can they trust me now?

How can they love me anymore?

I abandoned them, worried them, and scared them. Now, all of a sudden I'm back as if nothing ever happened. They must be so confused and dismayed. I have forever tarnished my status as a stepparent. I'm so sorry for what I put these kids through, and I have no idea how to tell them. I love them both very much and I hope I can find a way to repair our relationship. I hope we will all be able to heal as a family.

Hailey and I are not legally married, but I did tattoo her name across my ring finger years ago. We are partners in every sense of the word, financially, romantically, and of course in parenting. Paperwork and jewelry aside, I consider us husband and wife and I know she feels the same.

Am I a good husband?

I think I have been in the past, but not now. I'm distant, withdrawn, depressed, and carry a looming threat of taking my own life. Hailey is thirty-two years old and drop dead gorgeous... though I'm sure she'd disagree with me. She has blonde hair, blue eyes, and a body designed for me personally. More important is her unique, intelligent, and wonderful personality that allows her to deal with someone like me. It can't be an easy task... especially now.

We're currently in a terrible place in our relationship of nearly seven years, and it's my fault entirely. A couple of months ago I cheated on her with a woman that worked for me. I was guilty of having secret conversations with this person through text messages. We also shared awkward good-bye kisses at the end of our workday on two separate occasions.

In the swarming chaos of my mind, I became convinced I was falling in love with this woman. To this day, I can't understand why. I had never betrayed someone's trust before, and the guilt I felt keeping a secret of this magnitude from Hailey was crushing me.

I didn't have what many would consider a "real affair."

With the exception of those two kisses and a hug at the company Christmas party, we never even touched each other. There was certainly nothing sexual about it. I hid it though, because I knew it was cheating all the same. How would I feel if the tables were turned?

When Hailey found out what was going on, I got scared and ran away. I lived in a hotel for a little while, and then I signed a one-year lease on a condominium. Part of me really believed I was doing the right thing for my family. I knew I was coming undone, and I knew how crazy I could get. I was genuinely concerned that I would traumatize my family with my presence. I didn't think I was fit to be around people anymore.

I wanted to be alone.

Hailey was pissed off, and rightfully so, but she wouldn't let go of me. I spent all my free time with her, reminded of just how powerful our love truly is. It didn't take much longer for me to remember that I can't live without her. I turned my back on my condo, broke the lease agreement, and went back home where I belong. I was gone for almost two months.

I've never stopped loving Hailey, and I'm in awe of her ability to love me after I was so careless with her heart. I wish I could see myself through her eyes. I might see someone worth saving… worth loving. All I see now is a mental patient in a hospital gown, with a tired look on his face. A man searching for help, that he's not sure exists.

As I said, I'm fucked up in many different ways, and on many different levels. I am also many different things, to many different people. I have to figure myself out, heal myself, try to resolve the plethora of issues I've developed over the years, and salvage my life for the people I love.

3.

JOURNAL ENTRY
(Exploring My Mistake)

08 / 03 / 11

I'm sorry, and I make myself sick!

It's been months since I had my half-assed affair with that woman from work, but that's all I can think about lately. Not about her, I don't think about her at all. I just can't stop trying to figure out what went wrong inside my mind to make something like that possible.

It was not me!

I know that sounds like bullshit, but when I think about that time, the memories are alien to me. It's as if they belonged to someone else or were nothing more than a half-forgotten dream. The guilt is eating me alive... tearing me apart! All I want to do is punish myself, but I don't know how to do it sufficiently without affecting those who care about me.

I can only theorize about why I allowed myself to stray from my faithful path. It's a fool's errand perhaps, but I must take on the formidable task of rationalizing the irrational. No matter how carefully or diplomatically I try to do this, it's inevitable that I'll sound like I'm making excuses, but I'm not.

I'm just searching within myself for possible reasons behind what I did, for my own therapeutic benefit, if nothing else.

Here goes...

Stress from work was starting to have a bad effect on me, and I was coming to the difficult realization that in spite of how well I performed, I was not mentally capable of doing my job much longer. Although I'm good at it, I simply can't handle the burden. It took me far too long to admit that to myself, which prevented me from admitting it to Hailey.

She counts on me to be the breadwinner in the family, and she's pleased with the good paychecks I bring home, but I was unhappy. I've tried so many other avenues to make decent money, but all roads have always brought me back to the warehouse industry, where you typically have to run a department to bring home a sufficient check.

Between my Obsessive Compulsive Disorder, and the immense pressure I feel as a man to provide for my family, I had reached a point where I was always at work, mentally, if not physically. I just couldn't let it go, and even when I'd be home with my loved ones, I'd be worrying about my department. It was keeping me up at night, and I just couldn't find a way to shut it off. Extreme insomnia set in, paving the way for a fourth Cycle to disrupt my life.

I was working sixty hours a week, and traveling another ten. I became withdrawn at home, annoyed by my lack of ability to come up with something, other than my job to talk about. I was drowning in an ocean of stress, and I could see the shore getting farther and farther away. I didn't want to worry Hailey with my internal struggles. I didn't want to complain about what my success at work was costing me. I stupidly shouldered the burden alone, and that was a big mistake.

I wish I had opened up about the things that were keeping me up all night, but instead I allowed myself to grow calloused, feeling that the only option for me was to soldier on at any price, because that's what a "real man" does. I decided to drive it 'till the wheels fall off.

I fucked up, and let it go too far. I could feel myself getting lost, more and more, in my own mind. I wanted to be alone, and spent a lot of time sitting outside or in my basement... by myself, smoking weed and dreading my future.

Along with the insomnia, the Cycle always brings the ghosts of my past. They have only pain to offer and remind me of everything that has ever hurt me. Old scars start to bleed again. I started thinking about the horrible love triangle I was part of with Hailey and her ex-husband in the beginning of our relationship. I could feel the anguish and betrayal all over again.

Because of this, I stopped going to David and Amy's soccer games, or anywhere I thought their dad might show up. He was a living memento of a painful time. It snowballed from there into what would soon become another bout with agoraphobia. I started having bad feelings in places where I used to be comfortable, and then I just started going out less and less. I didn't even want to visit Hailey's mom or sister anymore.

The downward spiral was well under way. I thought I could keep my struggles with work to myself, but I knew I was going to have some explaining to do if I couldn't bring myself to function on a normal social level with my girlfriend anymore. Hailey was a big part of the last Cycle I went through, and it was a fucking nightmare! I was obviously heading into another one of these dark times, and I knew that she'd be just as scared as I was. I knew I should talk to her, but I couldn't make myself do it.

In the middle of the night, I would have imaginary conversations with her, trying to explain things that, I myself, didn't understand. I would tell her that I wasn't going to be able to do anything that made me feel mentally or emotionally uncomfortable for a while, because I was starting to fear for my sanity again. Her sister's wedding for example, was in the near future and I knew that I wouldn't be willing to put myself in that kind of environment.

I would practice explaining to her that I felt a strong need to step down from my current position at work, which would inevitably come with a substantial cut in pay. No matter how many different ways I pictured having these conversations, they never went well. Slowly and stupidly, I started to think that I could never talk to Hailey about these things. I was feeling alone, helpless and scared.

Depression set in and suicidal thoughts had begun peering up at me from the bottom of my soul. I stopped bodybuilding, and went from eating six healthy meals a day, to eating just once every day or two. I began dropping an average of ten pounds a month and smoking more weed and cigarettes than I had in a long time. I was cutting myself on a regular basis again, and having auditory hallucinations... strange whispering sounds that I knew weren't real.

Knowing how bad things got last time I went through this, I began questioning whether I would be able to survive, and thoughts of self-destruction started to invade my mind even more.

In the midst of all this turmoil, I was still able to operate in the workplace, but I was losing the ability to hide the signs of my struggle. I'd been studying Spanish in an effort to become more successful at the job I'd begun to hate. A woman I hired was also studying her second language, English. We started helping each other and eventually our study sessions became a daily routine. I honestly never saw what was coming. I was not at all attracted to this older woman.

After a while, this woman could see my obvious stress through my severe weight loss and rapid change in demeanor. More and more, she began asking me questions about my personal life, wanting to know what was troubling me. I opened up to her, and let her in. I told her about my anxiety and depression. I told her stories about the events in my life that still haunted me. I told her I cut myself, and often thought about taking my own life.

Her heart broke for me, and she always seemed to be understanding and non-judgmental. I know now that she was attracted to me all along, and I wonder how much that had to do with the friendship she offered. I was definitely not promoting myself as someone who would be a good catch, so I have to question her mentality in all of this too.

I got to know a lot about her life as well, and I did think she was a nice woman who seemed to mean well. When she eventually started flirting with me a little, I'm ashamed to say that I flirted back. It wasn't genuine, but I was on autopilot most of the time and extremely confused. She seemed like a classy person, and our behavior was never sexual or disrespectful. I would say things like, "You look beautiful today," things of that nature. Occasionally we spoke about our significant others, and it was always with love for them and shame for ourselves.

After a month or so, she wanted us to meet somewhere outside from work to talk, to figure out what was going on with us. I thought it was a good idea because keeping this secret relationship from Hailey was ripping away at me. I had become a total stranger to myself.

I was walking her out of the building one day, and when we said goodbye I leaned in and kissed her. There was no thought process whatsoever... I just did it. It was unplanned and awkward, lasting only a second, while I was looking out of the corner of my eye for anyone to come along and witness my infidelity.

I don't remember anything about the kiss itself, but I remember feeling utter disgust welling up inside. I contemplated driving my car into the river that ran adjacent to the parking lot instead of going home that night. A couple days later, she kissed me back and nothing felt right about it. I felt an incredible sense of urgency to figure out what the fuck I was doing.

I was Doctor Frankenstein, worrying about the monster I'd created. I asked her to meet me somewhere that Friday night so we could have our talk. I knew that I couldn't pursue any real romance with this woman, but I was afraid to hurt her, and add more stress to my work environment.

I just wasn't attracted to her like that and now I had to be honest with her. Nothing was real. We had said, "I love you" to each other a few times, but my world had become an ever-changing illusion, and my symptoms were rapidly overwhelming me. I was lost, and felt like I was unfit to be with anybody.

I didn't even have any hope of saving my relationship with Hailey. I just thought I was too far-gone. I was convinced the best thing for everyone would be if I were alone for a while so I could focus on my own personal survival (or destruction), and nothing else. At least I would be able to die in peace, without worrying about those who loved me finding my body somewhere.

I knew I made mistakes that had the potential to damage the people I loved. I didn't want anyone to get hurt because of my insanity, and I knew I was going to have to be careful.

23

Unfortunately, it's hard to be careful when you're a sleep-deprived basket case.

Hailey had gone to a soccer game, and to visit her sister, the night I was supposed to meet this other woman. I'd been texting back and forth with both of them, feeling nauseous and anxious. I wondered how the "players" of the world could not only deal with this kind of stress, but seek it out.

I didn't want to meet her anymore, but I didn't want to face her at work if I blew her off. There was no simple resolution. I pulled into a parking lot, having a panic attack and trying to figure out how to get out of my situation, when Hailey texted me that she was coming home early.

That gave me an idea for a way out, without hurting this woman's feelings. I decided to tell her that Hailey found out about our texting. That would get me off the hook for the night, and lay the groundwork for me to end the relationship before it began. It would have worked out fine, but when you suffer from various psychosis' you tend to be less than smooth.

I sent the text to Hailey by mistake, and when her perplexed response came back, I felt my loosening sanity unravel even more. I'd been teetering on the edge of a great precipice for so long, and now I could feel myself plummeting.

I went from one extreme to the other, from hiding the truth, to exaggerating it. Going completely off the deep end, I told Hailey that I was having an affair; I was completely in love with someone else and wanted to leave my family to pursue her. I took everything that I decided, threw it out the window, and told Hailey the complete opposite.

Why?

Maybe I figured the truth wouldn't be very believable. How many people have non-sexual affairs, and then end things before they ever get started? On the very same night, they happen to slip up and give themselves away...

"I know that message looked bad honey... but I was on my way to tell her I couldn't go through with an affair anyway." Yeah right! Nobody in their right mind would believe that shit whether it was true or not.

I also had a lot of guilt from getting away with being devious, and doing things I knew would hurt my girlfriend. I think I wanted to pay for my sins and suffer whatever wrath Hailey would rain down on me. I needed punishment for my actions so I embellished my story to make Hailey hate me as much as possible.

Another factor in my stupidity was feeling like I needed to be alone under any circumstances. Perhaps I instinctively knew it would be easier for Hailey to let me go if she was pissed off at me instead of worried about my health and sanity. I didn't want to burden her. I didn't feel like I deserved her love anymore, and thought that I'd be doing her an injustice if I fought for her.

Then there's the cold, hard fact that part of me doesn't want to survive, and is looking for any reason to end it all! I know damned well that the more mistakes I make in this state of mind, and the bigger they are, the sooner I can just give up and die.

I panicked and overreacted, going completely overboard in the process. I instantly had this horrible, "bring it on!" attitude, and I didn't take the time to consider the price myself and my loved ones would have to pay. I moved out and stayed in a run-down motel near my work, before eventually finding a place to rent.

In complete contradiction of what I told my true love on that wretched night, I ceased all contact with "the other woman" and began spending all my time with Hailey again. I tried convincing her that I wasn't in love with her anymore, but actions speak louder than words and we were inseparable.

It became obvious that she was determined to be there for me in whatever capacity I would accept. I still felt very strongly that I should be alone, but it didn't matter. I can't help myself when it comes to Hailey. My heart has been in her hands since the day I met her, and it's clear to me now that it's a mutual phenomenon.

We seem to have survived this, though the scars will remain visible for a long time. In a way, it provided us with a new beginning, and we seemed to fall in love all over again. Sometimes I believe what we have is indestructible!

I am sorry Hailey.

I'm so completely sorry. I've never felt anything like it, and its immense power is washing over me. Drowning me in my undeniable guilt, as I embrace the reflection of the pain I've caused. I now know that I've never truly experienced what it meant to be sorry until I broke Hailey's heart and turned my back on my family. I will carry this awful feeling to the grave with me, and it's rightfully so.

A grave that looms closer now, than ever before.

As I ride the plateau of the fourth Cycle, the guilt from what I've done has amplified my symptoms to frightening proportions. It's crushing me to death, and trying to prevent it feels wrong to me.

I need help, but I'm not getting any here. This hospital environment is not proving to be as helpful as I'd hoped, and all the medications I've been taking appear to be useless too. I need to feel medicated, before I tear my fucking skin off! I can't stand to be inside it anymore!

I need to get the fuck out of here. The walls are moving... bubbling and pulsing. It's hard to ignore that shit. I want this to end already! I want to go home and get high.

4.

MARIJUANA AND MADNESS

I started smoking marijuana when I was seventeen years old to help me deal with the immense sadness that embraced me. This was the same time I was waiting patiently for my mom to die. She had cancer for nearly five years at this point. It started as breast cancer, and then spread...

Her lungs...

Her bones...

By the time the death coach finally came for her she had tumors in her brain and didn't even know who I was anymore. Watching her suffer and deteriorate was tearing me apart.

Things were bad, and they were only getting worse. My ability to cope with the upcoming tragedy was dwindling in perfect proportion with my mom's health. I hated being alone with my misery, and my mom could no longer fulfill her duties as my best friend.

I had a close-knit group of buddies from the gym where I worked out and I started hanging around with them more than ever. Almost all of them smoked pot, drank, and even experimented with anabolic steroids. I didn't agree with their lifestyle decisions, but did a good job of not judging them for partaking in such damaging hobbies.

Up until this point, I was a health fanatic. I'd have a couple beers on occasion, but smoking anything was completely out of the question. A frothing-at-the-mouth Hulk Hogan roared, "Don't smoke it's a joke!" through my television set when I was a kid... and I listened.

I can't help but think to myself; *my, how times have changed,* pacing around my hospital room on the notorious fourth floor, daydreaming about intoxicating smoke inflating both my lungs, and my will to survive.

Politely, I used to go my separate way when my friends decided to "light up". More and more, however, solitude proved to be a formidable enemy. One I could no longer bear to face. I also hated being home with what was left of my mom, and the invisible clock ticking over her deathbed mercilessly discarding the final moments of her life as quickly as it did the ones above her crib.

Tick. Tick. Tick. I swear I could fucking hear it!

At first, I just hung out with Tim, Billy, and John while they did their thing. John was a long time childhood friend of mine, who had just recently begun experimenting with marijuana. He was an Italian kid, who looked a lot like Sylvester Stallone, and had a legendary reputation as a playboy.

Tim and Billy were my more recent gym comrades, and these guys were weed smoking professionals, if there could ever be such a thing. After a while, I started to feel a powerful sense of jealousy.

I was in awe watching them, as they played with the strange, dried up plant that somehow smelled good and bad at the same time. They removed the seeds and stems, preparing it for its fiery destiny in the multi-colored pipes and bongs produced from various hiding spots in Tim's basement. These things looked like some kind of extraterrestrial toys to me, and my friends were kids again. Playing and having fun.

They cleaned screens, poured water into tubes, packed bowls, and lit up. The process fascinated me. Apparently, there was a whole culture involved with smoking pot. I never paid any attention to the likes of Cheech and Chong growing up, and even though I was aware that my father smoked, I never witnessed anything like this.

Who could take the biggest hit? Who could hold their hit the longest? Who could smoke the most in one sitting? From the prep-work, to the actual smoking, to the long lasting blissful aftermath, I bore witness to this simple, entertaining, distraction from the real world and I wanted to try it... hating myself for the desire.

"Join the dark side." They use to tease me. Tim looked like the poster boy for sun and surf with his blonde hair, blue eyes, and year-round tan. He almost looked unnatural without a beach as his permanent backdrop.

Then there was Billy, who had an uncanny ability to look both chubby and muscular at the same time. He was a rich kid who had all the breaks, but he wasn't a snob in any way and could be wildly entertaining with his impressive menu of vocal impersonations. His *Kermit the Frog* voice was second to none. This was a great group of guys, and I always felt lucky to keep company with them.

They never put any real pressure on me to abandon my lifelong celibacy from drugs. After all, these guys knew me as a dedicated bodybuilder and martial arts enthusiast, and they had genuine respect for that. I don't think it even occurred to them that I might really partake in one of their "sessions", but I was closer than even I realized.

The laughter spoke to me... the hysterical, red-faced laughter that I wasn't capable of anymore. I wanted to laugh like that so fucking badly I could barely stand it. My laugh was hollow, and forced. It didn't come from humor, but from a voice in my head that did its best to coach me on normal social behavior.

I was suffering inside, but instinctively knew that displaying such suffrage would only be tolerated for so long before I was labeled a bummer, and left to wallow in my misery alone. Unfortunately, I would prove to be right about that repeatedly throughout my life.

It was getting hard to fake it. It was even getting hard to *want* to fake it. I was still just a kid in many ways, but I had a very grown up sense of impending doom. I desperately needed to get away from it. I wanted to laugh at stupid shit with my friends instead of ponder the cruelty of human mortality.

I wanted to be high!

It was just the third time I exposed myself to my friend's preferred method of unwinding, that I uttered those fateful words... "I think I want to try a hit." There was short-lived disbelief followed by raucous celebration and applause.

Billy packed a fresh bowl in my honor. Tim instructed me on how to manipulate the size of my hit by applying my finger to the carburetor on his "steamroller," and told me I was good to go. I was scared of the effect this drug was going to have on me, but if you weighed my fear against my desperate need for escape, the scale would tip over. I lit the bowl, took far too big a hit, choked, got tears in my eyes, and waited.

I took a second hit while my friends giggled like schoolchildren.

I took a third.

Then it washed over me, and I was gone... fucked up! I hated it, and I kept trying to ask how long it would last, but I could only make slurred noises as if a dentist had gone overboard with Novocain injections in every corner of my drying mouth. I was an invalid, and my friends had to prop me up on a toilet while I was lost in a hallucinogenic landscape inside my mind. I'll never forget the clarity of the false imagery my altered brain displayed.

All of a sudden, I was a glowing, blue-neon embryo floating in perfect blackness. The real world was nowhere in sight to me. I found myself tethered, not by an umbilical cord, but by endless beams of blue light that extended from my top and bottom. It reminded me of a lone carousel horse floating in space, with its braided bars stretching out farther than visual comprehension could allow.

I studied my tiny, incandescent hands in terrified bewilderment. I couldn't think. I was lost. Then, in an instant, the blackness seeped into the walls and I was in Tim's bathroom again. I was back, still stoned, but back in the real world, for better or worse. I splashed cold water on my face, and quickly relearned the English language. I hadn't laughed like I'd hoped, though I'm sure I doubled my audience's share with my rookie performance.

Overall, I considered the whole experience to be a nightmare. To this day, I've never heard of anybody having such an intense experience from weed, first time or not. I'm quite sure my reaction had a lot to do with suffering from sleep deprivation as well.

Never again, I lied to myself, but I was hitting the bowl a couple days later when Tim offered. I didn't trip out as I had on the porcelain throne that first time, but I remained fearful. It was definitely an acquired taste for me. It took me a few times to get used to the paranoia, cottonmouth, and warped perception, but once I did, I found what I was looking for. I started to laugh. I started to enjoy it... a lot. Then I started to need it.

I need it now, almost two decades later!

The kids I encountered back then smoked grass out of boredom, to party, or because their older brothers called them pussies if they wouldn't try it. For me, however, from that very first hit until today, it was medicine.

In retrospect, I know far better avenues exist to deal with suicidal tendencies, loss, grief, and severe depression, but I was ignorant to such things back then. Now, well a twenty-year-old habit is hard to shake. Especially when it's your most highly (no pun intended) developed coping mechanism.

It *has* saved my life in the past. I can say that with absolute honesty and the greatest sincerity. There's no doubt in my mind I would have taken my own life in 1993 on any given night after the death of my grandfather and my parents... after my girlfriend cheated on me, then left me.

I couldn't hold a job, had an eighth grade education, and eventually had to choose between living with a man I shared a mutual hatred with, my child-molesting sister, or in my dead dad's car on the cold, littered streets of Providence, RI.

I thought about killing myself all the time! I know I would have crossed that line if I hadn't traded some lonely nights of despair for stoned outings with my friends to the mall or movies, laughing at nothing instead of crying because of everything.

Everyone will argue there are better ways I could have survived, but I had no adults left in my life to steer me in the right direction. No one even tried. I was alone... no parents, teachers, guidance counselors, or doctors of any kind. There were no psychiatrists offering prescriptions for Prozac or Lorazapam to get me through the tough times. Therapy was a foreign idea to me back then. At seventeen, with no guidance and drowning in grief, I used what was immediately available to me. I got high with my fun-loving buddies... and I lived.

This new crutch found its way into my life none too soon. The first *Cycle* was oozing into my life, whispering *Pleased to meet you,* and extending its icy, skeletal hand. It had begun... the internal war that still rages inside me today.

Ever since I survived the brutality of those long-ago dark days, insanity seems to wash over me then retreat throughout the years like the ebb of the tide. I suppose in one way or another I'm always battling various demons, but for the most part, I believe I've been able to live a relatively stable and happy life.

Therefore, when I refer to my *Cycles,* I'm talking about periods of interruption in my life. I can no longer function in society. A time when I don't feel safe in my own company and my mind demands my full attention. This is a time when I endure insomnia, drastic weight loss, cutting, flashbacks, and hallucinations. I have increasing thoughts of suicide. I experience job loss, isolation, panic attacks, agoraphobia, and blackouts...

The worst part is, that sometime during the peak, I can always count on making a horrible and often life changing mistake. It's been a consistent factor every time. I remember an incredibly stupid adventure I went on the summer after my parents died, and I had just turned eighteen years old.

It was a dark and stormy night...

No bullshit, it was really a dark and stormy night. The setting is Hopedale, Massachusetts. I'm in the, *don't give a fuck about anything anymore,* stage of my grieving. I'm driving dad's blue Chevy Caprice Classic with no driver's license, or even a learner's permit. The car was unregistered and uninsured with an expired inspection sticker. In other words, there was nothing legal at all about this car, or me being behind the wheel.

I was cruising around with my friends smoking weed and hitting the drive-thrus. The characters in this tale are my friend Andy, three of his friends (I'll just refer to them as "the kids in the backseat"), and me.

Out of the five of us in the car, I was the only one who was legally an adult. One of "the kids in the backseat" was only fifteen. That didn't occur to me at the time, but hindsight is a motherfucker. All that mattered to me at the time was seeking adventure, or at least escape, with my buddies.

So back to the stormy night, it was raining, cold and quickly nearing winter. After smoking a blunt, or maybe two, we decided to seek out sunshine and warmth. We decided to head to Florida. It all started as a joke. None of these guys put any thought into it, but I was the one behind the wheel. I had no parents, no job, no school... no talking cartoon cricket on my shoulder to steer my conscience.

"Fuck it! Let's go!" I said stupidly.

We had an ounce of weed with us, a few hundred dollars collectively, and a unified goal to seek greener pastures. Andy made a phone call to his cousin, who said we could all crash in his basement in downtown Philadelphia on our way. This was getting better by the minute. We drove for six hours, smoking ourselves retarded the whole way, then landed in the ghetto of south Philly at one o'clock in the morning. To me it looked like something out of a movie.

Graffiti ruled the architecture. There were homeless people huddled around trashcan fires and I half expected them to start singing *"take it back"* like in the Rocky movie. Stripped cars littered the roads, and shady characters roamed the dark city alleyways. We stopped at a corner to use the payphone.

Immediately... a random guy in a black leather jacket, who appeared out of thin air like David Copperfield, offered us some crack. Another guy, who looked like he was going to explode, begged us to buy beer for him in an absolute panic. The store had banned him, he explained, and then assured us our age wouldn't matter. Something tells me he was probably right, but we refused him several times until he got the picture and left us to pursue other options.

The worst part was a car filled with gangsters that circled the block four times while Andy was using the phone. They were eyeballing us suspiciously and checking out my car. It was pretty fucking intense, standing there wondering if we were about to be confronted with some serious hostility so far from home.

Back in Hopedale, we would have called them "wannabe gangsters," but this was south Philly, and we were stoned out of our trees in the middle of the night. We were scared, but I liked it at the same time. I felt attached to the real world, pumped with adrenaline, and more clear-headed than I'd felt in a while.

Two of "the kids from the backseat," looked like they were making a strong effort not to embrace each other, and the other appeared as if he was going to shit himself any minute. The teen angst and weed that had motivated them to embark on this quest was wearing off quickly.

Finally, Andy got directions to his cousin's place and we crashed hard, literally, on a cold basement floor... rats and all. The plan was to get some rest, have some breakfast, then drive the rest of the way to Florida. It sounded good enough to me, but we awoke to a plot twist.

Andy's mother had called his cousin early that morning to tell him that I had some irate parents back in Hopedale fuming over my irresponsible actions. I had neglected to collect permission slips for my impromptu field trip. She wanted him to tell me that a couple of them had called the police. That morning I had a nationwide A.P.B. out for my arrest.

The charge... kidnapping!

"Dude, I think you're in a lot of trouble!" Andy told me in his thick Spanish accent.

I didn't consider the parents' point of view, because I lived in a world without parents. I instantly felt horrible, thinking about how frantic *my* mom would have been under the same circumstances. I filled my gas tank and watched Philadelphia disappear quickly in my rear view mirror, heading north instead of south. I white-knuckled my steering wheel the whole way home, chain smoking weed and cigarettes again.

I'm far from proud of this. In fact, the memory makes me feel sick. I was an inexperienced driver, in an illegal automobile, with minors and drugs. I was high and angry at the world. It's not lost on me that I could have hurt somebody, bombing up and down highway ninety-five. Unbelievably, I did something even more reckless during the first *Cycle*, but that came later in the early winter months of 1994.

I'm going to leave that skeleton in my closet... for now.

After surviving that first *Cycle*, I managed to get my shit together, for the most part. I met a girl, got a job, ate, and slept like a normal human being. I smoked pot on a limited and recreational basis, sometimes going weeks and even months without. For almost six years, I remained a healthy and productive member of society. I really thought I was fine until insanity tapped me on the shoulder again in 1999 and set the gears in motion for my next downward spiral.

During the next *Cycle,* I proposed to a woman named Paula, who I knew damn well I wasn't in love with... then I called it off... then I proposed again. It was like there was two of me, battling for control of my life's chessboard. The part of me that wanted to survive called it off and wanted to escape this damaging relationship, but I could not overcome the side that seeks self-destruction in the midst of madness.

When I finally broke through the chains of that psychological bout, I found myself with a wife who was crazier than I was. My feelings for her were closer to hate than love, but I did my best to survive in a hostile relationship for as long as I could. I did this out of a self-imposed sense of obligation to save Paula from herself. Of course, in the end, it was impossible.

The third *Cycle* began in 2005, just over five years after the second. I got Hailey pregnant during a time when I was still having serious trust issues with her. I left my job, had late night conversations with my dead mommy, and denied myself nutrition. Panic attacks and agoraphobia introduced themselves to me, and my cutting habit escalated to frightening proportions. A single, insignificant slice would no longer do.

Now, at the tumultuous apex of this fourth *Cycle*, I gave Hailey cause to second-guess her trust in *me* forever. I abandoned my loved ones and rented a condo where I could die alone, a social recluse. I've left my job... again. I've been starving myself... again. Now here I am, back in the hospital... again!

Through it all, I've self-medicated with marijuana. I'm convinced that, though it does damage of its own, and I don't want to be its slave forever, I have been better off with it than without. For me, and the symptoms that plague me, nothing else is its equal when it comes to dulling the edge of despair. As an adult now, I can compare it to many alternatives.

I'm currently on a prescribed menu of *legal* pharmaceuticals...

I take twenty milligrams of Prozac every morning to treat depression, panic attacks, anxiety, and Obsessive Compulsive Disorder. Along with the Prozac, I take one milligram of Klonopin. It's supposed to calm my brain and nerves as well as work with the Prozac against my panic attacks. It doesn't do shit as far as I can tell, but I take another milligram in the afternoon, and then one again at night with five milligrams of Zyprexa. The Zyprexa is also for depression, but can help with mania as well as hallucinations.

Throughout my career as a mental basket case, I've been on many different Prescription drugs, like Paxil, Effexor, Xanax, and so on. I've also seen my fair share of various shrinks.

My current therapist wants me to kick my nineteen-year weed-smoking habit, but it's so hard to give up something that works so well. I'll try to go a day and my symptoms become intolerable to me. The noises. Open spaces. People. Everything! I always cave and get more. It accomplishes everything that the pills fail to do with a couple of hits. My hopeless, and often irrational worries, dissipate in a thick plume of smoke.

There's no denying its immediate effect. When I get high, the buzzing chaos inside my mind calms. I can focus better. I have a more reasonable outlook on life and things are not always the end of the world. It also helps with my appetite, sleep, and gives me a little more control over my social anxiety and panic attacks. It's not a cure, or a solution by any means, but it quiets the call of suicide.

So, should I quit? I'm constantly asking myself that question. I think I can be a better version of me without it. I want to achieve peace of mind, and eliminate my never-ending desire for sedation. I want to find that "natural high". I want to quit because something substantial has to change to put an end to these fucking *Cycles* once and for all. Not to mention legal issues, long-term effects, and the bad example it sets for my children. It's inevitable they'll figure it out eventually. David and Amy are almost teenagers now.

Ultimately, quitting is what I want. For the immediate future, I still feel that I need to smoke weed to calm my stormy mind, but my days are numbered... in one way or another.

Why do I go crazy every five years or so, almost like clockwork? Every injustice and ugly memory from my past snowballing into a mind-crushing psychological avalanche that buries me in icy seclusion. I keep thinking I must have finally dealt with my issues each time I come out the other side, only to have it happen again with increased ferocity.

Why am I capable of being so fucking normal and highly functional the rest of the time? Being a good, trustworthy man, a disciplined employee, and dare I say great, husband and daddy. Will I eventually swing one way or another for the last time? Will I eventually *stay* normal... or crazy?

I'm arguably the perfect recipe for insanity.

Both of my parents had their own psychological issues and addictions. It's quite possible the first ingredient in this recipe is a genetic predisposition. My family tree is twisted and knotted, roots to branches, from generations of abuse and psychosis.

The second ingredient, perhaps, would be the traumatizing events and situations that have occurred throughout my life, leaving their black marks on my heart and mind.

If there's a third ingredient, it's just today's day and age. The economy is at an all-time low. Unemployment is at an all-time high. Everything you need is too expensive, and nothing you own is worth shit. Perfectly sane people are jumping off bridges and bathing with toasters.

I have a good, decent paying job right now and I'm lucky for that. However, I'm currently out on disability to deal with my problems, and I've been down this road before. I'm definitely fearful I could lose my job if I don't handle my situation perfectly and promptly. I have rent to pay, car payments, and kids... just like anybody else. Hell yes I'm scared that my mental illness will rob me of my ability to handle my responsibilities as a man.

All things considered, how could I not be a time bomb waiting to go off?

This is the fourth time in my adult life I've gone through this. One way or another, it has to end. The symptoms I suffer now are nearly impossible to withstand, especially when combined with enormous guilt from the things I've recently done. I don't want to know what a fifth time around would do to me, or the people I love. I do believe we'd all be better off if I were dead.

I know I shouldn't think like that. I know it's just an illusion that could end up a self-fulfilling prophecy. I can't help it. The lies I tell myself about my existence are so much easier to believe than the truth. I need to change, and I need to do it soon. My goal for right now, is to stay alive long enough to wake up from my current nightmare.

5.

JOURNAL ENTRY
(Leaving the Hospital)

08 / 05 / 11

Why am I this person? Why am I this thing, sitting in my hospital room, staring out the window at freedom and knowing it's out of my hands? This is my second stay at Butler Hospital... a mental institution.

The first time I was here was in 2006. I was in the off portion of my on and off relationship with Hailey. She'd just had the abortion and I was confused and devastated. I had always wanted a child, and thought that she was the right person to do that with, but I also knew I was a train wreck who could no longer take care of himself, never mind a newborn baby.

I was out of work for similar reasons to why I'm out now, hallucinations, panic attacks, agoraphobia, etc. I had locked myself in my apartment, and refused to answer my phone or doorbell. Hailey and one of my friends kept sending the police to my apartment to check on me. They were scared I was going to kill myself, so it got intense.

I would try to ignore the cops, but they would threaten to break my door down! When I would let them in, finally, they were always nice to me. They would ignore my bongs and the

41

pot smoke permeating the air. They complimented my pencil sketching's and admired my collection of medieval weaponry, while I sat nervously on my couch wondering if I was going to be taken away. There was never an arrest, and eventually they left me alone. I think they genuinely wanted to make sure I was all right and nothing more.

I wasn't.

I don't think I would have lived much longer the way I was going. Not eating at all, living on cigarettes and marijuana. I was getting less than eight hours of sleep a week, and hallucinating from sleep deprivation, having visions of my dead mother and neon spiders crawling up my legs. My mind was a freak show. I threw in the towel, called my ex-wife, and had her bring me to the emergency room. I used Paula, because I didn't want Hailey to see me like that. I thought she'd seen plenty already.

When I left my apartment, I did so with a jacket draped over my head so I couldn't see the threatening outside world. Later, when I was shuttled from the emergency room at the hospital to Butler via ambulance, I did so with a sheet pulled over my body from head to toe like a corpse. I wouldn't leave the building any other way.

I really felt like I was going to die out of the sanctity of my apartment, but I knew the opposite was the truth. This was the first time in my life I had such strong agoraphobic symptoms, and I truly felt like I'd gone insane. No drug I've ever taken has been able to warp my reality as convincingly as my own irrational fear can. I went to the hospital, in the back of that ambulance like a scared kid on a roller coaster.

The environment proved to be good for me at that time. I embraced the extreme lifestyle change, eating all the healthy foods and sleeping with the help of medication. I even *participated in every group therapy session and activity offered.*

While I was in there Hailey started visiting me and talking to me on the phone. We rekindled our romance while I was being the best patient I could be, and when I left the hospital, we decided I would move in with her and her kids. They released me after a few days and I got better at a gradual pace, started working again, and taking care of my new family. We had Chris a little more than a year later, and I lived a happy and healthy life for the most part, until this year.

I really thought I was all better... again! I see the pattern now, and it's about fucking time.

The difference in my experiences in the hospital that time, compared to now, is like night and day. My social anxiety, agoraphobia, and panic attacks are far more severe and cause me to perceive this place as hostile now. You'd think that just knowing it's all in your head would make you see things more clearly, but that's not the case.

I've been hiding in my room and refusing to participate in anything. I don't eat unless someone brings food into my room for me, and some of the nurses make it a point to make me feel like I'm being a pain in the ass... I suppose I am.

You're supposed to go out into the main corridor every morning for blood work and vitals, but I won't do that either. They have to bring everything into my room for me. I fucking hate it! Being here is making me feel worse. I can't handle feeling as if I'm being a burden in a hospital setting. The last thing I want to do is be difficult, but I'm physically incapable of crossing the threshold.

I also can't stand being away from my son, which is something I didn't have to deal with last time. Chris had to visit his dad in the loony bin yesterday... poor little guy. I can't help

43

but wonder if he'll be writing about the experience in his own journal someday.

Great... now I can't stop fucking crying again!

The only thing that's the same for me this time is Hailey coming to visit every day. She even snuck my cell phone in, so I could text her at night. It was cute and romantic, in a strange and sad way. I don't know what I'd do without her right now.

I've spent the last Five days writing. Without my weed, or a sharp object to open my skin with, it's the only thing left with the ability to keep me grounded. I've actually been enjoying it to some extent, filling an entire notebook already. Perhaps I'll find what I need in these pages someday. I'm certainly not finding it here, in room twenty-four.

I've been in this room for nearly a week now, and I think I've convinced the staff to release me. They realize I'll be resistant to help as long as I remain in uncomfortable surroundings. It was a mistake for me to come here this time, but I just didn't know what else to do. It helped before, but things are different now.

Things are worse.

I'll be leaving with an appointment to start seeing a resident here. At least one good thing came out of my visit. I would have to wait months to see a psychiatrist if I hadn't put myself in here. She doesn't have much experience, so I have some doubt she'll be able to help someone like me. Still, it seems like the quickest, most affordable way for me to get some kind of help. I'll be open minded and hope for the best.

It's hard to do that when you feel exhausted and demented. Scared to be alone with myself, but equally scared to be around people. Needing my family more than ever, but wrestling with the feeling that they'd all be better off without me.

My mind is a battlefield.

I want to leave right now! I don't even know if I can wait until morning. I feel like a scared little kid who misses his mommy, and I guess that's pretty close to the truth.

6.

MY BEST FRIEND

"Nathan
You are the sunshine in my life
The idea of <u>not</u> having a little boy never entered my head
I would have tried forever until I finally had you
Stay as sweet and loving as you are now -- Forever!

Love Mommy" 12 / 28 / 83

I got an autograph book for Christmas when I was eight years old. Three days later, I asked my mom for her autograph and that's what she wrote. I don't have the whole book anymore, but I have that page she wrote on almost thirty years later. I've kept it safe, hidden behind a picture of her in one of my photo albums. Her kind and beautiful words, combined with my persistent successful attempt to save them, are a fitting example of the love we shared.

It's a daunting task... putting pen to page and writing about my mother. It sounds cliché, but words can't possibly do justice to the love and friendship we shared, but I'll do my best.

Judy Daniels gave birth to me when she was twenty-six years old. She had five miscarriages, and my sister, on her mission to have the little boy she always wanted. So many times, she told me she never would have stopped trying until she had me.

I know my mom loved me with all her heart. In the seventeen years we spent together, she must have told me that she loved me a million times, and I always said it right back.

When I was an infant, my mom gave me all the nurturing care and loving affection that a baby needs. As I grew into a toddler and then a small boy, we did everything together. She was my mother, my teacher, my playmate. Like most children, I guess, my mom was everything to me. The kind of mom who could forget she had a debilitating fear of insects, if something buzzing or creeping was terrorizing her son in his room. She was the kind of mom that was the world's biggest fan of anything that captured my interest, even fleetingly.

At the same time, I had no relationship at all with the stranger in my house that I called daddy. I just knew to be scared of him. There were several times when I was little, when my mom would drag me out of the house in a mad rush, explaining to me in a panic... *"I think he's really going to kill us both this time!"* We would stay away; sometimes overnight at her sister's, until she was sure it was safe for us to return. My dad often referred to me as a "mama's boy." He was right.

My early years in school were a tough adjustment for both of us. It was standard procedure for me to cry my eyes out in the mornings before kindergarten, and when it came time to enter the first grade I had a serious case of separation anxiety. Many times when my mom would walk me to school, she would have to take me directly inside the building.

Meanwhile, the other kids... the normal kids, would play outside patiently waiting for that first bell to ring. Mom would bring me to my classroom with tears streaming down my face. My teacher would have to hold me, sometimes kicking and screaming, while my mommy walked away. I'll bet she had a tear-streaked face of her own. What a heart wrenching ritual for both of us to have to endure on such a regular basis.

This continued into the second, third, and fourth grades. I just hated being away from my home. I hated being away from my mother. What would happen if my scary dad hurt her while I was away at school? What would I do if I came home to a gruesome scene like the ones in the horror movies we watched in the middle of the night?

I think it's fair to say those early school years were a real bitch for both of us. Diagnosed with a stress-related ulcer, I had to take a big hit of Maalox with my Flintstone Vitamins before school every morning. I'd already had my first sexual experiences... with my sister! I was also in my first bar fight before I got to the third grade, but that's more of a daddy story.

My mom was my stability. She was the only person in my world that made me feel safe. The only person in my world that I knew would never hurt me. I was uncomfortable around everybody else. I didn't trust anybody else. My father, my sister, my other relatives, all made me feel awkward and tense.

I don't want to paint the wrong picture here. In spite of the nightmarish things that were often happening around me... or to me, I feel I had a happy childhood for the most part. That's a strong testament to how wonderful my mom was. It also helped, that for the most part, it was usually just the two of us. My dad worked a lot, slept even more, and was a frequent bar patron. My sister was older, and didn't want anything to do with me, not in the conventional sense anyway.

I was always at my happiest when I had my mom all to myself, and I know she did her best to make every day as special as she possibly could. She really shined when it came to holidays. Christmas and Halloween were her two favorites, but she loved to celebrate them all. Like any good mom, she kept me believing in Santa Claus for as long as possible. She made me feel the magic of Christmas.

When I was a child, it was tradition to open one present on Christmas Eve. Then we'd watch Christmas movies or cartoons, and listen to holiday music before falling asleep. We'd camp out beneath the flashing lights of the balsam pine in the living room. I was always sure to get the presents I asked for the next day, but I was never a spoiled child... far from it. Mom taught me to earn everything I had, but Christmas was definitely an exception.

We always decorated our house properly and extensively for the holidays. The walls had a thousand staple holes in them as Pilgrims and Indians replaced snowmen and reindeer. We didn't bother with outdoor decorations, but you always knew which holiday was approaching as soon as you stepped foot in our house.

One dimensional cupids or leprechauns brought the walls to life. Festive knick-knacks formed armies on all the shelf space in our home, banners hung, and theme music played. I was always her decorating partner, and it made me feel special to help her with the transitions from one holiday to the next.

Of course, I loved the magic of Christmas, what child doesn't, but Halloween was awesome too. All year long, my mom would collect novelty candles... skulls, black cats, spiders, and all things creepy. On Halloween, she'd burn them all. Ghosts and goblins cast their dancing shadows, over skeleton and bat infested walls. We would toast marshmallows over the candle flames and watch horror movies all night long.

My mom and I were the harbingers of each new holiday in our house. Easter, Valentine's Day, even St. Patrick's Day, were all big deals. Huge Easter baskets, valentines, corned beef with cabbage and mom making green beer with food coloring. I got green sprite so I didn't feel left out.

St. Patrick's Day, 1993...
That's when she left me. That's when she left all of us.
Now it will always be St. Judy's day for me. A bittersweet
holiday with bittersweet memories, but I digress...

Mom loved her "little vacations" too. New Hampshire was
a favorite when I was a kid. Sometimes we'd go for fun, and
sometimes for escape, but no matter why we went, she always
made sure we had fun and visited every tourist attraction we
could... Santa's Village, the Polar Caves, the Flume.

We'd have a blast and collect souvenirs, from t-shirts and
magnets to post cards and bumper stickers. We'd stop and
check out all sights, like the Man in the Mountain and Indian
Head. I also loved staying in the little roadside motels that we
randomly found in our travels, and eating in all the different
restaurants.

We were adventurers.

When I got a little older and my mom was re-married, we
started going to Plymouth, MA quite a bit. The Pilgrim Sands
Motel became her new favorite place, and eventually a new
Christmas tradition. This was right on the beach and had an
indoor pool and Jacuzzi that my mom and I loved. Several
years in a row, we packed up our presents and of course some
of mom's decorations, and headed to the Sands. We even had a
small tree for our hotel room.

We would still open a present on Christmas Eve, but now
we'd go swimming and relax in the Jacuzzi before falling
asleep to the enchanting combination of our flickering tree and
the sound of waves crashing on the beach outside. What a cool
way to spend Christmas Eve. Sometimes it even snowed for us.
I loved that place, and actually use to experience small bouts of
depression when we'd return home.

My mom was five feet, three inches tall with a healthy,
rugged build for the better part of her life. With her basic

wardrobe of t-shirts and stretch pants, she wore glasses and had long sandy blonde hair, usually pulled back in a ponytail. A "stay at home mom" who took great pride in the job. My mom was never harsh or overbearing, but quite the opposite. She was sweet and gentle with a strong love for life. Strict though. You ate what she made, cleaned up after yourself, and always had to help around the house.

"I'm your mom, *NOT* your maid!" She was fond of saying on the rare occasion I forgot to put my dishes in the sink, or left my dirty socks in the living room.

Warm and caring, with a great sense of humor, she had a deep sort of intelligence that transcended her middle school education. It helped that she had an insatiable love for both reading and writing that inspires me to this day. Observant and thoughtful, she was one of the easiest people to talk to about anything. We shared her love of music, movies, and all things dark and mysterious.

She was comfortable and non-judgmental, buying me a one-year subscription to Playboy Magazine when I was just twelve years old, because I had the balls to ask her for it. Knowing that I had become interested in that sort of thing, she knew I'd just end up with a secret stash of porn under my mattress like most boys my age if she didn't.

"Playboy's actually a pretty tasteful choice," she told me with perfect nonchalance. I think she was ahead of her time in certain aspects when it came to parenting. Undeniably cool, she would have been an interesting grandma to say the least.

I miss her so much!

Aside from some photographs, that page from my childhood autograph book is one, of only two mementos I still have from my mom. The other is a keychain that she left for me from a Pontiac Firebird she used to have. I'm not a car guy, so I don't know what year it was, but I know it was a badass car. White, with a black and gold firebird emblem sprawled out on the hood. Mom looked good in it, and my sister and I loved cruising around with her.

Sometimes, when she wasn't getting along so well with Michelle, she would drive around the popular teen hangouts with the windows rolled down. She had a twisted sense of humor, and played country "yodeling" cassettes at full volume, while my sister tried to disappear into the passenger seat. It was such an eye-catching car to have that wretched noise pumping out of it at full volume. As the little brother, I loved my sister's squirming discomfort, and mom was my hero.

I have so many good memories.

So many bad...

As far as my mother and father's marriage was concerned, it seemed troubled and on the brink of falling apart for as long as I remember. If my father was physically abusive to my mother, I never saw it and she never told me. She was definitely afraid of him though, and the threat of violence seemed to be a constant presence in our home.

My poor mother had to deal with an unfaithful husband. My father was totally blatant and disrespectful about it. I remember him bringing some strange woman home from a bar one night. He had the audacity to introduce her to my mom as his "new girlfriend," before disappearing into the basement with her for the night. According to my mom this was not the first time something like that happened.

He fucked my aunt too, right on our living room couch when he was drunk one night! My mom got up to use the bathroom and caught them in the act. When she told me about it later in life, she said he saw her and didn't have the shame to stop for even a second, because he was *"in some kind of trance"!* I don't know why she told me those details. I guess I was all she had, but knowing these things made being around my dad even harder than it already was.

Judy and Bruce Daniels were married for eighteen years before finally going through their ugly and bitter divorce. To me, I was ten or eleven at the time; it was a blur of holes punched in walls, police, lawyers, and scary words like restraining orders and custody battles. I don't know how any woman could stay in such a horrible situation for so long, but I think I understand why.

I know Hailey stayed in a relationship with a man that belittled and degraded her for far too long as well. I'm sure it's the same for lots of moms in bad situations. Fear of breaking up your family and not being able to take care of your kids on your own.

There's no real earning power, because you've spent years dedicating your life to your children. There are worries about the house, the vehicles, and providing necessities. A mother in these situations is standing up against seemingly impossible odds.

Eventually my mom and dad's divorce was final, and for a little while, I was the only man in her life. We were happy, but she was getting lonely and feeling insecure about our future.

After a short series of guys that she dated once or twice, she fell in love with the man that would soon be my stepfather, Steve Willis. I didn't like him from the start, and I'm quite positive it was mutual. He was a bear of a guy, whose salt-and-pepper bearded face was always in the shadow of his big, black cowboy hat. We got along with each other as best we could for the sake of the woman we both loved, but when she died, so did our ability to maintain any kind of civil relationship.

There was a stipulation in my parent's divorce agreement that she could continue to live in our house with her kids until such a time that she chose to re-marry. That seemed reasonable to me, and I was fully expecting to remain there until I grew up and went to college. What didn't seem reasonable to me was her contemplating marrying this jackass Steve, and ruining everything!

My mom presented her thoughts to me one night, and for the first time ever... I was pissed off at her. I swallowed the horrible feeling before I dared express it, and hid it deep within myself. I was ashamed of it.

My mom left the decision up to me, which I think was a little too much responsibility for a child to handle. It was clear that she wanted to marry this guy, but said it was my choice since I would be sacrificing my home and friends for her happiness. The big problem was that we weren't just moving, we were moving to the other side of the country to live with my grandmother in Texas.

I wanted to be selfish. Even though I was a big mama's boy, I had still developed a close group of friends that I'd grown to love during the course of my short life. I was comfortable in my school and very afraid of change. There had been so much in my life already. I wanted to scream no! No fucking way!

How could *I* be selfish though? It felt like I would be breaking my mom's heart if I begged her not to marry this guy so I could keep my friends and familiar surroundings. I didn't want to be like my father and hold her back from all her dreams. Stand in the way of her happiness. It was too much to figure out, and the confusion was dizzying. I didn't know how to act or what to say, and she was waiting with hopeful eyes.

I told her to marry him, and she was so happy and proud of me for making what she called "a very grown up decision". I tried to feel proud of myself too, but I could feel no pride beneath my deep sorrow and concern. I acted happy with hugs, kisses, and congratulations but I felt alone. I had a hard road ahead of me and for the first time in my life, I felt like I couldn't talk to my mom about it.

We packed our lives up into neat little boxes, and stuffed them into the back of our rented U-Haul. I said a tear-filled goodbye to my long-time friends and we were off to the lone star state. I was depressed about leaving my home and friends behind, but my mom did her usual great job of making life as fun as possible. Seeing her as happy as she was made it easy to forgive her, and as sad as *I* was... I was genuinely happy for *her*.

We drove to Texas, and took our time doing it. We stopped at every attraction possible along the endless highway. Mom was generous and fun, and we collected trinkets from every state we passed through, but when we arrived at my grandmother's trailer a week later, the party was over. Texas sucked! Nothing could change my mind about that, and I proceeded to downward spiral into a deep, dark depression.

I developed clinical insomnia, and made a new hobby out of causing myself physical pain. I refused to go to school because this was supposedly going to be a temporary stay. I didn't want to make a bunch of new friends just to lose them when we inevitably moved again. I was already having such a hard time missing my hometown. I wrote letters constantly because I had absolutely nothing else to do, but my friends did, so they seldom got back to me. Occasionally my best friend John would and I read his short letters repeatedly.

I think my mom started to feel a little worried about me shortly after we arrived. She didn't make me go to school like most parents would have. It may have been the wrong choice, and I'm sure she wrestled with it, but she must have been so desperate to please me and keep me as content as she could. Besides, I was adamant that I wasn't going to go.

For me Texas was complete and total isolation from any friends or peers for almost a year, with no school or kids in my neighborhood whatsoever. My mother wasn't only my best friend... she was my only friend. Any fun I may have had living there speaks volumes about her constant attempt to make her little boy happy. I know she did the best she could for me.

We went to plenty of movies, which throughout our life was always one of our favorite things to do. There were lots of restaurants, flea markets, and the mall occasionally. Once, we even went to the Dallas Arena to see my hero, Hulk Hogan, at a wrestling show. It was also when we lived in Texas that we took a vacation to Disneyland and Sea World in California. Therefore, it would be unfair to say some good memories didn't come out of living in Texas, but for the most part; it was a very dark time in my life.

We lived in Azle, a forgotten dirt road town that didn't even exist on most maps, and we lived in my grandma's trailer. I never cared for Deidre Swanson, a proud racist and religious fanatic, who used to have sex for money when my mom was a little girl. I don't think she cared for me much either, and I know she didn't care for the Miss June poster I hung in my bedroom.

Next door on the left were my Uncle Pete and Aunt Anna, and to the right were my cousins, Vick and Carly. Across the hard-packed soil road were my other aunt and uncle, Will and Janet. That's it! That was my neighborhood! My old relatives surrounded me, with nobody my own age in sight. Imagine being the only one in your community going through puberty! I swear it was like a retirement home set in an old western movie. At least Steve finally looked normal with his fucking ten-gallon hat, and my mom was with her siblings... but I didn't fit in anywhere.

I think a lot of my social awkwardness has roots in that dusty little town. My mom did her best to minimize the obvious damage happening to my psyche. I love her for it, but it was an impossible situation. Puberty and social isolation just do not mix well, and I couldn't even ride my skateboard because there wasn't any fucking pavement as far as the eyes could see.

Eventually our temporary stay in Texas did end, and we decided to move to Maine. We packed up our lives again and headed north. In another effort to make me happy, we took a detour to Hopedale so I could have a short, but much appreciated reunion with my childhood pals. We stayed a couple of days, and I loved it, but it just wasn't enough and it hurt when we left again.

I did find a little more stability and normalcy in Maine. We moved into a beautiful three-bedroom townhouse in the woods of Oldtown. There were plenty of kids my age in the little community we moved into and I instantly made some good friends. After that summer of bike riding and swimming in the local lake, I was willing to go back to school without much of a fight.

I joined the seventh grade, a year older than most of my classmates. The oppressive loneliness that I experienced in Texas left its mark, and I can't deny already feeling a little emotionally separated from the other kids, but I adapted and even fit in pretty well after a while. I learned to be happy again with the help of a few new friends.

By the end of the year, I wasn't necessarily popular, but almost everybody at my school liked me. I was developing strong bonds, and that was helping me let go of my old ones. There were also plenty of cute girls around. I started dating and having different girlfriends for the first time in my life. I even had my first *normal* sexual experience at thirteen years old in a playground... a quick hand job from my fifteen-year-old girlfriend.

My mom must have sensed where my relationships were heading. She bought me condoms for my thirteenth birthday and had a "talk" with me. It was a little awkward in spite of the open communication we usually shared, but it was a good talk, it made me feel somewhat grown up and I smile when I think of it.

The truth is I was far from ready for sex and broke up with my girlfriend because she wanted to take that step and I just didn't feel ready yet. I was content being a virgin for years to come and stuck with girls my own speed after her.

As far as my mother's personal life went, she was less than happy... again.

Steve hadn't worked in about two years. Mom had got a decent amount of money from the sale of our house and it was starting to run out after all our travels across the country. This guy was leeching off her and never contributing a dime. He waited until the well ran completely dry before attempting to find work. Then it was always temporary jobs that never seemed to last very long.

My mom started confiding in me that she really wasn't happy anymore, and my heart broke for her. I remember wishing so bad that I could quit school and get a job to take care of her so she wouldn't feel like she needed Steve. I even dreamed about it sometimes.

She never seemed to let her turbulent eighteen-year marriage snuff out her life-loving spirit. Now, she wasn't going to let her dead end romance break her either. The two of us had fun, as usual, and grew closer than ever.

I even neglected my friends sometimes because I'd be having so much fun with my mom, who had started to teach me how to cook. What a blast we had in the kitchen, preparing meals and baking cookies. We went to the movies almost every weekend, and enjoyed going hiking in the thickly settled woods surrounding our home.

Even though my mom and I had many good times together, and I was still having a lot of fun with my friends, I was definitely feeling a high amount of stress poking away at my joy.

My mom was no longer in love with my stepdad, who I never liked to begin with, and our bank account was usually bone dry. She wanted to leave him, but soon his meager and infrequent income would be all we had. I felt frustrated and helpless. I wanted more than ever to be able to take care of my mother by myself; hating the father figures, I had.

Things were bad.

Then they got worse...

"Feel this." She said to me. We were in the hallway. She lifted her right arm up over her head.

"Feel right here." She lifted her blue t-shirt up to her armpit... gesturing.

"Do you feel something here... like a lump, maybe?"

I did. It felt like an almond beneath her skin, and I felt an instinctive dread almost instantly.

"What is it?" I asked, knowing it was something serious, but not knowing *how* I knew.

"I don't know... it's weird." She smoothed her shirt back down to her waist and shrugged, but I noticed her hands were shaking and her smile wasn't quite *real*. "I'm sure it's nothing... "

It *was* something. It was cancer.

Her doctor diagnosed her with breast cancer at thirty-nine years old, and I started worrying about her dying again at the age of thirteen. First we found out she had cancer. Then we found out it was malignant.

They tried radiation therapy, but the tumors kept growing. I kept hearing the phrase, "terminal illness" and was thinking about what that really meant. I would say I was crying myself to sleep almost every night for a while, but my insomnia was back so there wasn't much sleeping going on in my room. I spent the nights crying and worrying about the possible... no! Impossible death of my mom, and I started cutting myself for the first time to quiet the screaming in my head.

I stayed silent at night, keeping my insomnia, cutting, and fear to myself. During the day, I was supportive and rallied behind her fight. I was amazed and impressed by her optimistic attitude and did my best to emulate it. With the spirit of a true warrior, she wanted to fight and she wanted to win. Relentlessly, she began studying everything she could about cancer and its various treatments and success stories.

Together, my mom and I watched countless movies about the horrible disease in the place of the scary movies we use to enjoy. She researched everything from the best diets to the most healing atmospheres and climates. As it turned out, a hot and dry atmosphere was the most conducive for healing a body with cancer. Here we were in the cold woods of Maine, and my mom was about to wedge me in between a rock and a hard place.

She wanted to move back to Texas with her mom again!

I was devastated. It was decision time again, and I felt the weight of the world on my adolescent shoulders. It was clear that she felt the best choice for her health was to move back to Texas. Moreover, living with grandma again would be good for our worsening financial situation. Once again, she told me the decision was up to me. Once again, I would be letting go of my friendships and giving up what had become my home. The choice was mine, but really...

There was no choice!

I was terrified of the social exile I would experience in Azle again. I was depressed about the idea of having to miss *two* groups of friends now. Mostly, however, I was scared my mom was going to die... off to Texas we went.

The only thing that was different this time was the cancer. Steve still didn't work, and I didn't go to school for another year. Everyone on the street still shared my bloodline, and again, I missed having friends my own age.

Good ole Texas.

Mom had some small victories with the new diets and treatments. Sometimes the tumors didn't grow, and sometimes they even measured a little smaller. After almost a year though, the cancer was still winning... still spreading through her defiant body. Being less than happy with how her treatments were going, me sulking around the trailer twenty-four hours a day, and Steve now mooching off her *and* Deidre, she made the decision to move one more time.

Some cousins of mine, who lived back in Hopedale, were soon to be moving out of their apartment. My mom talked to them and had them ask their landlord if we could move up there and have their place. The idea was to trade the good climate for a better hospital, and a chance to see her son happy again in his old hometown. In a matter of phone calls, it was a done deal and I got the best news I'd gotten in a long time.

We were going home!

It really was great news in my little world, but it was bittersweet too. I was elated to be moving back to my old town and friends, but I was moving back with a very sick mommy.

I started the eighth grade in Hopedale, now two years older than most of my classmates. Steve started looking for work again, and mom started chemotherapy at Hopedale Whitinsville Hospital. After all the time that had passed since her initial diagnosis, she started to look like she had cancer. I felt torn between trying to enjoy my life as a teenager, reunited with his long lost friends, and spending as much time as possible with my mother... whose days were quite possibly numbered.

She fought hard, and usually kept her sense of humor and love for life. When her hair fell out, she bought wigs of all different styles and colors and acted comically glamorous, adding big sunglasses, wild handkerchiefs, and blowing kisses to people like a movie star. When she lost a third of her bodyweight she told people it was because her new diet was working. "The cancer diet," she'd call it. I'm sure she had plenty of private moments where she came undone, but her spirit was strong, and I was in awe of her.

I thought about the great strength that I knew she possessed. When I was five years old, and begged her to give up her long time smoking habit, she agreed without any fuss and never had a cigarette again. As a smoker myself now, I'm impressed and have already failed to do the same thing at my own son's request. My mom was stronger than I am, stronger than all the men were in her world. She's the reason I have infinite respect for good women, especially mothers.

For some reason she didn't drive for most of my life. That firebird was the last car she ever had, and I'm not sure why. I think, in retrospect, she may have had many of the same issues I experience today. She never worked or had any friends aside from her siblings and myself. It's quite possible she had some social anxiety. We walked everywhere together, and it was one of my favorite things to do. We even walked to her chemo appointments.

One time I didn't want to go. I bitched that I was too tired, and didn't feel like it. She left, visibly upset, and I regretted it immediately. That only happened once. I was sixteen, but I still feel like a jerk when I think about it. She was dead a year later. It was normal teen behavior, but it haunts me nonetheless.

When she was getting close to the end, my mom and I had an important and painful talk. This was shortly before hospital beds, visiting nurses, and brain tumors. In other words, mom was still mom but not for much longer. She told me she was in pain twenty-four hours a day, and she told me that she loved me...

"I love you too." I said.

She told me she wasn't afraid to die, that she didn't know what was out there, but she thought it would bring her peace, and she said she loved me so much...

"I love you too mom!"

She asked me to do her a favor, *"as a man"*, is how she put it...

"Please don't cry at my funeral, Nathan." She took a long, noisy breath... wheezing. She struggled through her words. "Promise me... you won't cry... so I know... you understand... that I'll finally... have peace after... after all these years... of fighting so hard." Her voice was cracking, she was having trouble breathing, and getting emotional. I closed my eyes against the sight of her struggling to breathe, and clung to her deformed but loving words.

I promised not to cry at her funeral.

She told me that I'd grown to be someone she was very proud of, and she loved me with all her heart. She said she could rest easy because she knew she raised a good man. I was seventeen, and scared! I didn't feel like a man at all, wondering how I was going to survive in the great big world without my mommy! I asked her...

"Can I cry now?" I already was.

My mom hugged me with every ounce of strength she had left in her frail body. "Yes." She whispered. "I love you, Nathan, and when I'm gone I'll love you still." She kissed me.

We both cried, and our hug lasted forever.

My mom died a few months later. We were poor, and my stepdad and I could no longer hide our mutual hatred for each other. He still barely worked, and now he was trying his hand at being a drunk. I had dropped out of school at sixteen, and with my eighth grade education, I'd been working various jobs for minimum wage for over a year.

I began experimenting with pot a couple of months before my mom passed away. I was out all the time with my friends, smoking weed and hiding from reality, as I've mentioned before. I tried to forget about the hospital bed in our apartment, where the shadow of my best friend waited patiently to die. A skeleton under a thin sheet, wheezing through dry, cracked lips beneath sunken eyes and a hairless skull.

I came home after partying all night on St. Patrick's Day, 1993. I came home to an unwelcome, forced, and sloppy hug from Steve and I didn't have to look in my mom's room to know her bed would be empty. I felt myself go numb from head to toe.

I didn't cry at my mom's funeral. I kept my difficult promise to her. All my friends cried, which touched me deeply and reminded me how loved she was by all who were lucky enough to know her. My cousin sang Amazing Grace and it echoed, hauntingly, throughout the funeral parlor.

When it was my turn to approach and say my goodbyes, I didn't see my mother. I saw death, and I didn't say goodbye because there was nobody there to say goodbye to. I left in a state of terrible shock, and stayed that way for quite some time.

She was gone...

She has been gone for more than half my life now and I still miss her severely. I wish she could know my son, and I like to tell myself maybe she does *somehow*. Perhaps she's still aware of me and *with* me in some mysterious way. It's a beautiful thought.

I would love to make my mom proud of me again, and conquer my illness before it defeats me.

Her passion for living, even in times of great turmoil should be an inspiration for to me to love my own life... and save it! I have to honor her memory and hold tight to the fact that she would want her little boy to survive, and be happy.

7.

JOURNAL ENTRY
(The Wedding)

09 / 11 / 11

I've been out of the hospital for over a month, struggling to get better, but getting worse instead. The hour-long weekly therapy sessions and various medications are no match for my problematic mind. I feel very strongly that I need more help than I'm getting, but I don't know what else to do. My options seem so limited.

During the last few weeks, I've been writing about my parents, my childhood, my problems and their possible origins. I wrote an essay about my mom and spilled more tears on the pages than ink. I've always tried to keep my pain at bay, even ignore it whenever possible. This approach hasn't served me very well, and has become a problem all its own. It hurts to look at my memories and relive the grief in my past, but something feels right about it. I suppose, ultimately, I'm searching for closure. I hope it works, but for now, I remain as fucked up as ever.

I had to go to Nancy's wedding yesterday... Hailey's sister. I had been dreading the event for weeks. Well, since the engagement to be honest. This wedding was one of the things I use to fret about in the middle of the night, when I first started losing my mind again last spring.

To somebody in my condition a wedding, or any type of social gathering for that matter, is a virtual assault on my senses. I'm agoraphobic.

Hailey and the kids left early to go to her sister's house for the preparations. I stayed behind to wait for her mom's boyfriend, Rick, to come pick me up and bring me to the church. The whole family was in the wedding party except for me. I appreciated that and wouldn't have had it any other way.

I took a shower and tried to wash the fear away. Every time I started to think about what was in store for me I could feel the panic welling up inside. Of course, I couldn't think about anything else, leaving me in a perpetual state of escalating terror.

After my shower, I went downstairs to the basement with shaky knees, and got dressed slowly with unsteady hands. I got stoned and took two Xanax, and paced around the house waiting for my ride to bring me to my inevitable doom.

It's no exaggeration. You can't know what it's like to feel like you're going to go completely mad in front of a crowd of unsuspecting bystanders. There's a massive sense of internal compression, and you feel like you're going to explode. I picture myself in these situations. I picture myself screaming at the top of my lungs, turning on my heels, and running away like a lunatic.

I'm lonely in the sense that no one around me can relate to this kind of suffering.

I felt like shit in my clothes too! I've lost so much weight. My pants and shirt don't fit right. They're baggy and hang on my body in an awkward embrace. My face looks drawn and unhealthy. I used to be huge and muscular. Now I feel, quite literally, like less of a man. I'm a shadow of my former self. I feel disgusting and embarrassed for my girlfriend!

I am a lowly thing.

The weed and pills seemed to have calmed my frayed nerves somewhat, but when Rick arrived, I immediately started having trouble breathing. Defining reluctance, I got into his truck and rested my forehead against the passenger side window, concentrating on breathing, and nothing else. We headed to the church.

The building was foreboding and seemed bigger than should be possible. I crossed the street staring at the front entrance, my vision a kaleidoscope, twisting and turning everything I saw into colorful bursts. I slipped two more Xanax into my mouth, felt my heart start kicking hard in my chest, and walked up the front steps to the church with dream-like difficulty as if I were knee deep in quicksand.

I walked through the doorway, a hungry mouth looking to eat me up, and I started sweating. There was too much open space and my eyes began playing tricks on me as everything in my peripheral vision began melting away.

The sunlight crashed through the stained glass windows and sent colors flying through the air before me. The notes from the monstrous pipe organ stomped on me and made me wince. Voices became hostile and gained weight inside my head forcing me to brace myself. It was an angry choir yelling and screaming at me as I resisted the urge to take flight from the holy nightmare.

The wedding procession was a stream of madness inside my twisted mind. Somehow I was able to see through the fog long enough to watch my son grace the isle with his adorable presence. He looked so cute in his suit, and for a fraction of a second, I felt like a normal, proud daddy.

Watching Chris, however, depleted my reserve ability to focus, and I gave myself a mental ass whipping for missing Hailey's walk down the aisle. I was looking forward to seeing her in all her glamorous, glittery pink glory.

The ceremony itself was too much and I kept my eyes shut tight, most of the time gripping the sides of my chair like a pilot who just hit the emergency eject button. I pictured shattering the stained glass windows with telekinesis, and slitting my wrists with the colorful shards!

When it finally ended, I stumbled out into the afternoon, drunk from the sights and sounds from within. Disoriented, I avoided the wedding party lined up outside. I shook no hands and gave no hugs, kisses, or congratulations. I stood off to the side, hiding behind my sunglasses and stared in horrible wonder as I watched the flight of stairs dissolve into the street.

Who needs acid or mushrooms when you have overwhelming social anxiety with a heaping side of agoraphobia?

Hailey left the wedding party and came to stand by my side. I loved her for that and appreciated the gesture. It made me feel warm and safe for a little while. Very shortly, however, she had to leave in the limo and go with the rest of the party to take pictures. I hated being apart from her.

It was too early to go to the banquet hall for the reception, so Rick and I went to a local bar, and I pounded a couple of beers with my last Xanax. I wanted sedation, as if I were going into surgery.

Between the weed I had smoked beforehand, all the pills I ingested, and then the alcohol, I was as relaxed as I could possibly be. I continued to drink throughout my dinner and even managed to maintain a couple of conversations... about what, I have no idea.

Hailey was the best. I could tell she was making every possible effort to make me as comfortable as she could. She kept leaving the head table during dinner to sit on my lap and share my drinks with me. When the wedding party was supposed to dance amongst themselves, she danced with me instead of her assigned groomsman. She made me feel safe somehow in an impossible situation. I couldn't help thinking... this woman really loves me!

By the end of the night, I couldn't handle the noises and lights anymore. My drugs and alcohol were wearing off and I had reached my absolute limit of stimulation. I spent the last half hour of the party waiting patiently in the hallway for it to end.

Overall, it went surprisingly better than I thought it would, as I was expecting a waking nightmare. It wasn't easy, but I'm glad I went. Hailey deserved the effort and I'm proud I was able to do that for her. I wouldn't do it for anybody else in the world.

I'm happy for Nancy and her husband too. I've always liked her, but we've never been very close. It's my fault. I have many walls around me, but I'm sure if I can find a way to reduce them to rubble she could be like a real sister to me. I hate that I was so absorbed in my own world while they celebrated their love for each other.

I do feel a small splinter of hope, having gone through this and survived, unscathed. Hope that Hailey and I will be all right regardless of my recent shortcomings and intense problems. Hope that I'll be all right in the end, and able to endure anything with the support of my family. Only time will tell.

In the meantime, I remain a mess.

I can't help but wonder if I'll be able to return to work before they decide to replace me. In all honesty, I don't want to go back. There are too many reminders of how I came undone, but I know I'd be a fool to lose my job in this economy. Not to mention, the prospect of starting all over again somewhere new is nauseating. I feel like I've held a thousand different jobs since I dropped out of school twenty years ago.

8.

JACK-OF-ALL-TRADES

I turned sixteen the summer after I completed the eighth grade. My mom was well into her battle with cancer, my stepdad wasn't providing for us, and I felt a responsibility to be able to fend for myself financially. I thought maybe I could even help with the bills if I dropped out of school and started working full time. That's what I did, and in the last twenty years, I've had more than my fair share of jobs.

Even though being at school was hard for me, I always did well and it came easy to me. With minimal effort at school, and maximum problems at home I got A's and B's on my report card every year. I was in all the high-level classes, and frequently made the honor roll.

In spite of doing well, I hated going to school every day and I was more than happy to call it quits. I didn't have a problem with the education. I've always loved learning. It was the social aspect of it, the intense interactions with students and teachers alike. I've always been more comfortable being my own teacher. I taught myself how to swim, ride a bike, and even drive.

I continued learning even after dropping out of school. When I wasn't working, I spent a great deal of time at the local library, reading for fun or studying one subject or another on my own. I've read thousands of books, and written thousands of pages in journals.

As my friends and girlfriends went through high school without me, it was always my pleasure to take on various assignments for them and score them A's from behind the scenes. I got my G.E.D. immediately after I turned eighteen and scored a ninety-three on the test without even studying for it. Learning and retaining information has always been a talent of mine, and I can't help but wonder how far I might have gone if I wasn't such a lost soul.

The first job I had, when I was sixteen, was as a telemarketer making minimum wage. Yes, I was the asshole interrupting your dinner to ask for some of your hard-earned money. It wasn't even a real job. We were supposedly calling people to ask for donations benefitting aids and cancer research, but it turned out to be a total scam.

I only worked there for a couple of weeks, and couldn't stand it. Repeatedly, we had to read this pre-written script to annoyed people over the phone. It was so robotic. Shortly after I quit, I heard the place closed and the guy running it went to jail. That was my introduction to the work force, taking part in a telephone swindle to rip people off. "Dial and smile," that was our motto.

During these teen-age years, I was heavily into my bodybuilding and martial arts training. I was the top student at the Shaolin Kung-Fu Academy in Hopedale and I quickly formed a bond with my instructor, who also owned the place. He gave me a key and named me the school's manager. It was my job to open and close the place. I also had to keep it clean, and sign up potential students that walked through the door.

I even taught my own class on Tuesday nights when the owner couldn't be there. It was a lot of responsibility for someone who wasn't receiving a paycheck. I worked in exchange for instruction and unlimited training, but I was dedicated to the school as if I was making top dollar. I even kept a hot plate there so I could eat my meals and keep the school open as much as possible. It was cool, but it wasn't putting any money in my pocket. I needed a paying job.

Everyone knew me to be a disciplined athlete at the gym where I worked out. Many of the older bodybuilders seemed to like me and made an effort to take me under their wings. One of these guys owned his own construction company and offered me a job as a laborer when he found out I was looking for work.

I jumped at the chance to make some real money. I would be paid eight dollars an hour under the table and work about fifty hours a week. That's not bad for a sixteen-year-old kid in the early nineties. For a while, I enjoyed bringing more cash into the house than my stepfather, which was something I always dreamed of doing.

The lifestyle was challenging, but I enjoyed the work and learned a lot about building houses. Every morning I would get up at four o'clock, eat, and then go to the gym to lift weights for an hour. My boss would pick me up there at five-thirty and we'd be on the work site everyday by six. We did it all, from framing houses and offices, to roofing and siding projects. We even painted and did some renovations.

I would pound nails for nine or ten hours, and then my boss would drop me off to open the Kung-Fu school, where I would stay for the next five hours. Every night, around nine, I'd walk home through downtown Hopedale... exhausted from a grueling seventeen-hour day. I kept this up five days a week until the construction business got a little slow and my boss couldn't justify keeping me on any longer.

I stopped going to the kung-Fu school around the same time. I had developed tendonitis in most of my major joints from years of intensive training in both martial arts and bodybuilding. My doctor recommended giving one of those activities up, so I said good-bye to my career as a martial artist. I have a lot of love for the training, but I love the gym just a little bit more. In any case, I found myself with a lot of free time on my hands and the need to find another job.

I filled out an application at the K-Mart in Hopedale, and they hired me with part-time hours, making minimum wage again. I went from bringing home four hundred dollars cash every week to getting a check for eighty bucks, if I was lucky. It was a depressing adjustment. Not only did the money suck, but I also hated the work.

The people employed there were miserable and I didn't like dealing with the customers either. I rode my bike to and from work, put in my four-hour shifts stocking the shelves, and started to worry about my future. I didn't last very long at that department store. Customer services, and the hustle and bustle of the retail world, are not for me.

I took a job at Stop and Shop not long after I quit working at K-Mart. I found no difference at all in the transition to grocery store. Minutes felt like hours as I tried to stay busy keeping the isles full and avoiding stupid questions...

"Is this *ALL* the peanut butter you carry?"

"Of course not lady... we keep a secret stash of special peanut butter in the back."

In a shirt and tie, nametag and apron, I bagged groceries and collected the shopping carts from the parking lot. I would dream of a better life, a life where I was worth more than four dollars an hour... a life where my mother wasn't dying from cancerous tumors at home. Meanwhile, my friends were studying chemistry and getting ready for the prom.

Not long before my mom died I managed to hook up with the same guy that had hired me to do construction. He still owned his own business, but focused more on siding. He took me back as an apprentice, and I started making good money again. The two of us spent our days hanging wooden clapboards on newly built houses.

I loved the smell of sawdust, and the sound our power tools made. I might have been happy to keep doing that forever, but my mom passed away and I became increasingly fucked up. I took some time off when she died, but when I tried to go back to work, I was only able to hang on by a thread for a short time. I was depressed, and never slept. I was constantly telling my boss that I couldn't make it to work and he eventually had to let me go.

Next was the most short-lived job I ever held. My stepdad, Steve, who became a raging alcoholic after my mom died, did most of his drinking at a local bar called Richard's Pub, formally known as the Red Vest Pub. I'd been going there most of my life with my mom and dad, and then my mom and stepdad. This was the place they met, and supposedly fell in love.

I don't know what I was thinking, taking a job in the same place that this man liked to be liquored up. I lasted a record-breaking four hours before I walked off the job, never to return. Try bussing tables while your drunken stepdad takes turns between busting your balls and slobbering all over you in front of his equally drunk and annoying friends.

My friend Tim got me my next job and I loved it. He and I got to work together under the table for an advertising agency called Checkers. It wasn't work at all. Different companies would hire this agency to do special promotions for their products for a certain amount of time.

Our first mission was to represent the Butterfinger candy bar. Every morning we'd go pick up the big, yellow Butterfinger van and load it with cases of candy bars. Tim did all the driving since I didn't have a license, and still wouldn't for quite some time. We had to go to college campuses where they were having special events or parties, set up a table, and just give out free candy bars to everyone that walked by. Our uniform was obnoxious yellow pants that said Butterfinger down the legs in big, blue letters and a Bart Simpson T-shirt that warned... "Nobody better lay a finger on my Butterfinger!" We made it a point to wear that shit to the office, but we always changed into our regular clothes whenever we got to our destination. I remember playing a lot of Frisbee, tanning on the roof of the van, and entering an outdoor bench press competition.

It was great, driving around while we got high, partying with college kids, and being paid for it! Unfortunately, that job was temporary. They offered us another gig dressing like the Keebler elves, green tights and all. Handing out cookies at fairs and amusement parks, but Tim was all set and I didn't have my own transportation so that was the end of the advertising game for me.

After my father died unexpectedly, a few months after my mom, I was feeling lost and hopeless. I no longer had parents, and Steve and I weren't getting along at all. It wasn't lost on me that I had an eighth grade education and was racking up quite a list of jobs that I only held for short periods. That never looks good to potential employers. My future was looking bleak.

My mom had left me her secret stash of money that she had hidden in her bedroom. It was over two thousand dollars. On top of that, when I turned eighteen I received six thousand dollars from a life insurance policy that my father had.

Having this money bought me a little time to figure things out and make some kind of plan for myself, and that's exactly what I did. I decided to spend all the money on keeping myself high and trying to have fun with my friends, then I would kill myself when the cash ran out.

My sister had moved back to the area after living in Florida for a while. With both of our parents dead, she wanted to rekindle some kind of relationship with her little brother. We hadn't seen, or talked to each other in years. She knew I couldn't stand Steve and offered me to move into her new apartment in Providence with her and her dysfunctional family.

I was willing to try putting our past behind us and spend some time hanging out with her, but the thought of living with her made me sick. Living with my stepdad made me sick too. I moved out and spent a cold winter as a homeless guy living in his dead father's car. I did crash at my sister's place occasionally and that's how I met Paula, who would someday be my wife.

Paula worked at the convenience store adjacent to my sister's apartment. This woman is a different story all together, but I'm bringing her up because she's the reason I didn't kill myself when that money ran out. She seemed to like me even though I was a burnt out homeless guy with no job, who had just blown through eight thousand dollars. I thought that maybe I was giving up too soon. I thought maybe this girls saw something in me that I'm in too much pain to see myself. I decided to live a little bit longer, but then I needed a job again.

I started working third shift, for minimum wage again, at a local newspaper press. I worked in the mailroom inserting ads and coupons into the paper. It was a mind-numbing, tedious job, but I wasn't qualified to get anything better.

Meanwhile, I had started living with Paula at her mom and dad's house, and the two of us were desperate to get our own place. The eighty dollars a week I was making was never going to cut it, so I took a second job at another grocery store.

I would work all night at the press, then throw a shirt and tie on and go take care of the produce department. My work schedule was different every week, and impossible to adjust too. I knew from experience I wouldn't be able to keep it up for very long.

Paula and I ended up moving into our first apartment while I was working these two jobs. I felt like the pressure was on. I had just wanted to end my life, now all of a sudden, I not only had to take care of myself, but someone else was depending on me too. All of a sudden, I felt the need to "man up." I was desperate to find a real, full-time, first shift job with benefits. I was desperate to feel like a grown up.

I ended up quitting my job at the store unexpectedly. I filled out an application at a temp agency, left the printing press as well, and started working full-time hours at various manufacturing jobs, assembling random things like valves and picture frames. My third assignment with the agency was at a local beverage company, picking orders in their warehouse. I felt like I found my niche'.

The money was decent and the warehouse environment seemed to fit my personality pretty well. After working there for three months, the company took me on as a full-time employee and I started to feel like my life was coming together. I had my own place with my girlfriend, a good job, and I had taken up bodybuilding again. I wasn't even getting high or cutting myself anymore.

I ended up staying with that place for six years and when I left, I had experience in just about every aspect of the warehouse industry. I started out picking orders, and then had the added responsibility of doing all the company's UPS shipments. I learned how to make the labels and receive incoming items using the new on-line computer system.

When one of the delivery drivers had to take time off for surgery, I volunteered to fill in for him and took over his route for the next three months. I delivered coffee, in a cube van, all over New England. When it came time to go back to work in the warehouse I took a new job checking the completed production from the different departments, and putting the finished goods away.

I spent my days on a forklift and soon knew the location of every item the company sold. Because I was working with food products, I had to be mindful of expiration dates. I developed a card catalogue system for the company that ensured our products would leave the building in the order they were made. I took ownership of my job and eventually they changed my title from "stock clerk" to "physical inventory control person". I got a big raise to go with it, and I felt mildly successful.

As the company expanded, it started to experience growing pains and we were running out of room. It was becoming impossible to work around the hundreds of new products we made, because there was just nowhere to put them. As they began exploring the option of getting another warehouse, I stepped up and volunteered to redesign our current location.

I promised I'd be able to organize the mess and make the order picking a much more efficient process. One of the guys covered my duties for me as I spent the next few weeks walking around the isles making a blueprint for new racks and product locations. Once I had a plan, I set it into motion. I spent weeks relocating older products to make room for new ones, and built all the new racks myself.

My mission was a huge success and when the smoke cleared happy employees were picking orders in half the time with none of the aggravation they were experiencing before. I became "employee of the quarter" for my efforts, and they wrote some flattering things about my work ethic in the company newsletter. It felt good to play such an important role in the company, and I was feeling like I had come a long way from the kid sleeping in the back of his father's car.

I spent years mastering the position I held, and received several more raises, but eventually got bored. I had become the forklift instructor for the company, was on the safety committee, and worked on several problem solving task forces. I took a new job within the company, as a service technician and learned how to repair and rebuild the various coffee machines we sold.

Soon I was on the road again driving around with other technicians installing and repairing machines on site in restaurants, hotels, and hospitals. I enjoyed working with the machines, but didn't like all the driving around. When a job became available working for the maintenance department, I jumped on it.

I got to work with an infinite supply of power tools and quickly started to gain experience working on all the machines we had in the different manufacturing departments. The maintenance manager liked me a lot and began filling my head with a plethora of mechanical knowledge. He sent me away for courses on industrial electricity and taught me different styles of welding.

He also sent me to a three-month night school program to learn how to operate high-pressure boilers. I took the state exam after I completed the schooling and scored a ninety-eight, making me a licensed high-pressure boiler operator. The woman who gave me the license said I had the highest score she'd ever seen. I was happy, and continued learning everything I could about electricity, plumbing, and machine maintenance.

After nearly a year, my boss gave his notice to leave the company. His replacement didn't like me very much, and gave me a new job as a preventative maintenance tech. I walked around the building with a rag and a grease gun keeping the machines clean and lubricated. I wasn't learning anything anymore, and all of a sudden, I found myself in a dead end job. I made the decision to cash in my 401K and leave the company in search of something new.

I took a little time off from working to train for a reality show that I had successfully auditioned for, but I'll get into that later. When I did return to work, I did so in a completely different atmosphere. I took a job at a fast paced, gourmet deli making sandwiches for the hungry masses. It was a fun job working with some cool people. They became good friends of mine, at least for a little while. I worked plenty of hours and the pay was surprisingly generous. This particular deli had three locations at that time, and I worked at all of them over the course of the next two years.

Paula, who was my wife at this point, was working a regular, Monday through Friday, first shift job. My hours were more towards the evening with weekends as well. I liked my schedule just fine, but Paula hated it.

She suffered from severe depression and couldn't stand being alone as much as she was. Our conflicting schedules were a constant source of arguing, so after much debate she convinced me to seek out a more compatible shift. I decided that returning to the warehouse industry would be my best bet, considering the amount of experience I had.

It wasn't long before I found myself back on a forklift and picking orders, this time for a company that dealt with food products. I started on the ground floor, but very quickly was able to climb the ladder. I became a nationally certified forklift instructor during my time there and was once again on the company's safety committee. They gave me multiple promotions, as I went from "crew leader," to "team leader," and finally "department supervisor."

I was the boss for the first time in my life. I had regular employees, temporary workers, and convicts that were bussed in every day as part of a work release program, all answering to me. I was making better money than I ever had, but I hated the pressure of being in charge. I didn't feel comfortable being responsible for anybody but myself in the workplace. I felt proud and overwhelmed at the same time.

My wife and I separated during my time at this company, after being together for over ten years. Eight months later, I became involved in a devastating love triangle that would change my life forever. I started dating *my* boss's wife, Hailey... the very same Hailey that I'm still with today.

The drama created during this turbulent period of my life gave me my first experiences with panic attacks, as I worked with a guy that I knew was fucking the woman I was falling in love with. The third *Cycle* was born from this. I was living alone in a new apartment, and found I could no longer take care of myself.

I left my job, and collected temporary disability benefits, but I never went back. I'd been there for two years, and doubled my hourly rate, but I just couldn't return. I locked myself up in my apartment, and was in the mental hospital shortly after that. When I got out, I moved in with Hailey, anxious for a new beginning. I collected unemployment benefits for a while and decided to try my hands at a new trade. I wanted to be a tattoo artist.

I don't consider myself an artist really. I'm not capable of creating original art, but since I was a child, I've had an uncanny talent for being able to recreate any picture I look at. I see all the individual lines that make up a picture, and I can perfectly reproduce them in any size on paper.

I decided to trade in my pencils and pens for tattoo guns and needles. I was a natural. I practiced on soft, white leather at first, then on myself, before I started drilling ink into my friends and family. I'm proud to say that I've never done a bad tattoo, and have actually done some impressive ones.

The problem was that I wasn't a licensed tattoo artist, making my work technically illegal. It's a federal offense to tattoo somebody in Rhode Island without a license. I tried to become legitimate and get a job in a real shop, but I found it to be an incredibly tough industry to break into. You have to be an apprentice first and then it's up to the discretion of the owner when you get your license. There was no pay, and I'd be at the mercy of someone else telling me when *they* felt I was ready.

I think I went to every tattoo shop in the state looking for something that made sense, but it wasn't working out. Hailey found out she was pregnant again and this time we wanted to keep the baby. I needed a job that paid, but I was reluctant to return to warehousing. I knew I would have to be a supervisor again to make comparable money to my last job; I just didn't want the stress that came with those responsibilities.

Out of desperation, I took a job that I knew wouldn't fit me. I became a door-to-door vacuum cleaner salesman. I wore a shirt and tie, and went into people's houses to do a live, ninety-minute infomercial demonstrating the multi-use vacuum cleaner.

You have to be somewhat of a performer, and definitely a people person. I'm neither one of those things, so I didn't even last a month. I did sell a couple of vacuums, but I knew my personality type would never thrive in that line of work. I needed to find another warehouse to work for, so I went to a temporary agency to fill out some paperwork and they had a job for me the next day.

Once again, I started in an entry-level position as an order picker, this time for a stationary distributer. Once again, I made my climb at a record pace. I only had to pick orders for about two months before they trained me as the company's back up receiver and full time Quality Control Person. Once again, I found myself the forklift instructor. They didn't have a safety committee, but they did send me to a seminar and gave me the title of "safety officer".

I was there for less than a year when they fired the assistant warehouse manager. His primary function was to run the production department, so they created the new position of "production Supervisor", and offered it to me. I wasn't as familiar with that aspect of the business, but I accepted and embraced the challenge.

I did well and made many improvements, but I could feel the stress of my growing responsibilities starting to take a toll on my psyche. Just when I started wondering how long I would be able to deal with the headaches that came with being the boss again, my body decided to give out on me before my mind had a chance.

I had a birth defect, a vascular anomaly in my right leg that that caused me some minor discomfort throughout my life, but no real problems. It became a problem and I started experiencing pain, a limited range of motion, and a horrible numbness that traveled from my foot to my hip. I saw three different doctors, and found out I was in danger of having an aneurism at any time. They told me I would have to stop working immediately, and be prepared to stay out for quite some time. I required surgery and was afraid for my health.

At the same time, I did enjoy the break from my supervisory duties. I was collecting temporary disability insurance again, intending to return to work in a matter of months. As it turned out, I was gone a lot longer than I expected and the company could no longer hold my position for me. Laid off, I had no idea that it would be two years before I worked again due to the suffering economy and the lack of jobs available.

I made good use of the time I spent out of work. First healing, and then educating myself in a couple of areas that always held some interest with me. I played the role of "stay at home dad" and formed an unbreakable bond with my son. As I healed from my operation, I began studying full time for the American Council of Exercise's board exam to become a Certified Personal Trainer.

I studied relentlessly for eight months... anatomy, physiology, biomechanics, etc. It was challenging and almost felt like learning a second language. I was developing high hopes for a career in the health and fitness world, and when I took the exam, I passed with flying colors.

I got a reality slap when I started looking for work at various gyms in my area. It turned out being a personal trainer with no field experience required you to be more of a salesperson, working for commission to supplement a miniscule hourly wage. I filled out an abundance of applications and had a couple of interviews, but soon had to face the reality that I didn't want to be a personal trainer anymore.

I was frustrated and didn't know what to do with myself next. I was discussing my dilemma with Hailey one night when a commercial for a truck driving school came on the television. We had one of those moments where we looked at each other and knew what the other was thinking. I knew what I was going to do next.

I called the school the next day, set up an interview with a recruiter, got a student loan, and that was all she wrote. I had to give up my recreational marijuana use for random drug testing, and attend the school for twenty hours a week for five months. You spent ten weeks in a classroom, and then ten weeks driving the big trucks in preparation for the Rhode Island Commercial Driver's license road test.

I graduated with a 4.0 GPA and was proud of the fact that I only got one question wrong out of all the tests I had to take. I also passed my road test on the first try, which was a rarity. When I left the school, I had my Class a CDL license with endorsements to drive double and triple trailers, tanker trucks, and to haul hazardous materials. I had work lined up through the school's job placement program to start driving cross-country, but I didn't take it. I was only interested in working locally.

It was time for more harsh reality. You couldn't get a good local truck-driving job without cross-country experience, and I wasn't willing to leave my family for weeks at a time in pursuit of less money than I was making as a warehouse supervisor.

Here I was a skilled tattoo artist, a certified personal trainer, and a heavily licensed truck driver, yet it seemed I was destined to return to a warehouse. The problem was I couldn't even find a job doing that. My unemployment benefits were running out, and I was starting to wonder how I was going to support my family. I ended up going back to the stationary company, much to my dismay.

I was depressed and felt like a failure. I'd made so many attempts to better myself, and my family's situation. I applied myself and always did better than average, but none of that seemed to matter. The worst part was I had to start all over again as an order picker making fifty percent less than I made when I left. The last thing I wanted to do was claw my way to the top again, but that's what I had to do.

In two months I moved up to a quality control position, then in a twist of fate, the company fired their production supervisor. My previous position became available to me. I got my old job back at my old salary, which I guess made me somewhat of a successful-failure. I accepted my fate and grabbed the bull by the horns, making rapid and substantial improvements in what had become a broken department.

They noticed my efforts and gave me a promotion from supervisor to manager, with a three dollar an hour increase in pay. Unfortunately, I was falling apart mentally. The stress was eating me alive and I couldn't seem to stop thinking about that stupid production department. I started to feel like work-related stress would be the death of me someday. I was losing my mind, and didn't want to admit to Hailey that the job that was supporting our family was too much for me.

It was in the midst of my lonely, internal struggle that I had an affair with a woman in my department. I was out of control. I couldn't think straight or function well in public anymore. I started hearing whispering voices that I couldn't understand. I didn't want to leave my house anymore, and I couldn't even go to work unless I got high first. I went from having perfect attendance for nine months to taking more time off than I had available.

Hailey and I split up, and I moved out for a little while. I told that woman from work that I wanted to be alone and wasn't fit to be in a relationship with anybody. Then I rekindled my romance with Hailey in spite of myself, abandoned my apartment and lease, and moved back in with my family, all within two months. Regret, guilt, frustration, and confusion flipped my world upside down and inside out. I was losing it!

I ran out of weed one weekend, and when the alarm went off that Monday morning, I knew I was going to have trouble. Hailey drove me to work, where I talked to my boss briefly. I was in the hospital the next day, and I haven't returned to work since. I'm not sure if I will. I've reached a point in my life, again, where I don't know what to do with my future. I feel beat-up and tired, well beyond my years.

This pattern of achieving success, only to keep losing it all, and starting all over again has added a great deal of frustration to my life. I don't know how much more of this I can take.

9.

JOURNAL ENTRY
(The Birthday Party)

I fucked up again! Amy's birthday party was last night and I couldn't handle it. I can't even handle an eleven year olds birthday party. What the fuck is the matter with me. I'm so sick of this shit.

I don't know how to be me anymore. The line between right and wrong has become so blurry. I stressed out all day over whether or not to make an attempt at going. If I were normal, it would be a no-brainer. The obvious right thing to do would be going to my stepdaughter's party, but I'm pretty fucking far from normal and nothing is obvious to me anymore.

I have to worry about embarrassing her. I have to worry about how I'll look to her, and her friends, if I start having a bad panic attack at the roller skating rink. Will the kids, and their parents alike, think I'm drunk or crazy if I put my head down on the table and start rocking back and forth, because the lights and sounds are freaking me out!

What will happen if my symptoms get out of hand? I totally black out and start acting like a complete maniac, counting and tapping my fingers to a primal rhythm that only I can hear. People might try talking to me, and I won't be able to understand them. I might respond by babbling some kind of gibberish back at them and making a fool of myself. I can just imagine Amy's friends asking her at school the next day, "What's wrong with your stepdad? He was acting really weird!"

With these things going through my mind, I couldn't help but wonder if the right thing to do was not going at all. I felt like I had to try for her. I just didn't want to let her down or ruin her night. What a fucking disaster!

I was imagining the skating rink with its multi-colored strobe lights, disco balls, and pounding music that would dilate my ear canals with each rhythmic thud. There would be a hundred kids screaming and laughing, while their parents itched for empty conversation. I had to sit on the edge of my bed, and rock back and forth, just thinking about it.

I had to try though!

Of course, I was having a full-blown attack by the time we pulled into the parking lot. The trees that lined the parking lot were attacking our mini-van with their twisted branches. Trying to tear the roof off and get me. Nobody else seemed to notice, so I just shut my eye and recited the definition of hyper-vigilance, inside my mind... or maybe it was aloud. Hailey did give me a funny look.

I couldn't breathe and I felt like I was going to throw up on myself. I saw some of our relatives gathered outside, and absolute horror overwhelmed me. Why was everyone wearing those terrible masks? Was I wearing one too, I wondered? Then it occurred to me that there were no masks... I was hallucinating. I had a strong urge to jump from the moving vehicle and make a run for it, but as usual, fear held me in a paralyzing grip.

Hailey was un-phased by my state of mind; unfortunately, she's used to it. She gave me her blessing to just sit in the van and try to go in after I calmed down. Her understanding tends to make things more painful for me. If she was a bitch about it, I could just say fuck her and not worry, but her kindness makes me want to try as hard as I can for her. Then, when I inevitably fail, I feel so much worse having let her down.

I saw all these same people at Nancy's wedding, but it doesn't matter. I'm worse now than I was then. In addition, Amy's dad was there last night, and he is a walking reminder of one of the worst times in my life. The mere sight of him can cause me to downward spiral in record speed. I just sat there, in the van. Hailey came out to check on me a couple of times, but nothing was going to get me inside that building.

My crazy ass sat in that passenger seat for an hour and a half, lost inside myself. I weaved in an out of awareness until I finally made the decision to walk home. Soon the party would be over and I was worried about everyone coming outside, seeing me, and knowing that I just sat there that entire time. I thought that would strike people as just as strange as anything I might have done inside.

Briefly, I considered hiding in the hatchback. Then I imagined it opening, with the whole family standing there ready to pack it full with Amy's presents. I would be in the way. I'd look completely insane. I would kill myself! Instead, I made sure the coast was clear, and then I snuck away as if I were leaving the scene of a crime. It was a crime to miss my little girl's birthday.

It wasn't a long walk, but I was concerned that when Hailey came out she'd be worried or upset that I just left like that. I was wrong though, and she wasn't upset at all, or at least hid it very well. When she got home, she was very pleasant as usual and I felt a huge sense of relief mixed with my usual dose of guilt.

Amy wasn't upset with me either and I was happy about that. She had a blast at her birthday party. I wish I could've been there. Now I've missed two parties this year. I missed my own son's too and I don't know if I can ever forgive myself for that one. I hate to think back on it.

Every year I've videotaped Chris's party, and intended to do that for his whole childhood, but I blew it. His birthday came during the brief time that I had moved out and was living in an apartment by myself. I couldn't make myself go to Hailey's for his party because I was afraid of everyone. I paced back and forth in my stupid condominium, twitching, and falling apart instead.

I waited until nine o'clock to head over, when I was sure everyone else would be gone. I brought him a bunch of presents, but by the time I got there, he was asleep, and the sight of his peaceful face squeezed at my heart. I wanted to kill myself! I'm sure he had fun, but I'm also sure he was wondering why his daddy didn't show up for his special day. I'm such a fucking loser!

I hope I can get my shit together soon for all the poor souls who are stuck loving me. I'm trying, I really am. I need to stop disappointing myself by disappointing everyone around me. I need to heal and regain control of my life. I have to keep telling myself that I'm not a bad father, I should know, I had one.

10.

THE STRANGER IN MY HOUSE

"Nathan,
A son that makes his parents extremely proud of him.
We know that you will give it your best shot to reach each and
every goal you set.
Wishing you the best of luck in all your quests.

Love Daddy 12 / 28 / 83

My father wrote this to me in the same autograph book that my mom wrote in. The words are kind, and might even represent how he really felt about me, but for most of my life, my dad seemed distant and unapproachable. His favorite nicknames for me included pussy, fag, and mama's boy. He was a master of verbal emasculation, and carried with him a constant looming threat of physical violence.

He was fond of folding his leather belt in half and making a loud, intimidating, snapping sound with it to let you know what would be coming if you made him mad. I was honestly scared to death of him growing up. My mom was too, and the fear that she couldn't hide was all the proof her little boy needed to know that his father was a dangerous man.

Bruce Daniels was a hardworking, blue-collar man, who served his country in the Army National Guard. I was born on my Dad's military base in Ft. Tacoma, Washington. I had a double hernia, making even my birth, a stressful event.

When I was three years old, my father relocated his family of four to Hopedale, MA, where we remained for almost a decade until my parents got divorced. During that time, he worked on an assembly line, building cars and trucks for the General Motors Company. If I had just one good thing to say about the man, it would be about his incredible work ethic. He always worked long days, and never stayed home when he was sick or hurt. Our family always had financial security with him. He was a good provider.

It's amazing how few memories I have of a man that lived under the same roof as me for over ten years. Most of what I know about my father I learned from my mom's horror stories about him. I tried to live my life, invisible; to someone that I should've had an unbreakable bond with, it was an unfortunate way to grow up.

I'm enough of a realist to accept the possibility that some of the things I heard about my dad might have been embellished, or exaggerated. My own personal experiences with the man, however, leave me with little doubt that he had a deeply disturbed mind.

It was almost as if there was an invisible line dividing our home, with my mom and I on one side, and my sister and dad on the other. They weren't as close as we were, but they had compatible personalities. My mom told me that my sister, manipulating and pitting them against each other, was the source of a lot of my parent's fighting. It definitely wasn't all her fault; I already mentioned my father's blatant infidelity.

My dad was an alcoholic, and his red and white Budweiser cans were a regular fixture in our house. He typically had *the king of beers* in one hand and a Marlboro burning away in the other. Under the couch was the tin where he kept his pot, or his "funny cigarettes", as mom would say. I never thought anything of it when I was a kid. It wasn't until years later when I started smoking weed myself, that I realized what he'd been doing. I probably have more in common with my father than I'd care to admit.

He was five feet, ten inches tall just like I am today, but he was a lot thinner than I am. He wore jeans stained with grease from working on cars, T-shirts, flannels, and old spice after-shave. I loved the smell of that stuff when he'd put it on. He always wore boots that he kept meticulously shined, and I used to sit "Indian-style" on the floor and watch him, quietly polish all his combat and cowboy boots.

He had dark brown hair that he wore like a 60's greaser, which combined with his facial features, made him look an awful lot like James Dean. There was an eagle tattooed on his left arm. I don't know if he just got it because that's what soldiers did back then, or if it meant something more to him. As a tattoo guy, I wish I could ask him about it. I'd like to ask him many things.

I knew my mom's side of the family pretty well, but my father's side was a different story altogether. It was much more dark and mysterious. His dad died when I was a little kid. I'm not sure how old I was at the time... four or five maybe. Apparently my father had some daddy issues of his own because he was arrested a couple of years later at his father's gravesite. He was drunk, had a gun, and was threatening to kill himself.

I'll never know what that was all about, but as someone who wrestles with suicidal tendencies of my own, I wish I had a better understanding of what might have been going through his mind. Did my dad suffer some kind of abuse? Was he angry with a man who fucked his head up and made life tougher to live than it needed to be? Were dark family secrets haunting him? I just don't know. Maybe he just loved his dad and felt an unbearable loss that kept eating at him until he couldn't take it anymore. I can only guess.

My grandmother, on my father's side, disowned me when I was a kid. Her name was Ellen Daniels, and she felt that I got too much attention at home and could do with one less relative. It wasn't a legal disowning in the courts or anything, but it was final.

The woman methodically let everyone in the family know, via phone and mail, that she didn't want anything to do with her grandson anymore, and that was truly the end of our relationship. She was clearly not a rational person, and I wonder what kind of mental damage someone like that could do to her own child... my daddy. Was she the reason he was as fucked up as he was? These are family mysteries that, unfortunately, I'll never be able to unravel.

My dad had three brothers. My uncles Bill, Wyatt, and Randy and I don't think I'd be able to pick any one of them out of a line-up. I don't even think I ever met my Uncle Wyatt, and all three of them seemed to spend their lives in and out of prison for rapes, assaults, and robberies. My Uncle Randy sexually abused my sister and started a chain of events that inevitably ended with her molesting me.

It's a frightening thought, that out of the four boys, my psychotic dad was the good son. Perhaps he was just lucky enough to avoid the law. To the best of my knowledge he was only arrested a couple of times in my life. Once for marijuana, then the infamous cemetery incident, and again for violating a restraining order my mom had against him when he started stalking her after the divorce.

My dad belonged in jail, if one of the most-told stories about him was true. I heard it several times from my mom, other relatives, and friends of the family. My dad had a pistol-grip crossbow, and he liked to shoot people with it. When he felt like he needed to blow off some steam, he would drive around in his pick-up truck, drinking beers, and looking for "fags" to shoot at.

My dad defined fags as guys who had long hair, wore earrings, or looked feminine to him in some way. He would pull up, start harassing them, and if they'd talk back, he'd shoot them in the leg with his fucking crossbow! My mom said she witnessed this once. These stories not only scared me, but also filled me with a certain amount of hatred. When we left him I grew my hair long, and I got my ear pierced too.

Another story that made me hate my own father involved a kitten. My mom and I loved cats, and had them as pets our whole life. I guess my dad didn't care for the animals very much and would have preferred not having them around. This particular incident happened when I was a baby, and I wish my mom never told me about it.

The kitten was climbing around on my dad while he was trying to relax. That pissed him off, so he picked it up and threw it against the wall as hard as he could. It died instantly! My mom was horrified and devastated. So was I, hearing about it years after the fact. I can't stand people who are comfortable hurting animals in any way. I don't even like to kill insects, and usually refuse to do so. I'm the guy that bring spiders outside to set free, rather than squashing them underfoot.

There was a story about a mouse too, more proof that my dad was psychotic. He was in the bathroom for quite a while and my mom heard a horrible squealing noise coming from behind the door. She walked in and saw my father with a crazed look in his eyes, cutting the arms and legs off a mouse with his buck knife, over the bloody bathroom sink. She told me that he was so lost in what he was doing that he didn't even notice she was there. He didn't even notice her screaming at him to stop!

He personally victimized me with his need for sick entertainment on more than one occasion too. He took me to a bar once, when I was about eight years old. It was rare for my dad and I to do anything, just the two of us, so I felt uncomfortable and scared long before I had any idea what was in store for me. I don't know what the deal was with this place, but there was nobody there except for my dad's drinking buddy, and his three sons.

I sat at the bar and had a soda while he and his friend pounded beers. The other three boys were running around, acting rowdy and knocking things over. They were wrestling with each other, and their dad was bragging to mine about how tough they were. I don't know if that's what planted the idea in his head, or if he'd brought me there with these intentions to begin with, but cash was being laid on the bar and I was about to be thrust into my first bar fight whether I liked it or not.

I was secure in my knowledge that when my father told me to do something, I better fucking do it. Therefore, when he told me I was going to fight his friend's three sons one at a time in a little tournament and make him some money, I knew that was exactly what was going to happen. It went against my peaceful, non-confrontational nature to fight, and fear welled up in the in the pit of my stomach.

As scared as I was to take a possible beating... or three, I was far more scared of what repercussions I might face if I upset my drunken daddy. It was a survival moment, and I just had to pick the lesser of two evils, so to speak. That was all the motivation I needed to turn my little hands into fists and do what I had to do.

My dad asked me which one I wanted to take on first, and I can remember very meekly saying, "the big one." I wanted to sound brave, but the reality was I wanted to get the worst of it over with as quickly as possible. Maybe he would just lay me out with one punch, and it would all be over.

The other boys were eager for battle, but their love for roughhousing was no match for a scared little boy's primal survival instincts. I recall one of them calling me a pussy, my father laughing, and then it was over in minutes. It wasn't pretty, but I ended up beating the shit out of three older boys that night, and going to school with dried blood on my knuckles the next morning.

Mounted on the wall was a stuffed deer head. It wore an army hat adorned with shiny medals and pins. A ridiculous sight to say the least, but all us kids thought the hat was cool. When I finished fighting for my dad's amusement and financial gain, he took the hat down and placed it on my head, crowning me the "champion."

Bruce Daniels looked in my eyes and told me he was proud of me. I didn't feel proud of myself... far from it. I felt abused, victimized, and deeply confused by the relationship between my father and I. It's a sad fact, that for the rest of my life, no matter what I accomplished, my dad never looked at me with such beaming pride again.

There was another incident a couple of years later where my dad tried to get me to fight for his amusement. It ended rather differently, and I'm not sure if that was because I was a little older or if it was because a friend of mine was involved instead of complete strangers.

I was having an intense argument with my friend Jimmy, in my backyard. We were yelling at each other, calling each other names... nothing unusual. A typical "boys will be boys" moment until dad decided to interject himself into our childish quarrel.

"Is there a fucking problem out here?" My dad was bursting through the back door, beer in hand, yelling at my friend and I. Paralysis embraced me instantly. This was always my reaction when daddy had a few beers and started to get loud, especially when I was his focal point.

"The two of you sound like a couple of little girls, screaming and yelling!" It was unusual for him to show his true colors when we had friends over, but he was obviously in rare form on this particular occasion. My buddy seemed frozen as well, but it was more likely out of the normal shock a kid experiences when adults start yelling, rather than the justifiable fear that gripped me.

"If you two have a problem... you're going to settle it with your fists like men, *not* yell at each other like little girls!" He took a long, hard hit off the red and white can, and then gestured like a referee starting a boxing match.

"Go ahead... fight!" Neither one of us budged. I started to cry and my father gave me a sharp glance of disgust, calling me pathetic with his cold eyes. "I said fight, god damn it!" His attention had shifted completely to me, and he crushed me with his heavy gaze. I just could not bring myself to take a swing at my friend, but I'm guilty of wanting to.

I'm guilty of desperately wanting to turn my father's look of disgust into one of pride as I'd seen a couple of years ago, in that bar. I'm guilty of wishing with all my might that I had it in me to hurt my friend, so my dad wouldn't hurt me, even if it would only be with his eyes and his words. I just couldn't do it. Jimmy had started to cry a little too, from the sheer awkwardness of the situation.

My father looked me square in the eyes and called me a pussy. He walked away, shaking his head, as he lit a cigarette and disappeared back into the house. My friend Jimmy never came back to my house again after that. I'm sure he went home, crying to his parents about Nathan Daniels' psycho dad. I don't blame him one bit. I spent the rest of the afternoon, curled up under the porch, waiting for my dad to pass out drunk inside.

My entire childhood was corrupted by the stress and fear my father instilled in me. Fueled by the images I saw in my mom's horror movies, and the stories I'd heard about my unbalanced daddy, I had trouble falling asleep at night. I felt a strong need to maintain constant vigilance. Frequently I wondered... *would this be the night we died.* When I did sleep, the nightmares came.

Other kids worried that the boogeyman caused the things that go bump in the night. I wondered if the noises I heard were my dad bludgeoning mommy with a hammer, or her gasping for air beneath his strangling hands. These are the things I dreamed of, and the terror and exhaustion I suffered lead to my problems going to school, and planted the seeds for a lifetime of insomnia.

It was these fears that turned me into the freak that never wanted to leave his mommy's side. I was a kicking, screaming, sideshow that had to be restrained inside the school building, more mornings than not. Sometimes my mom couldn't take it and she'd let me stay home, even though she knew, my dad had no tolerance for that. I would hide under the stairs until he went to work... until it was safe.

I remember sitting on the floor in the living room, watching television once. My dad was sitting on the couch staring at it, but not really watching it. I kept looking at him out of the corner of my eye. That was usually the only way I dared to look at him. He spoke softly all of a sudden, and his words chilled me to the core.

"Sometimes... I want to kill every last one of you." It was quiet, almost a whisper. Mom was in the kitchen, and he didn't say anything more, but just kept staring *through* the television.

I swallowed hard and wanted to cry, but I was afraid of breaking his trance and gaining his attention. All of a sudden, I had to pee. I wanted to get up and flee the room, but couldn't make myself move. I didn't even want to breathe.

When my mom came in, I took advantage of the distraction and got up to run for the bathroom. I didn't quite make it, soaking my pajama bottoms instead. I stripped and sat naked on the bathroom floor, crying and rocking and hugging my knees, until my mom came to check on me. I didn't go to school the next day... nightmares, again.

My father was abusive; there's no doubt about that. He was intimidating, threatening, and mean. He wielded his harsh words like dangerous weapons, and threatened physical violence toward both my mother, and I, on a regular basis. He never did lay a hand on me though... not even once.

Why?

My dad was constantly getting into bar fights. Violence and rage seemed to emanate out of every poor of his being most of the time. So why did he never follow through? Was he strong enough, or did he love me enough, to repress the urges he felt and never cross that line? I wish I could know. Was it my mom's expertise at subtly protecting me, combined with the fact that I stayed extremely quiet and never got into trouble? Was our unified mission to fly under his radar what kept us untouched?

It's possible he just liked holding the fear over us, like the sharp-angled blade of a guillotine. I don't commend the man for never hitting me. He might as well have. I've become an expert on pain and suffering, and I can say quite adamantly that physical pain and discomfort pale in comparison to mental and emotional anguish.

I think I would have preferred a father who skipped the verbal assaults, and just gave me a good backhand occasionally. The pain would dissipate in minutes as opposed to the never-ending burn of insults and degradation. I suppose abuse is abuse, no matter what form it comes in, and the torture of it is infinite, when it's at the hands of someone who's supposed to love you.

I do have a couple of good memories with my dad from my childhood. He took me to go see "Bambi" when it came out in the movie theatres, and "Rocky II". I remember him holding my hand in line, and smiling at me a couple of times. When I reflect on this, I get a warm and loving feeling that is completely uncharacteristic of most of my memories with my father.

I can also recall a time when we went to run some errands together. We went to the bank and he sat me down in a chair to wait for him. For some reason, I became extremely uncomfortable sitting next to a couple of strangers, and I started bawling. Within seconds, my dad was scooping me up out of the chair and holding me tight against his chest. I was very little and have no idea what he said to me, but it was soothing instead of aggressive and when I think back on it, a rare feeling of safety and security washes over me. It's a haunting glimpse of what my relationship with him should have felt like.

It's depressing... grasping at straws trying to come up with a couple of fond memories of my dad. It hurts to search through my entire childhood and only be able to come up with a couple of trips to the movies and him holding me tight once when I was upset. I have to be honest though... that's really all I have. It's the result of doing my best to avoid him whenever he was around, and remain as non-existent in his world as possible.

When my parents were nearing the end of their relationship, my father seemed to be losing control. He was constantly drinking and growing increasingly violent. He told my mom, at one point, that he would track her down and kill her if she went through with her plan to leave him. She was more frightened of him than ever, and truly believed he would be capable of following through with his threats.

Our living situation had become unbearable and mom decided to take me away for a few days to New Hampshire. While I was in the car waiting, my dad pinned her against the wall in our living room, and punched a hole through it, inches from her face. That was the last straw for her, and in a hysterical panic, she took a stand against him and called the police immediately.

Meanwhile, out in the car, I had no idea what had transpired inside and was working myself into a ten year olds version of a panic attack. My imagination was running wild and I was starting to picture my dad, murdering my mom, in a multitude of different ways. I wanted to go inside and help her... save her! I had seen little kids in movies carry out similar acts of heroism to save a parent in a life-threatening situation.

It was unquestionable to me that I loved my mom far more than these fictional children loved their parents, yet I was stuck to my seat, unable to move. I felt like a coward sitting there, and I started to cry. I decided that if my mom died in that house it would be because I sat idle, and allowed it to happen. False guilt started to grow quickly inside of me, but at last, my mom emerged from the house unscathed, and ready to save me from my father, and the images flashing through my mind.

She got into the firebird, shaking, and told me what had happened in the house just as the police pulled up with their lights flashing intently. She could see I had become terrified and did her best to comfort me, as we both let the flood gates open, and cried together harder than we ever had before. It was a life changing moment, and we could both feel its overwhelming intensity as we hugged each other in the front seat of the car.

The police made my dad pack a few of his things and vacate the premises while we waited, somewhat patiently. Before he left, the cops let him approach our vehicle briefly, to speak to his wife.

"Are you sure you want to do this?" He asked her, leaning his face in through the open passenger side window, inches away from me. He struck me as being unnaturally calm for this situation, and I found that more frightening than if he'd been visibly irate. I remember trying to summon the power to become invisible, but to no avail. My mom responded with a nod of her head and a tear in her eye. He responded to that with a strange grin that sent chills through my spine, and then he turned and walked away from us.

The divorce proceedings were hard for me. My father wanted visitation rights with my sister and I, but I was scared to death to be around him. I'd lie awake in bed at night worrying that the courts would force me to be with him, alone, without the protection of my mother. I worried about what he might do to me if we were ever by ourselves. Would he direct his anger toward my mother, at me? Would he push me into a wall and smash holes into it next to my small face... or worse?

I had good reason to be afraid. My dad was no less threatening since moving out of our house. He was irrational and went through a brief stalker phase where he harassed both my mother and I by phone and in person. He would drive to our house late at night and park on the street. Getting out and just standing there, chain smoking, and staring at our home. It happened several times, even after she got a restraining order against him. She called the police every time and it became his ritual to stand there waiting, ever so patiently, for them to come tell him he had to leave.

Even my sister was scared of him at this point, and the three of us would huddle inside, peering through the curtains, in nervous anticipation of what he might do next. We were scared he'd bring one of his guns some night, and the police would prove to be too little, too late. After all, he did keep calling and threatening to bring death to our doorstep!

My mom and I went to lunch one afternoon at the Red Vest Pub. We sat there together having a good time, after doing some shopping at the plaza up the street. We were sitting at the bar and I was laughing at something my mom had just said. I turned around, and there was my dad standing ten feet behind us, just staring at me with his awful, blank expression. His eyes like a shark. Then he acknowledged me with a twisted sneer, winked at me, and walked out of the place. I started crying as I tugged at her sleeve, and told my mom...

"Daddy was just here!" I gestured to where he was standing, and she went to the window to see him getting into his car to leave. She called the police again, they took her report as usual, and my dad spent the night in jail for violating the restraining order again.

One of the hardest things I had to do during that time was sit in a judge's chambers and explain to him, in my own words, why I didn't want the court to grant my father visitation rights with me. I cried my way through it and made quick work of getting my point across. All the while, my mom rubbed my shoulders, standing behind me, and whispering to me that everything was going to be all right.

After the divorce, very gradually, things began to settle down between my father and us. He managed to get some kind of control over himself, before the situation escalated to a point of no return. He left us alone after a while and disappeared from our lives. I should point out that, never once throughout the entire ordeal, did he falter in supporting his family on a financial level. The checks came in like clockwork every week and mom gave him credit for that, if nothing else.

Almost a year after the divorce, my father wrote me a very long and touching letter, that expressed some feelings of regret for having failed his family. He admitted in his writing, that he was an alcoholic, and that had a lot to do with his bad behavior towards us when he was there. He told me that he had quit drinking and had been sober for several weeks. He said he wanted me to be proud of him someday, and he hoped I would eventually give him a chance to spend some time with me.

The letter was long, emotional, and surprisingly well written. I wept as I wondered what might have been, and what still might be. He acknowledged having been a monster, and was suffering from the memory of his behavior. I just didn't trust him, and I felt like the man that wrote that letter was a complete stranger to me. I was intrigued though, and before long, I opened up to communicating with him through the mail, and then occasional phone calls.

By the time, Steve had moved into our house, I had agreed to try short visits with my dad. We would go out for a couple of hours twice a month to have lunch or see a movie. I'll never forget the first time we went out together. I was obviously incredibly nervous because of our dark history and the fact that I hadn't seen him in almost a year.

We got a couple of blocks away from my house, and my dad pulls into this empty dirt lot, with nobody around, and stops the car in a cloud of dust. Mortal fear struck me like lightening, and I honestly believed my father was going to kill me in the front seat of his car. I remember hoping it would be a gun instead of a knife, imagining a bullet might be quicker and less painful.

"Do you want to drive, buddy?" he asked me. I was sitting there in shock, wondering if kids could have heart attacks.

"I don't think I'm ready for that." I answered him, with shaking words, after a couple of much needed deep breaths. Little did he know I felt like I'd just had a near-death experience. Before he pulled back onto the road, he told me that he'd been sober for almost a year. I told my dad I was proud of him, before I had a chance to figure out if I really was or not, and for the first time I was the one to make *him* cry.

We went for lunch that day and my dad was on his best behavior. In spite of this, I never had time to learn how to trust him or get over the fear he used to instill in me. The limited visits during the next few months were often pleasant, but always awkward, and in no time at all my mom remarried and we were off to Texas.

I'm sure this pissed my father off on many different levels, but he harbored no more grudges as far as I'm aware. Our relationship slipped back into the abyss and only partially survived through infrequent phone calls and letters, as I traveled the country with Steve and my mom.

Years later, when my mom was less than happy with her new husband, she began some sort of pen-pal relationship with my father. I knew a little bit about it but didn't pay much attention to it until she asked me once, when we were living in Texas the second time, how I would feel about the possibility of them getting back together someday. My first reaction was that she lost her mind.

I knew my father was a different man than the one from my childhood. He remained sober, and was retired, living a quiet and lonely life. I also knew how miserable my mom had become with Steve. I honestly wasn't sure how I felt about it, but I told her I would always support whatever she wanted to do. Strangely enough, we didn't talk about it much after that. I think my mom was confused about having feelings leftover for my father.

When we wound up back in Hopedale, cancer and all, we were close to my dad again... geographically speaking anyway. Steve stayed with his mother for a few weeks, while my mom and I stayed with my cousin and his wife, until they vacated the apartment for us. During this time, we made a habit of going to visit my father at his condominium in Franklin.

He was so different from my painful memories of him. He loved to cook and could be funny. He had discovered the joy of reading, and liked a lot of the same music I did. We enjoyed hanging out with him and kept the excursions a secret from my step-dad, which I looked at like some kind of bonus. Sometimes I imagined my father, kicking my step-dad's ass... but he just wasn't that guy anymore.

Steve eventually moved in with us, and our lives became all about my mom's illness, as she got progressively worse. Both of our relationships with my dad fizzled out, as we tried to brace ourselves for her inevitable death. He was respectfully distant towards the end, probably not quite sure how to fit in. I thought about him occasionally, but allowed us to lose touch. He'd been such an erratic presence for most of my life; I just couldn't reach out to him. I chose my friends for comfort instead, and lost myself in the constant pursuit of sedation.

Shortly after my mom passed away, I was going through some of her stuff and came across the letters my dad had written to her when we were in Texas. They were sweet and supportive, and I was in awe. With my mom gone, and Steve and I at each other's throats, I felt lost and alone. The letters gave me a small bit of hope that I might still have somebody out there who loved me.

I sat down and poured my heart out to my dad, as I never had before in a letter of my own. I explained all the mixed emotions I felt about him after the fragile relationship we had maintained over the years. I told him about how bad I was suffering with the loss of my mom, and that I needed and wanted him in my life more than ever. I told him that Steve and I couldn't stand to be around each other, and asked him if he would consider letting me move in with him.

I mailed the letter and three days later, my father died, unexpectedly, due to complications from bronchial pneumonia. I have no idea if he received it or not, if he read it, or what he thought of it if he did. I hadn't talked to him in several months, as my whole world had become my dying mother, and I deeply regretted the loss of contact. That unanswered letter of mine will remain a loose end for the rest of my life, a fact that is nearly unbearable.

When I think of my dad these days, it fills me with pain and confusion. It's confusing because he left me with so many unanswered questions about who he was and what drove him to do both the good and terrible things he did. It's as if, when I think of him, I have to think about two completely different people. Both a mystery to me, like Dr. Jekyll and Mr. Hyde. It's painful because in a strange way I mourn his absence more than my mother's.

My love for her was the most powerful force I've ever felt, mirrored now by the way I feel about my own son. She died far too young and it was a tragedy in every sense of the word, but my time with her was wonderful from beginning to end and left me with a lifetime of beautiful memories. I never had anything even close to that with my father.

I studied and analyzed the letters he'd written me in the past, as well as the ones he wrote my mom, I was able to learn more about his true feelings. He expressed pure regret for the horrible role he played in our lives, and described himself as a monster. His words, laced with a deep self-hatred that I find all too familiar now. There were no excuses, just admissions and apologies. He loved us, and when he was convinced he really lost us, he miraculously started to heal himself.

He explained in these writings that he would always be there for us, but knew the damage he'd done had been severe. He never pressured me into any more of a relationship than I wanted, and he genuinely seemed to cherish our limited communications. In the letters, he explained that he sometimes wanted to cry and beg for my mom and I to come back to him, but knew he didn't deserve us enough to put up a fight. I can relate to similar feelings.

He was able to create a better version of himself and the potential to have a real father weaved in and out of my life until he died. Bad timing and worse circumstances, kept us estranged throughout the years. I had hope for us to get to know each other as adults. To bond and perhaps help ease each other's burdens, but all hope was lost. I think that's why his death vexes me far worse than my mom's does. In regards to him, I'm condemned to spend the rest of my life wondering... what if?

11.

JOURNAL ENTRY
(Another Wedding)

11 / 10 / 11

I had to go to another fucking wedding a few days ago! This time it was Hailey's cousin, none of my family was in the wedding party, and I really didn't want to go. It's not like I wanted to go to her sister's either, but I felt an obligation to the whole family to show my support, especially to Hailey and Nancy.

I knew all day that things were going to be different... worse somehow. I was right. On the way to the reception, I was sick and dizzy, staring out the window and watching the world go by in an overwhelming blur. I felt like someone who was about to be thrown into a lion's den.

I had four Xanax left in my prescription bottle and took them, greedily, all at once in the parking lot when we arrived. Hailey expressed some concern that the pills were going to "knock me on my ass," but I knew that they weren't going to phase me in that state of mind. I was right again, and the pills proved to be useless.

I tried to tell myself I was just going out to dinner... no big deal. Mind tricks, however, were not going to work for me either. I could feel myself losing it, and it was happening fast!

It felt like there was an imaginary cliff in my mind and I was being pushed backwards toward it, knowing I was about to fall off any second. It was a horrible feeling and there was no way to run and hide from it.

I vaguely remember getting my food, and hazily recall beginning to eat it, but somewhere during the course of that meal I disappeared, and became lost in the endless catacombs of my mind. It's all just warped flashbacks after that. I was there for hours, but remember only seconds.

I can see myself sitting at the table, with Chris sleeping in my lap, rocking back and forth.

I can see Hailey and her mom dancing and having a good time on the impossible-to-look-at dance floor.

The bride is talking to me at one point, but I have no idea what she's saying. The words coming out of her mouth sound like abrasive, guttural noises. Her face twists and contorts into something demon-like, and I have to look away.

In a moment of clarity, I know I need to get outside, and ask Nancy if she can help me. I couldn't find Hailey. I didn't dare look out at the maddening dance floor again, where people appeared to be devouring each other. I felt like letting out a loud scream, but swallowed it instead, along with my pride and dignity. Hey, look everybody... the freak show's about to lose it again.

The fresh air felt good when I got outside, but the Earth tilted and I had trouble balancing myself on it. I was mentally and emotionally exhausted. I didn't go back in, but just stood on the sidewalk waiting impatiently for the world to make sense again. I might be waiting for that forever.

When Hailey finally came out to leave, she seemed different to me. She's usually so unshakable when it comes to my many drawbacks, but there appeared to be a chink in her armor. I certainly don't hold it against her, and I know I could never ask for a better support system. It did catch me off guard though, and I struggled between desperately needing her after the night I had, and knowing that she desperately needed a break from me.

I can only imagine that she might have been going through a similar struggle in her own tired mind. Knowing she needed a distraction for the benefit of her own sanity, but feeling guilty for having fun instead of catering to her psycho boyfriend. I say good for her! I survived, and she needed it.

We had a quiet ride home, and I think neither one of us knew what to say. As we lay in bed that night, she started crying. It was stupid of me to ask her what was wrong, and her response proved it... "Do you really have to ask?"

I could feel the rise of another panic attack, brought on by the incredible guilt I was feeling. I knew right then that neither one of us would be able to comfort the other, so I gave up for the night and went to lay on the couch in the living room and watch a movie.

I fell asleep and had an extremely vivid dream...

I was in my basement, sitting at my desk, with a dirty razor blade in my hands. I wanted to cut myself with it, and my mother's ghost was standing at the foot of the stairs crying, and watching me. Even in the dream I knew she wasn't real and would disappear once I started bleeding, so I ignored her and carved the letter L into the inside of my left calf.

Normally I try to be sterile when I cut myself, but this wasn't real, so it didn't matter. I etched the letter O into my leg. It was much deeper than I usually cut and was bleeding quite a bit, but that didn't matter either and I couldn't feel anything anyway. Drops of blood were collecting on the floor as I sliced an S into my skin.

I took a second to glance at the stairway to make sure my phantom mother had vanished. Of course she had, and I finished with the letter T. Writing actual words on myself has never been something I've done, but everything seemed different to me. I felt lost all night, and my sub-conscience was telling the tale in gaping wounds. I feel lost most of the time and in my dreaming mind, I decided to express that on my flesh.

It all felt so real...

It was!

The mother-fucking dream was real. I woke up the next morning with a bloodstained leg and the word "LOST" spelled out in deep, open gashes. I felt the most nauseating mixture of pure confusion, terror, and disbelief I've ever felt in my life. I kept telling myself, "this can't be happening," but the evidence is undeniable, and will be with me for the rest of my life.

I cut myself again the next day. I was feeling depressed and down on myself. Hailey went to dinner at her mom's house and I decided to stay home. I was in a fugue state, close enough to being mentally present to be aware of what I was doing, but too far away to do anything about it. I must have started a trend the night before, with the word thing.

Using the same dirty razor, I cut another word into my leg. I'm a broken man, and beneath the word LOST, I spelled it out with my blade... BROKEN. I've become so scared of myself. I've been having visions of cutting my left pinkie finger off with a meat cleaver, and I'm starting to wonder if there are any limits to the pain, I'll inflict upon myself. Perhaps I need to do something extreme like that to get some real assistance. I can't help but feel like my medication and therapy sessions are a joke. I'm getting nowhere fast.

I feel more insane than ever, having blacked out and done that kind of damage to myself. I fear the possibility that these events could escalate. In a dream-like trance, I could open a vein or slit my own throat. My family would hate me for my suicide. My image, tainted in their hearts forever, but it wouldn't be my fault! I think my death may be inevitable at this point.

I hadn't left my house since the wedding; I've been far too depressed and symptomatic. This morning I wanted to perform a couple simple tasks. I promised Hailey I would bring Amy to school, I wanted to go to the post office to mail a package, and I wanted to get myself a coffee. Simple errands, and yet I got dressed as if the end of the world had arrived.

I cried hysterically, and wanted to wake Hailey up, but I just couldn't bring myself to disturb her. I smoked a cigarette, and when I was done I grinded its burning, orange head into my leg. The same leg I'd been torturing all weekend. I focused on the pain from the burn, and it bought me some time to go out into the world and do what I needed to do.

I hadn't smoked weed in a couple of days, and that was clearly not working out for me. Hailey got some for me this afternoon, and I was pathetically happy about that. I'm stoned as I write this and it feels so surreal to look back on the last couple of days. Looking at my leg, you'd think a madman held me captive in a basement somewhere and tortured me. I guess that's at least partially true, but what do you expect... I'm LOST and BROKEN.

I'm not sleeping, and the lonely nights are killing me with their unnatural length. Voices in my head recite the reasons I shouldn't kill myself, while other voices argue that I'm only stalling. How can I sleep with the constant bickering?

I watched one of my mom's favorite horror movies the other night, An American Werewolf in London. It's an older movie, but the special effects were good for the time. I could almost feel the pain that guy was experiencing when he transformed for the first time. I remember lying on a couch thirty years ago, with my mom's arms wrapped around me, watching the same film. Her protective embrace is so distant to me now.

The monster dies at the end, and I felt the sickest sense of envy. Nobody could blame me for killing myself if I were a werewolf.

12.

A POEM

LYCANTHROPE

Vanquish my soul... the somber night
Wicked moon... such a woeful light
Shackled to this curse, I remain forever
Its undaunted clutch, I cannot sever
A lifetime ago, I was lost in the forest
Hiking the woodlands, an innocent tourist
When the sunlight left me, I was truly alone
With the darkness came howling, I was chilled to the bone
Wind whispered secrets through the cold night air
Secrets of evil, but I roamed... unaware
I was trying to escape that horrible sound
Instead, I made circles... as if I were bound
Exhausted and frightened, I leaned back on a tree
A beast's crimson eyes were examining me
It lunged at me, threatening with claws, teeth, and eyes
I was deafened, at once, by my own useless cries
Its breath in my face... its claws in my skin
It bit into my throat then it howled again
I remember falling... the earth hit my back
I screamed one more time and it all faded black

When I woke the next morning, my skin stained with blood
I felt the sun on my face, as I lay in the mud
Elated to live... I just laid there and cried
Now I know better, and I wish I had died
My wounds healed in days, though the gashes were deep
While nightmares of monsters were haunting my sleep
Creatures, feasting, on flesh in the dark
Clawing, biting, and leaving their mark
Each night it got worse... 'till the month passed me by
When the full moon exposed my flesh as a lie
Heart wrenching pain knocked me down to the ground
My screams turned to howls, an unnatural sound
My bones all felt broken, my skin started to burn
I writhed on the floor... I felt my blood churn
Coarse strands of fur stretched my pours open wide
As a deep-seeded evil was rising inside
My fingertips bled, as claws took their place
My jawbone shattered... distended my face
Blood filled my mouth, with the arrival of fangs
My stomach was plagued with ravenous pangs
My backbone exploded... extended its length
Beneath all the pain, I felt ominous strength
No longer a man, I was replaced by a beast
I searched for an exit, I longed for a feast
I crashed through my window, my reflection a blur
Revealing to me, a black streak of fur
Embraced by the darkness, I hunted the night
My senses enhanced, my jaws poised to bite
One by one, I found victims to rip at and kill
They screamed and they bled 'till death made them still
Scenes of destruction were left in my path
As all who beheld me suffered my wrath
Innocent people were nothing but prey

And I gorged until nighttime surrendered to day
Month after month, the curse tightened its grip
As soul crushing guilt made my sanity slip
The ghosts of my victims screamed in my head
A constant reminder of the blood that I shed
Gnashing my teeth, and soaking my tongue
In the blood of the people, I made die too young
My monstrous memories... destroying my soul
Where my heart used to be is an empty, black hole
The creature controls me... I can take it no longer
I'm fading away while the demon grows stronger
I used to just change by the light of full moon
Now I change when I'm hungry, the time's coming soon
I've ceased to exist... it's gone on too long
I'm now just a mask for the werewolf to don
Why was this fate bestowed upon me
I have only one way I can set myself free
I've gathered my silver, and I've fashioned a bullet
My finger, grips trigger... I cry as I pull it
I vow, never again will I go on the prowl
Then the gunshot silenced my tormented howl

PART TWO
TREADING WATER

13.

HE-MAN, BRUCE LEE, AND HULK HOGAN

Various types of physical training have been a huge part of my life since I was a little kid. Much like my ability to learn quickly on an academic level, I've always had a knack for learning how to manipulate my body to do whatever I wanted it to do. My original motivation had a lot to do with my father and the intense environment where I grew up.

I've been clear about the fear I felt towards my dad when I was a child, and the threat of violence that I always expected to rear its ugly head. I suffered from great anxiety going through elementary school, worried that my dad would hurt or kill my mom while I was away. I tried to remain unseen at home to avoid his attention, and the possible abuse I was always waiting for.

My older sister was constantly picking on me and pushing me around... at least until I got a little older and was able to defend myself. Michelle loved to hurt her little brother and make him cry, either by administering physical punishment or with harsh words. My dad and my big sister, both seemed to get a kick out of making me shed tears, and the two of them together could be relentless.

When my mom was around, she cast an aura of protection around me, shielding me from the abuse I would suffer from my other family members. If she was there, she always found a way to defuse potentially explosive situations. I don't know what I would have done without her. I always felt like my mom would take a bullet for me, and I'm sure I'm right about that.

I was an extremely sensitive little boy who cried on a regular basis. I was soft, and I knew my mom worried about my ability to take care of myself during the times when she wasn't present. I felt like she had enough on her plate, and I should find a way to take some of that stress away from her. I had to somehow make myself stronger and grow into the kind of man who would always be able to protect not only himself, but his loved ones as well. I was afraid of everybody, and I wanted to be able to defend myself as well as my mom.

A line of toys came out when I was young, *He-Man and the Masters of the Universe*. The He-man action figure was like nothing I'd ever seen before. He was a man who had muscles on top of muscles, a big sword, and a desire to snuff out the evil forces in the universe. I wanted to be him! If I grew up to be like He-Man, I could laugh at my father's threats. Humble him, instead of trembling in his presence. If I was like He-Man, my mom and I would always be safe.

Eventually a cartoon came out to represent the toy line, breathing life into my hero. It was an inspiration to me, and opened my eyes to the possibility that "good" could be more intimidating than "evil". I watched the show religiously, and to this day, I can recite the opening sequence word for word.

My love for this new hero, and my desire to become just like him someday, lead me to have a conversation with my mom that quickly turned into a conversation about bodybuilding. She told me about a guy she'd heard of named Arnold Schwarzenegger. My mom blew my mind, telling me that there were really people out there as strong as my cartoon idol.

I had to see it for myself, and begged her to buy me one of the "weightlifting magazines" that she told me about. Of course, she did, and introduced me to a world that changed my life forever. The people in the magazine really did look like my action figures, with bulging biceps, and tree trunk legs. I hung pictures of Arnold and Lou Ferrigno all over my walls to inspire me.

When my dad saw the new decor, he told me I was a bigger fag than he thought, and laughed at me while he spilled beer on the floor. I was sitting on my bed, wearing my Batman pajamas. I imagined Lou Ferrigno coming out of a poster and throwing my dad through a wall. I'd seen him do that kind of thing on the *Incredible Hulk.*

I discovered Bruce Lee around the same time I started exploring the world of bodybuilding. The feats he was capable of amazed me. He was small but muscular, and seemed indestructible. He would beat the shit out of twenty guys without even breaking a sweat. I wanted to be able to fight like him, and quickly developed an obsession with the martial arts.

I got into Chuck Norris, David Carradine, and eventually every ninja movie I could get my hands on. Hooked, I fantasized about being a real-life superhero someday. Huge and powerful like Arnold Schwarzenegger, with the fighting skills of Bruce Lee, or maybe even a ninja! I would never have to be afraid of anybody again. At six years old, I vowed to myself that I would embark on a life-long quest for my idea of physical perfection.

I found even more inspiration, while flipping through the channels on the little black and white television I had in my room. I saw the 6' 8", three hundred pound, Hulk Hogan, tearing his tank top off his massive body while he yelled into the camera about what he was going to do to his next opponent.

I had heard of him, but never paid any attention to professional wrestling until this point.

The intensity in this guy's eyes me pay attention, talking about training, saying your prayers, and eating your vitamins. He was obviously a "good guy", but he was so intimidating and almost scary with his need to destroy the next villain that dared to challenge him. I had a new hero, and a new passion, Professional Wrestling. As I grew older, I wanted to be a wrestler more than anything else and constantly dreamed of that career path, while the other kids wanted to be soccer players or rock stars.

My father represented everything I *did not* want to be when I grew up, and I was never able to look up to him as a male role model as most kids get to do with their dads. Instead, I looked to the larger than life heroes on television like He-man, Bruce lee, and Hulk Hogan to pattern my life after, and use as an example of how to behave like a man.

My mom and I were shopping once, in the local department store. Feeling generous, she gestured toward the toy department and told me I could pick out whatever I wanted, as long as it was less than ten dollars. In this store, the toy department was right next to sporting goods, and as I went to browse, a set of small dumbbells caught my eye. I wanted them, and decided to forget the toys so I could get started on building my muscles.

When I found my mom elsewhere in the store, I had already started to struggle carrying the six-pound box, and my mom started laughing when she saw me.

"What have you got, Nathan?" She asked me. Her amusement wasn't mean-spirited like my dad's always was. In fact, it was contagious, and I remember laughing a little bit myself. I was persistent though, and explained to my mom that

I didn't want a toy. I wanted the weights instead, so I could begin my first training regimen.

Mom was feeling playful and made a deal with me. She wouldn't allow me to put the weights in her cart, because it was silly for a seven year old to start working out she said. However, if I could carry them the whole time she shopped without putting them down, she'd know I was serious and buy them for me. We had fun with my challenge. Mom took her sweet time shopping, but in the end, there was no denying me and we headed home with my new three-pound dumbbells.

Unfortunately, I didn't know what to do with them beyond lying on my couch and pressing them up and down. It became routine for me to lay there and do hundreds of repetitions like that every morning before school. My mom showed me a couple of different exercises... most likely things she saw on an aerobics show. It wasn't good enough. I wanted to learn how to train my body like the professionals in the magazines. I began studying the various training tips and articles.

The next time we were in a bookstore I asked my mom to buy me a big, black book that I saw on the shelf, *The Weider System of Bodybuilding*. This book would become like a bible to me over the next several years. I read it from cover to cover, but at my young age, probably understood less than half of it. The vocabulary was beyond me, but I persisted and read that book many times, always improving my understanding.

After a while my mom stopped thinking my desire to get into shape was a cute little phase I was going through, and she became impressed with my relentless pursuit of my new interests. I would hear her telling anybody who would listen about how strong and tough her little boy was getting.

When my eighth birthday was on the horizon, I wanted more weights, so I could add to my meager training program. Mom was happy to oblige, and I was happy to unwrap my twenty-five pound, junior barbell set. From that point on, I spent a huge amount of my time training in my basement with a growing collection of weights.

While the other kids were playing for their little league teams, I was in that cellar pressing, curling, rowing, and squatting my barbell and dumbbells. I started to acquire other things too... jump ropes, punching bags, and different devices to squeeze for improving your grip strength. Occasionally my dad would interrupt my training and force me into a game of "mercy". Staring me down, he would crush my fingers and my spirit, until I would cry and run away.

"I thought you were a tough guy now?" He'd yell after me... "Still look like a pussy to me!"

Even though my father humiliated me, and degraded me every chance he got, I never let him deter me. I continued my obsession over the years, surviving until he was out of the picture.

When Steve moved in with us shortly after the divorce, he brought me his neglected workout bench to add to the gym I'd created in our basement. One of the few things he did that made me happy. It was my first bench and I was excited to be able to add to the exercises I could do.

Throughout my youth, my discipline remained impressive, and I had the full support of my mom. In my Easter basket would be things like workout gloves, martial arts magazines, and vitamins because I didn't like eating candy anymore. By the time, we moved out of our house, she had helped me transform our basement into my own personal gym and karate dojo. All my friends thought I was weird because I always wanted everyone to workout out with me instead of playing or indulging in activities that were more childlike.

After leaving our home, traveling, and staying in different hotels, I always wanted my mom and Steve to find places that offered a gym. I couldn't care any less about an arcade or pool as long as I could work out. They did their best to accommodate me and when there was no gym available, I would make do with sit-ups, push-ups, and running laps around the building.

In Texas, I set up another small gym in my bedroom. In Maine, I made one out of our storage unit in the apartment complex where we lived. Finally, when we moved back to Hopedale I was able to join my first real gym. I'd been dreaming about training with other bodybuilders since I got that first book years ago. At this point, my library of exercise manuals had grown substantially, and I was becoming somewhat of an expert.

I trained my ass off, and knew a lot for a fourteen-year-old kid. I quickly gained respect at my new gym, and became well liked by all the hardcore regulars. They adopted me as one of their own and I spent the next couple of years soaking up all their knowledge and experience as a supplement to my own trial and error efforts. I talked to all the personal trainers that worked there and was becoming a fountain of information on all things diet and exercise related.

When I was sixteen years old, I had sixteen-inch arms. At seventeen, they measured seventeen inches, and they had grown to eighteen inches during my eighteenth year. I read an article in a magazine about a bodybuilder that they referred to as a child prodigy because he had those exact same measurement statistics. It made me feel good to think that my personal accomplishments might be respectable to the professionals I admired. I was strong too, and could bench-press over three-hundred pounds while I was still a teenager.

My muscles made me popular in school, compensating for my introverted nature, and by the time I was in the eighth grade I was bigger and stronger than most of my classmate's dads.

Two things started to happen around that time, which would prove to follow me wherever I went for the rest of my life. First, people started to regularly seek out my advice on diet and exercise and ask me to design workouts for them. This would continue into every place I would ever work, and was my main reason for thinking that being a personal trainer would be the perfect career path for me.

The other thing I started to have to deal with on a regular basis was rumors about steroid use. Sometimes I saw it as a compliment, as if people were saying that it would be impossible to look like I did without some kind of pharmaceutical assistance. Other times, people's insistence that I had to be "cheating" could get very annoying and offensive. The truth is I've never experimented with steroids and never will. This is the main reason I never wanted to be a professional bodybuilder, in spite of how passionate and dedicated I've always been.

It's just something that I do for me. It has given me the gift of self-discipline, perseverance, and confidence. I love the daily challenge of pushing myself to the limit and beyond. I love the goal setting and the achieving of those goals in direct relation to how hard you work. I'm also addicted to the pure exhaustion, pain, and natural high you get to experience from an intense workout.

At thirty-six years old, I've been involved in the world of bodybuilding, off and on, for almost three decades. I've never competed in a show, but if I had a "bucket list" that would be on it. I'm positive it will remain something I'm involved with, to some extent, until the day I die. It's a huge part of who I am.

My martial arts training ran parallel to my pursuit of size and strength. I would watch any "karate movie" I could get my hands on, and not just for entertainment. I would study them. Even to the point where I'd watch certain fight sequences in slow motion to better understand what the action stars were doing. Then I'd spend countless hours in my basement emulating the different moves, and training methods.

After a couple years of self-instruction, when I was about nine years old, mom poked her head out the back door while I was playing with one of my friends and announced that she had just signed me up for lessons at Fred Villari's karate school. I had been begging her to find a school for me, so I was thrilled with her news. I immediately started imagining what it would be like and wondering how long it would take me to earn the much-coveted black belt.

I attended two karate schools when I was a kid, Fred Villari's and then the Iron Dragon School of Self Defense. I never did get my black belt, and I quit taking karate all together when the drama between my parents was escalating. I consistently trained and practiced on my own, however, whether I was attending a school or not.

In Texas, I had nothing to do but practice and train. I would jog the dirt roads of Azle early in the morning; do my bodybuilding workout in the afternoon, and then my martial arts training in the evening. I had started the process of becoming less than sane, for lack of a better term, and added something I called "pain tolerance conditioning" to my nightly regimen.

I would lie on my back and hold a ten-pound barbell plate over my stomach, and then continue to drop it on myself a hundred times, to simulate punches to the midsection. After that I'd sit Indian-style on the floor of my bedroom, meditate, and then punch myself in the face twenty-five times on each side. I would often end this ceremony by hitting myself in the groin, and trying to endure the pain without showing any signs of it.

Picturing a twelve-year-old kid doing that type of shit to himself is a disturbing image, I know. My mom walked in on me once, wondering what the noise was, and walked away with a worried look on her face. Later I assured her I was just training. I did have a legitimate theory that if I conditioned myself to absorb that kind of abuse on a regular basis, it would be harder to phase me in combat.

I also started collecting different types of weapons while I lived in Texas, and would practice daily in the field behind our trailer, with my staff, nunchaku, and various swords. My mom allowed me to have these things because she had gained respect for my skills, and knew I wasn't just "playing around" with dangerous items.

In Maine, we lived deep in the woods, which allowed me to live out some of my ninja fantasies. Mom made a deal with me, and gave me free license to acquire whatever weaponry I wanted as long as I didn't show them off to my friends or ever let them touch the stuff. It was wise on her part. It might have been hard to explain a blowgun or throwing star mishap to another parent.

I put a lock on the closet door in my bedroom and I agreed that I would keep my growing collection in there and only practice in the woods by myself. I thought it was cool to have a secret ninja arsenal behind the locked door. I had it all set up like a display, so when I opened it up; all the glistening blades would meet my eyes.

I had everything from grappling hooks and climbing claws, to blow guns and throwing spikes. Numerous swords and weapons made out of wood, rope, or chains. I would disappear into the woods for hours, climbing trees and making targets for my throwing weapons. I loved living in the woods and found that they provided a great training environment.

When we moved back to Hopedale and I was in the eighth grade, a Kung-Fu school opened up in the downtown area. I joined right away and made friends with the owner. I helped with all the renovations. We built and decorated the altar, put stretch racks up together, and mounted a wide array of traditional weaponry on the vast wall space.

Mark Macgill was a tiny guy with an earring and long, black hair that he wore in a ponytail. He looked exactly like the kind of guy that my father would've enjoyed picking on. It would have been a mistake though. This little man could do a standing back flip, counter almost any attack, and reduce a brick to pieces just by dropping his hand on it.

I attended classes six days a week and was always the first one there and the last one to leave. It became daily routine for me to be waiting patiently on the front step for my instructor to arrive. He eventually just gave me a key to the place, as well as a job.

I loved the atmosphere. You had to bow to the altar, as well as the teacher, whenever you entered the school. All the counting and instructions were in Chinese, and you were required to study the history of the art. I took great pride in memorizing our study-book, and being able to quote its contents whenever called upon.

We did Tai Chi, gymnastics, weapons training, and an abdominal workout that I would classify as torture. We bruised our shins, kicking cement columns, and then followed suit with our forearms. After these exercises, we had to rub a Chinese ointment called Dit Da Jow on our bruises to prevent the formation of blood clots. It was all very traditional, and I couldn't get enough.

After about six months, I trained for the one and only tournament I would ever do, the Rhode Island Karate classic. I competed in the teenage division and did well, taking third place overall. My mom was in the audience and told me how proud she was of me when I was done.

Next, I began doing something called iron palm training. It was the necessary conditioning needed to perform *Dim Mak* which translates to, *the death touch.* You develop your hands to be able to smash through boards, bricks, and even cinder blocks... an intensive ritual that carried with it an air of mystery.

You had to perform a special breathing technique designed to channel your body's energy into the palms of your hands. After a while, you could really feel them get hot and start tingling. At this point, you would begin repeatedly dropping your hands, with full momentum, onto a canvas bag filled with iron pellets. You had to perform hundreds of repetitions with each hand, three times daily, for one hundred days.

I was disciplined, but not perfect, and I never finished the training. It was difficult to do it at the right times. You're supposed to do it during the times of day when your body's energy is at its strongest. In addition, you weren't supposed to have an orgasm at all for the first one hundred days. Supposedly, it would drain vital "chi" needed for the training. In the end, I became no more than a proficient board breaker.

After a year with the school, Mark received permission to start teaching a new style... Wah Lum Tam Toy Northern Praying Mantis. A monk named Pui Chan, from the shaolin temple in China, was the grandmaster of this style. He had opened a temple in Orlando FL, while his brother, Nelson Chan, operated a private school in Natick, MA.

This was where Mark pursued his own training, and it became my honor to join him for his weekly sessions with the Grandmaster's brother. He was an impressive old man who had an aura that commanded respect. It was a privilege to watch this master demonstrate pressure point manipulation and expert swordsmanship. It was a full contact environment, which sent me home bloodied and bruised, on more than one occasion. I loved every minute of it, and learned a lot in these long, tortuous sessions,

Eventually, my physically demanding schedules lead to tendonitis, and put an early end to my martial arts career. I miss it sometimes, and might just pick up where I left off someday. At that time, however, it became too much and I put my full attention back into the gym and daydreaming about being a wrestler someday.

Almost all of my involvement in professional wrestling has been from the standpoint of a fan, or perhaps a fanatic would be more accurate. Hulk Hogan really turned me on to the spectacle, and I was the biggest "Hulkamaniac" in my neighborhood. Many of my friends liked to watch it too, but I was passionate about it. There was a magnetic attraction for me, and much like my karate movies, I studied it with intense interest.

I wasn't stupid. I got it. These guys were working together to put on a show, but there was no denying the athletic ability needed for these three hundred pound guys to do the things they did. They're able to simulate realistic looking combat while protecting each other at the same time. If you think about it, that requires more skill than *real* fighting.

They get hurt every night, but no matter how bad they suffer if things go wrong, they always finish the match. Their "show must go on" attitude is inspirational, and I've witnessed wrestlers over the years finish matches with everything from separated muscles to broken necks. There are no sidelines and no seasons. These men and women travel the world year round, entertaining the masses while putting their bodies on the line.

As I grew up, I did what came naturally... I studied it. I read everything I could get my hands on that had anything to do with my beloved non-sport. I collected magazines, posters, autographs, toys, videos, and books. I absorbed it, and for some reason felt a much stronger attraction to it than I did for any other interests. I knew that, more than anything that was what I wanted to do when I grew up. My mom was as supportive as always, helping me think of possible names and gimmicks for my future career, and making me costumes and title belts to play with.

I continued being the biggest fan I knew as the years went on. More times than not, my bedroom looked like a wrestling museum with wall-to-wall posters, framed eight by ten autographed pictures, and toys set up like displays. I idolized the superstars, and felt emotionally invested in the storylines. I cried my eyes out when the Hulkster lost his title for the first time to Andre the Giant.

In the eighth grade, I got a taste of "real wrestling". The middle school had an introductory, ten-week program, to prepare you for the team try-outs in high school the following year. I had very little interest in the legitimate version of the sport, but knew many of the pros wrestled in high school and college. I thought it would provide a good foundation for my future career as a superstar.

I showed up on the first day in a sleeveless, Brutus "the Barber" Beefcake shirt. I had a mullet with the sides of my head shaved bald and extremely long hair in the back. Some of it braided, and decorated with beads like the British Bulldog. The coaches had a good laugh at my appearance, and warned me to lay off the dropkicks and sleeper holds. I did earn their respect though, after easily performing all the drills and learning advanced moves after one or two tries.

I enjoyed the ten weeks, and felt like I'd added a new fighting style to my growing repertoire. I'm sure I would've joined the high school team, but my life ended up on a different path after the eighth grade ended.

It was during that summer that some local independent wrestlers, who worked out at my gym, took an interest in my obvious obsession. I always had some kind of crazy-ass hairdo going on. Spikes, mohawks, or designs shaved into the back of my head. My wardrobe consisted of more than twenty wrestling t-shirts and jerseys, and that's all I wore to the gym. I was also training harder than most of the adults there, and had a well-known work ethic.

I was familiar with these guys, and had seen them on a couple of WWF television shows. They'd work for the company whenever it was in town, which I thought was pretty fucking cool. They seemed to be on their way to capturing the same dream I had. I began working out with them on a regular basis. Picking their brains and reveling in their backstage stories. Eventually they invited me to check out the wrestling school where they prepared for the shows in their independent circuit.

I met the owner, and my newfound friends tossed me around the ring a little bit. I felt the most incredible sense of satisfaction being between those ropes and feeling the impact of my body against the canvas. At the end of the day, they told me I should join them in their training, but the fee would be fifteen hundred dollars. I would be licensed in three to six months, and have at least one live match... guaranteed. I went home to my mom filled with hope and excitement.

Money was tight, as mom's health was deteriorating at a more rapid pace. It just wasn't possible, and I could tell that she was genuinely broken-hearted for me. She knew that a dream of mine might be within reach or at least a step towards it, and she had no choice but to deny me. I felt bad for both of us, and was depressed about the missed opportunity for a long time afterwards.

My life took some drastic turns as I moved into adulthood, and though my dreams of being a pro wrestler seemed to flicker and fade, I always remained a loyal fan. It's my secret passion and my guilty pleasure.

In 2001, at twenty-five years old, I got one more shot to live out my dreams when the WWF introduced a new reality show called *Tough Enough.* The premise got my attention immediately, and I knew I had to go for it. They wanted you to make a three-minute audition tape, explaining and showing off why you should be a pro wrestler. Then you had to send it in with a forty-page application, a photo of yourself, and a bunch of signed waivers.

From the videos, the most promising applicants would be selected and receive an invitation to New York City to stand before a live WWF audience. From there the wannabes faced rejection until twenty-five remained, and ultimately, thirteen would appear on television. The prize for the sole survivor would be one hundred thousand dollars, and more importantly, a one-year developmental contract with the WWF.

This happened right around the time I had left my job at the beverage company. I decided to live off my 401K for a little while so I could concentrate on getting ready for a possible audition. I had an unjustified sense of confidence that I would make it to New York City.

I put together a decent video that captured a variety of my skills. I did flips, splits, and various gymnastics. I demonstrated some Kung-Fu weapons, and broke through a stack of five boards with the palm of my hand. I did a posing routine to showcase my physique, and then addressed the camera with deep sincerity. The company loved my tape and quickly called me back... I almost hung up on them!

My wife Paula and I were newlyweds at this time, and celebrating our first valentine's day as a married couple. We were having dinner and a couple glasses of wine when the phone rang. Paula answered, but then handed the phone to me. "I think it's a telemarketer... you should just hang it up." she said.

Normally that's exactly what I would've done, but since my wife suggested it, I decided to take the call instead.

"Hello?"

"Hi is this Nathan Daniels? The voice asked me.

"Yes." I responded. I was getting annoyed and preparing to explain why I didn't need whatever it was the voice was selling. They could "dial and smile" for someone else.

"Hi Nathan, this is Christina with the World Wrestling Federation. How are you this evening?"

I almost fainted.

The mother fucking World Wrestling Federation was calling to tell me that they loved my audition tape, and would be sending me an official invitation package to go to the big city as a semifinalist. Over four-thousand people sent in tapes, and less than four hundred received invitations. I was one of them, and my dream was alive and well again.

Paula started fucking with my head. One day she would act excited at the possibilities that lay before me... exhibiting false pride at my minor accomplishment, and boasting about me to friends and family. Then she'd be miserable and crying, laying a guilt trip on me for wanting to leave her behind to seek fortune and fame. Laying it on thick, she would tell me how fucked up it was for me to want to travel the world, while I had a wife at home. "You know I'll kill myself." She'd warn. "Are you going to be able to live with that?"

I couldn't keep up with her mood swings, and the guilt trips were having a seriously negative effect on my training.

This mental and emotional warfare would prove to be my downfall, and when I arrived in the big apple, I wasn't physically or mentally ready for it. I maintained an impressive physique, but my heart had grown numb and I was running on empty.

I slipped into a deep depression as my date got closer, feeling as if I had to choose between my wife and my destiny. I knew what I wanted, but I felt like if I made it into the competition, my failing home life would be too much of a distraction for me to be successful. By the time I hit the ring, I knew my heart wasn't in it enough and I just wanted to put an end to the fantasy and go home.

I was number forty-two and had to wait in a holding area at the entertainment complex, with a hundred other hopefuls for six hour, before it was my turn to go on. Someone from the production staff finally called my number and led me out to a waiting area closer to the ring. I could see and hear the crowd of over five-hundred people enjoying the auditions.

I bounced up and down, in nervous anticipation, shaking my limbs and head. Trying to wrap my mind around the fact that I was about to enter a WWF ring, speak in front of an audience on a WWF microphone, and put my fate in the hands of a panel of real live WWF superstars. It was all too much to bear. Colorful light bulbs were flashing, video cameras on cranes were floating through the air, and busy crewmembers were babbling insistently into their headsets. I started to question if I could really go through with it. I did, but my motivation and confidence were scarce and it wasn't exactly pretty.

I had planned to make an impression, so I vaulted myself over the ropes instead of climbing through them like everyone else. It was harder than it looks on TV. The ropes had more give than I thought they would, and for a split second, I thought

I was going to trip and fall flat on my face. It scared the shit out of me, but I pulled it off.

My heart was pounding as I picked the microphone up and introduced myself. I guess my entrance looked better than it felt, and a wrestler known as Tazz asked me where I went through my training. I assured him that I had no previous experience, but was hopeful for an opportunity to earn some. It got weird then, and Tazz started getting pissed off and calling me a liar. He said I clearly knew exactly how to grab the ropes and jump into the ring, and I had obviously done it many times before.

I didn't know what to say, and could feel my heart rate quicken even more as I began to feel very self-conscious. I told him about my visit to the wrestling school in my teen years, but insisted I had no formal training whatsoever. He called me a liar again, and said he was done with me, tossing his pen down on the table. That killed off any lingering hope I had left, but they kept interrogating me anyway.

I provided extensive information about my entire life in the monstrous forty-page application. For some reason, a wrestler named Al Snow picked the death of my mother as the jumping off point for my conversation with him. The personal and awkward nature of his question caught me off guard and I stammered through an unintelligible response. The verbal portion of my audition was over. I felt emotional and just wanted to go home, but it was time to get physical. I had to take my shirt off and move around the ring so they could get a look at me.

I jumped rope and performed a series of drills, which I executed with a fair amount of precision. Unfortunately, I forgot to breathe through most of it, and when I finished I was gasping for air. Tazz couldn't resist one more opportunity to make me feel like shit and proceeded to yell at me for my poor cardiovascular conditioning. To this day I have no fucking Idea what that guys problem was. I guess something about me just rubbed him the wrong way.

Once I was free to leave, I went back to my hotel room for a sleepless night of waiting. They would post the results on the door outside the audition complex the following morning. I knew there was no way in hell I was going to be on that list of twenty-five, and I was right. I headed back to Rhode Island the next day in a far different frame of mind than I had when I'd arrived. I had a t-shirt, a story to tell, and a little more resentment towards my wife as souvenirs.

Today, I have no regrets at all about my experience with *Tough Enough*. I know that there's no way I'd be able to handle the lifestyle of a professional wrestler, with all the psychological deformities that plague me. I won't be living that dream, and that's all right. I tasted it, and that memory will last a lifetime. I failed in New York, but it was a hell of an experience, and I'll remember it for the rest of my life.

Almost ten years later, with Hailey and our newborn son by my side, I found myself training with greater discipline than ever to compete on *The American Gladiators*. How could I resist... Hulk Hogan was the host! I was in the best shape of my life, and had the greatest support system. Hailey was just as excited as I was, preparing meals for me, and keeping me motivated to train. She genuinely wanted me to compete... and win!

It wasn't in the cards though. This was when my leg started going numb because of the vascular malformation I had developed from a birth defect. I had to cease and desist all of my training efforts, and it would be almost a year before I began exercising again.

I built myself back up, but mellowed out on the intensity level, feeling like I was getting too old and beat-up for sports-related reality shows. I stuck with just working out, because I enjoy doing it. I was healthy, and thinking about getting involved in some cage fighting for my next endeavor. Everything was going great until I lost control of myself this year. Now, survival is my only goal. I don't know what comes next, but I imagine that He-man, Bruce Lee, and Hulk Hogan are all very disappointed in my current state of being.

14.

JOURNAL ENTRY
(Officially Unemployed)

12 / 05 / 11

So many things have changed.
I received a certified letter in the mail from my company, letting me know my position no longer exists, and I no longer work there. Hailey has no income whatsoever right now, and the five of us are living off my temporary disability insurance. Our van needs six hundred dollars' worth of work on the front end, and we're behind on the payments, rendering us vulnerable to repossession.
We've grown used to not having cable television over the last couple of months. Our phone service was shut off; we had to start a new one, and are already behind in those payments. We're getting letters threatening to turn off our water, and our electricity is off, due to our thirteen hundred dollar debt to them.
All five of us are currently living at Hailey's mom, Lori's house. We have an air mattress that takes up the whole living room, where Hailey, Chris, and myself all sleep. There are usually some dogs and cats as well. Amy folds up half a dozen blankets and comforters for a makeshift bed on the floor, and

David takes the couch every night, its tight quarters to say the least.

In the midst of all this, I have gone off all my prescription medications. I'm currently un-medicated with the exception of my marijuana use. I've also ceased all therapy sessions and doctor's appointments. Being unemployed now, I no longer have medical insurance, and just can't afford to keep up with the cost of my treatment. That shit wasn't helping me anyway, and I seem unchanged.

As far as losing my job goes, I have mixed feelings as usual. It's not a good feeling to get a letter like that in the mail letting you know that you're services are no longer needed. It sucks to have the decision made for me, and the finality of it is a like a bad taste in my mouth. I knew it was going to happen, but I never allowed myself to think about it. I created a black hole inside my mind that swallowed my work-related thoughts. I have to admit though... It's exactly what I wanted.

That job, the building, even the people there, would all remind me of the stupidest thing I've ever done. It was the biggest mistake I ever made, the craziest I've ever felt, and one of the darkest times of my life. Of course, there's a massive sense of relief that goes along with knowing I never have to return to that landmark of self-destruction.

I don't want to be the boss anymore. I don't want to bury myself in stress, fighting for that next disappointing raise for the rest of my life. I'm so sick of always feeling like my paycheck is two steps behind my performance. I'm tired of draining myself... exhausting myself, for companies and products that I don't give a shit about, leaving me with little left over for my family.

I need to simplify. I need to rearrange my priorities, and put my focus more on being a better partner and father. I want to put in an honest day's work and be able to financially support my family, but I need to stop chasing that extra dollar an hour, and losing myself in the process. Money is not everything.

At the same time, it's killing me to think about all the training, education, and experience I've acquired over the years. All the different avenues I've explored in an effort to make myself more valuable. The seminars, certificates, and licenses... were seemingly, all for nothing. I'm banging my head in frustration at the idea of being at the bottom again. I just don't know if I'm capable of much more.

Meanwhile, living with Hailey's mom isn't as bad as I thought it would. It seems to have brought us closer as a family. To the kids, it's almost as if we're on vacation. We're all camped out together just trying to get through this tough time. We eat dinner together every night, and entertain ourselves with movies, games, and homework. The kids are loud, but well behaved, and somehow I feel relaxed and at home in this environment.

Hailey and I spend our days running errands and seeking out assistance with food and utilities. I guess we're officially white trash now. The state is going to pay to have our electricity turned back on, but we'll have to wait a few more days.

It sucks knowing that I need help taking care of my family. I'm going to experience a lapse in pay very shortly when I transition from collecting temporary disability to collecting unemployment. Christmas is sneaking up on me all too quickly too, and I am worried about how much I'll be able to do for my kids during this time of poverty.

I would have thought that I'd be incapable of handling everything that's going on, especially without any type of therapeutic support, but I feel like I've gone numb to all my problems instead. I thought I was going to get sick when I came off all my medications so abruptly, but that didn't happen either. I honestly didn't notice any difference at all when I stopped taking all those stupid pills.

In a way, I feel better. I'm not worried about getting back to a job that made me uncomfortable. I don't have to worry about pouring my heart out to different doctors and therapists to no avail. No more extensive menu of pharmaceuticals to fit into my daily routine, while I stress out about potential side effects. I'm not a fool. I know I'm still an extremely fucked up person, I just have a few less things to worry about.

I've been avoiding crowds, and staying in the van when we go out. Even though I feel good now, I'm concerned the reality of our current bleak situation is sneaking up on me. It's hiding just around the corner, waiting to blind-side me with the force of a tidal wave, and knock me into oblivion. I haven't blacked out in a while, or had any serious episodes, but I remain leery of my psyche.

I will stay stoned for now, and continue writing for therapy. I'm trying to arm myself with self-awareness, while I find weakness in the armor of my illness. I'm delving deep into my past, and it hurts, but I know I should keep going.

Exploring the relationship I had with my father was an emotional tempest, but I feel like I see a whole person now. I haven't allowed myself to feel love for him in a very long time. I had a vision of a monster, with a belt in his hand and beer on his breath, frozen in my stubborn memory. I never allowed myself to think beyond the pain he caused. Now I feel closer to him, twenty years after his death, than I ever could when he was alive. I feel like I understand him better. It's sad, but not as sad as hating him has been.

I know I have to continue my journey, and I dread what comes next. My father was not the only monster wreaking havoc on my childhood innocence... there was Michelle too.

15.

MY BIG SISTER

"Nathan! Come see this! It's really cool!" Michelle was yelling at me from the tree in the corner of our backyard. I was five years old and I always got excited when my big sister paid attention to me. I went running... "What... Shelly? What?

"Look stupid." She was pointing at something in the tree. There was a buzzing noise, and I saw something weird and grey stuck up in the branches. I took a step closer, while Michelle was stepping backwards. I didn't notice the rock in her hand.

"What is it?" I saw bees now and started to get scared.

"It's a hive, idiot!" My sister threw the rock, with precision accuracy, into the hive that dangled precariously over my head. She ran for cover, into the house... laughing like a cartoon witch.

I was screaming! The hive fell, quite disturbed, and smashed before my feet. The angry bees swarmed and stung, in a whirlwind of buzzing chaos. My arms flailed, and I spun in deformed circles. In my child's mind, I thought I was going to die. The tiny black and yellow monsters attacked my ears, mouth, and cheeks.

I saw the world in wild, spinning pictures, all filled with angry, buzzing, bees! My feet were turning and turning... the old, rickety fence... the tree... my sister's laughing face, through the screen door in the house... Finally, my mom coming to the rescue with a hose and a look of scared determination!

I was stung eleven times in my face, and sixteen more times below the neck, before gallons of harsh water sprayed my enemies away. Then I was rushing to the emergency room in shock, because I was allergic to bee stings... Michelle knew that.

It wasn't the first time I went to the hospital, compliments of the cruel hands of my big sister. A year before that, she sawed my index finger to the bone, in the sharp-toothed hinge of a folding lawn chair. I needed several stitches to repair the damage, but I don't remember the incident very well. My mom was furious, as she would tell me several times throughout my life. She saw my sister do it, from across the lawn, and she swore she saw purpose in her eyes.

For the next several years, Michelle would continue to beat and bully me. She made my life miserable with her wicked ways, and ultimately stole my innocence.

It's a sad and disturbing fact that my earliest memories of my sister, and my first sexual experiences, are one in the same. These painful memories are fragments and often attack me in the form of vivid flashbacks. It's happening now, as I write this. I can see the horrific images in my mind's eye as if I witnessed them through an out of body experience... I often wonder if I did.

Throughout my entire adult life I've been plagued by a terrible mental slideshow, playing on a continuous loop. When I'm at my worst, knee-deep in one of my vicious *Cycles*, my haunted past can be debilitating and make functioning in public close to impossible. It's hard to carry on conversations with people while your troubled mind flips through the pages of a pornographic family photo album inside your head.

151

"Are you even listening to me?" Ask annoyed people, who catch on to the fact that I'm definitely not listening to them. They can't know that I'm not present, because I can see my naked body pressed against my sister's a lifetime ago. I can feel the anguish and despair as if it's happening to me right then and there. Sometimes I can shake it off, and apologize for being rude, and sometimes I can't.

My sister did a lot of damage.

Michelle Daniels was born seven years before me, and when I came along, she hated my guts. My mom had been trying for so long to have a boy. She was jubilant when she was successful, regardless of her failing relationship with my father. They didn't get along well, and my sister stood by our dad for the most part. She exploited their fragile relationship, and liked to add fuel to any fires that would ignite.

My mom loved her, but learned not to trust her, and resented the extra problems she caused. Their relationship ranged from, not much more than cordial, to downright hostile at times. An invisible line divided our family. It felt unnatural to me, and I longed for my whole family to love me, and each other, like those lucky bastards on the *Cosby Show*. There were times when I literally begged my sister for attention. I got it sometimes, but it was never what I had in mind.

I know its normal for older siblings to torment the younger ones. The problem was there was no balance. Much like my relationship with my dad, virtually every interaction I had with my sister was a negative experience. I lost hope for my father's love early on, but I thought I could eventually win my sister over if I tried hard enough.

Michelle loved our dad's side of the family and they loved her too. She always went to visit his mom and brothers with him. I was personally uncomfortable around them, especially my uncles, and I usually avoided going unless my mom went too. It was fine with them; they didn't want to be bothered with a spoiled little mama's boy like me anyway.

I was right to be leery of my uncles, but my sister had to find out the hard way. Our uncle Randy sexually assaulted her in the shed behind our grandmother's house. This undoubtedly changed the course of her life, and in a few short years, she would pass the burden on to her six-year-old brother. She molested me for almost a year until our mom walked in on us, putting an end to my secret nightmare... or so I thought. It's probably for the best I didn't realize I would still be suffering from the abuse three decades later.

I hate my uncle for the perverse atrocity he committed against his own niece. I understand it's the reason behind what she did to me, but I also understand there's a big difference between a reason and an excuse. Nothing will ever excuse what she did to me, just like nothing will ever excuse what he did to her, and once you cross that line between being a victim and being a violator there's no going back.

I can close my eyes, and be right back in her bedroom... or the basement, as if I had a time machine fueled by the power of pain and suffering. She wanted me to be her "practice boyfriend," that's what she told me. It would be a new game for us. I didn't understand, and the more it progressed the more it felt gross and wrong.

I was torn.

I had always wanted my big sister to play with me and spend time with me, but I didn't like her games. After a while, I became increasingly difficult to coerce, and she'd bribe me by playing with my toys in exchange for doing what she wanted to do after. If that didn't work, she'd threaten to unleash our father on me, and tell him our secret.

"Dad will kill you if he finds out you're a little perv." She'd warn. "He already hates you. I'll tell him you touched me like a little pervert, and he'll kill you for sure!"

"But... it's always *you're* idea." I'd say, quietly.

"You know it doesn't matter 'cause he won't even listen to you, and if he did, he'd just think you were a liar too. Then he'll kill you twice." She had a solid argument as far as I was concerned. Mom would believe me, but it wouldn't matter. If my daddy were that mad, he'd probably end up killing her too, if she got in his way.

"Come on already! Just let me do it and get it over with!" She said impatiently.

"*o.k.*," I whispered.

I see myself sitting on a stool in front of the TV in my basement with my pants pulled down around my ankles. My sister tells me to just sit still and watch my cartoon, while she practices a new way to kiss boys. I don' t remember feeling anything, and I know I was afraid to look at what she was doing with her mouth, but I recall the strange smell of saliva-soaked skin and the funny slurping noise that terrified me.

On occasion, she would say things to me along the lines of... "Aren't you glad we're finally getting along after all this time?" Shit like that really fucked with my head. She manipulated my emotions and made me feel like I was as willing a participant as her. After a while, I was convinced I'd be in just as much trouble as she was if our secret saw the light of day. Irrational guilt, shame, and fear tortured me from the inside out.

I can see us now, writhing on the floor in the cellar together... the musty carpeting, abrasive against my skin. She's sweating and has a sour smell I don't like. She's making disgusting noises that I don't like either. Her hands are doing something, trying to get me to move the right way, but I don't understand. I'm not inside her, and she's frustrated... swearing. She says something that makes me feel stupid, so I start to cry.

Michelle gets dressed and heads for the stairs, reminding me of the trouble I'll be in if our secret gets out. I was so fucking confused! I was so fucking young! I had heard words like sex and virginity, but I didn't understand what any of it meant or how it applied to my horrible secret. I was lost in my confusion and alone in my suffering. There was no one I could talk to about it.

My sister played tortuous mind games with me. She would give me choices...

"Do you want to kiss *me* between *my* legs, or do you want me to kiss *you* between *your* legs?"

I had to choose one way or the other. She'd make me ask for it, and I get chills to this day just thinking about it. Later she'd be mean and tell me I was a dirty little pervert and she couldn't believe I asked her to do that sick shit. I started to feel like I *was* a pervert, and there *was* something wrong with me.

It became so twisted and convoluted, with her acting as if she was doing *me* a favor with these unnatural acts. I started to believe it *was* my dirty little secret! I was six fucking years old, and I spent nights lying awake in bed, trying to figure out what was wrong with *me!*

Now I can see us in her bedroom... lying in her bed. I'm dressed, but my sister is naked from the waist down, beneath her sheets. My head is in between her legs, and her hands are on the back of it, forcing my face into her. It smells bad and I can't breathe. I feel like I'm suffocating.

"Stick your tongue out, stupid!" She instructs, but I don't know what I'm doing, and the taste of her is making me want to vomit. It gets rougher, as she gets more agitated with her little brother's inexperienced cunnilingus. Her hands grip more harshly on the back of my head, and she starts grinding her pubic bone against my face... nails digging into skull! It's as if she gave up on my tongue and is trying to make do with my nose, chin, forehead, or whatever else she can violently rub against herself.

It hurts a lot, and I'm starting to fight against her but she's much stronger than I am. I'm getting more frightened and starting to wonder if you can die like this. She's smothering me, and I try to yell out for her to stop hurting me, but she selfishly bucks even harder.

That's when her bedroom door opens up, and my mom walks in.

I didn't know... I was still under the blankets and couldn't see or hear. My sister's body language changed in an instant, her hands let go of my head, and I was free. I tore the sheets off me and was ready to jump out of the bed and run for my life. Then I saw my mom standing in the doorway with her jaw on the floor and horror on her face. I went from terror, to relief, to shame in less than a second.

I didn't even have time to jump out of the bed, as my mom snatched me up and threw me across the room. She was just trying to get me away from Michelle as fast as she could, but she hurt me a little in her haste, and I was scared she was going to start hitting me.

My sister had me so fucked up that instead of feeling relieved my mom had stopped her, I was worried about being in trouble. Our mom yelled at me to go in the living room and wait for her, as she started screaming, crying, and yelling at my sister. I sat on the couch blocking my ears and crying... thinking I'd be next.

I was not in trouble. When my mom came to me with tears in her eyes, she just held me, rocked me, and told me that my sister would never touch me again. She wanted to get me out of the house, so she took me to a restaurant for lunch. I could sense how worried she was about me; she kept looking at me with such sadness. My mom was tender and loving, but I wish she got me some kind of professional help after that, even if I didn't want it.

I don't know what my sister's punishment was, and I don't remember anything about how my father reacted to the situation, but she never did touch me like that again... at least not in reality. In my broken mind, however, she still molests me every chance she gets through my foul memories and lucid flashbacks.

We had no relationship to speak of for the next several years. We just stayed out of each other's way. After our parents got divorced and Steve had moved in with us, my sister went to go live with one of her friends. She didn't want any part of our changing family, and like me, did not want any part of moving to Texas. We went our separate ways, and I only saw her sporadically from that point on.

When our parents died, Michelle moved from Georgia to Rhode Island, in hopes of rebuilding a relationship with me. I was a grown man, and had transformed myself into an intimidating presence during my teen years, but it didn't matter. Whenever I was around her, I became that scared, confused, six year old boy again.

Am I condemned to be her victim for the rest of my life?

I tried to put our sorted past behind us so we could start over as adults, but it didn't work. She wanted me to move in with her and her family, but I couldn't do it. I felt physically ill around her. The prospect of living under the same roof as Michelle was no better than staying with Steve, so I chose to be homeless and live in my dad's car on the street. I spent some time with her, but it never felt natural or healthy.

After I met Paula and moved in with her, I went more than ten years without any contact with my big sister. We both live in Rhode Island, and I have bumped into her on occasion. It's always uncomfortable. I know she wants me to forgive her, and be part of her life, but I still don't feel like I can do that.

Michelle has gone on to have six children of her own from multiple partners, bad guys, who weave in and out of her life. She supports herself and her kids by working minimum wage jobs, while collecting welfare and food stamps from the state. I know she's miserable, and I know she thinks having her brother back in her life would be helpful, but I can't oblige. I don't owe her anything, and I refuse to sacrifice my fragile mentality for the benefit of hers.

Part of me loves her... she is my sister. I feel bad for the little girl, whose own uncle assaulted her in that shed forever ago. I can relate to her struggle to be happy, and I hope she is someday. Unfortunately, I can only love her from a distance, because I hate her so much too.

To this day, I'm still trying to get beyond the abuse I had to endure at her hands. My mind is rotting soup and my early experiences with her are a key ingredient. Sometimes I feel like I forgive her, and sometimes I don't. I guess I'm still trying to figure that one out. Even if I did, I don't know if it would change anything between us today.

I can't help but wonder if she forgives our Uncle Randy for what he did to her. Has she offered him the same understanding that she craves from me? Has she been able to let it go, or does she still see it happening in the back of her mind, as part of her own mental slideshow?

I wish I had some nice things to say about her to add some balance to how I feel, but I don't. I have no fond memories of bonding with my big sister. I don't remember her ever sticking up for me or helping me out. I can't recall ever feeling like she even liked me, never mind loved me. When I think about my sister, I think about bees, being bullied, and child molestation.

16.

JOURNAL ENTRY
(Remaining Issues)

01 / 12 / 11

Our electricity is back on, and we've been home for about a month now, after spending more than two weeks at Lori's house. Regardless of the fact that negative circumstances put us in that situation, we all viewed our time there as a positive experience, and agree it brought us closer together as a family. Tough times tend to do that.

Still, I can't help but notice a feeling of distance between Hailey and I, on a romantic level. We're not connecting like we usually do. She doesn't deny it, but she's more honest about what the problem is after she has a couple drinks in her.

I cheated on her, lied to her, and hid things from her. I betrayed her trust and disrespected her with my actions. She's still pissed off, and has every right to be. After all, it's been less than six months since I came undone.

It's a tough situation for both of us. I knew it would be, and that caused me a lot of hesitation when I decided to move back into the house. I hurt her bad, and it's only natural that I should have to absorb a certain amount of punishment for that. Unfortunately, I'm so thin-skinned right now that she constantly has to bite her tongue in fear of triggering my self-destruct mode.

I'm sure this unfair situation is causing a lot of resentment to build up inside her, and I'm sure she's doing better than most would, keeping it at bay.

When she gets a little intoxicated, I get a more uncensored version of her and her feelings. Questions about the affair start pelting me like hail. Some real questions and some designed to cause pain. It gets tough, and she'll ask the same series of questions endlessly. It starts to feel like I'm being tortured, and I'm sure of two things.

One... I deserve it.

Two... I can't take it.

I hope we're able to figure this out before there's too much damage. I told her I wouldn't be able to withstand the drama that I rightfully deserved, and it could be what finally pushes me over the edge. Several times, she has promised me that she was done bringing it up. Her heart's in the right place, but it has proven to be a promise she just can't keep.

I have put her through hell, and that knowledge pokes and prods at me. This poor woman has had to find me, crouched behind the boiler in our basement, hiding and raking my arms against the bricks. Drawing blood and trying to find my way back to reality. Trying to get away from things, she couldn't see.

"I JUST WANT TO DIE!" I screamed so loud the house shook and my throat hurt for days!

I put myself in her shoes, and see myself in those situations... through her eyes, and it's ugly. I hate knowing Hailey has seen me like that, and I know how painful it must be.

I hurt the kids a little more indirectly. Children are more forgiving than adults are, so my relationships with David and

Amy are stronger than ever. Our bond has proven to be powerful, and I feel like we're closer than we've been in a while.

Amy gives me a lot of love, and she and I have a tendency to laugh our asses off, to the point that it annoys everybody around us. David is far from affectionate, but he and I are like a couple of buddies that like to bust each other's balls, and watch action movies together.

On another positive note, Hailey did find a job and I think it's going to be good for us, and take a little of the financial stress off me. It will get her out of the house, cause us to miss each other, and bring us closer again. It will also force me to do a little more around the house as far as daily chores are concerned.

I need the forced motivation right now, a reason to rise to the occasion, and do what I have to do. I'm not a lazy person by any means, but these Cycles bring such lethargy. There are times when all I want to do is lay in bed for hours, with the blanket pulled up over my head, and at those times that's exactly what I do.

I played the role of "stay at home dad" before, shortly after Chris was born. I honestly loved it. I kept myself busy with housework, taking care of my new baby boy, and studying one thing or another. I'm a firm believer that taking care of a household and children is not only a real job, but also one of the more difficult... and most rewarding.

I'm really looking forward to the one on one time with my son again, as Hailey returns to the workforce. When I'm alone with him there's not much room for my problems, and he helps me harness my focus to give him the best possible care I can. Deep down inside, I do believe I'm a good dad.

I like to imagine that I'm getting better. I like to imagine how good my life might be if I wasn't such a distraught person.

I have the best family I could possibly ask for. I know they all love me.

Now I have to learn how to love myself so I'll be able to heal, but first I have to forgive myself, and I'm not sure I can. I wish I could make myself forget how I've behaved this year, and bury the wicked memories in the soil of my mind, but I know that's not the answer. Sometimes, buried memories dig themselves free.

17.

SKELETON IN MY CLOSET

I didn't realize it at the time, but the first *Cycle* occurred when I was eighteen years old, shortly after I'd lost both of my parents. My sister was back in my life temporarily, bringing with her many painful memories. Broke and homeless, I had ceased all training activities for the first time in my life since I was seven, and had withered away to one hundred forty-nine pounds. I didn't know who I was anymore.

I missed my mom intensely, mourned lost opportunities with my dad, and was learning to hate my big sister all over again. I would stay up all night sitting in the backseat of my father's car staring out at the cold, empty streets of Providence, or I'd be working at my third shift job at the newspaper. I was suicidal and having trouble staying high enough to numb the pain.

I was supposed to work one night, but was feeling as low as I'd ever felt, and decided to blow it off. I was about to hit rock bottom. Incapable of working, and having nowhere else to go, I was just roaming the streets in a zombie-like daze. I needed to get high, but I had run out of pot again. As I walked around, I started to think about different ways I could kill myself. I started searching within, for the intestinal fortitude to carry out the task. I wanted a cigarette, but I'd run out of those to.

It was about two 'o clock in the morning and I was making my way slowly, down Main Street. I saw a middle-aged man sitting on a bench smoking, and I decided to bum a cigarette off him. I approached, and he was happy to give one up, a little too happy. We were exchanging some meaningless banter when he got a strange look on his face and laughed a little to himself.

"What's so funny?" I asked him.

"Nuttin'… I was gonna ask you if you wanted to make some money... but you're all set with that... right?" Then his expression got serious. "You *wanna* make some money?" He asked.

I immediately got the feeling I was being hustled, but I had nothing else to do and I was curious what this guy had up his sleeve. I didn't think this stranger would really have any money for me, but I thought he probably got high and there might be a chance I could get some weed out of him.

"What are you talking about?" I asked him. He was starting to look at me as if I was a big piece of candy.

"Look, I'm not gay or nuttin'... I love pussy, but once in a while, I like to suck a little dick too. Ya know?" I didn't know, and I felt a burning sickness deep in the pit of my stomach, as if hot coals inhabited it. I should have gotten the fuck out of there, but I didn't. I felt like I was slipping into the back of my mind and someone else was taking control of my actions. I felt the sensation of falling, yet my body remained standing on the street.

"You wanna let me suck your dick a little... I'll give you some money." He continued.

Feeling like a bound-and-gagged hostage in my own mind, I couldn't believe what I was hearing when I started to negotiate with the guy on the bench. I was screaming at myself, internally, to shut my fucking mouth and start moving my feet in the other direction.

"Save your money. I don't think I could do anything like that... besides I'm busy trying to get my hands on some weed right now... You don't know where I could get some at this hour do you?" I was hoping he just happened to have some on him, and would get me high out of the kindness of his heart.

"Oh, you don't think you could do some shit like that... huh? You lookin' for some weed though?" He smirked at me and I felt the urge to start beating the shit out of him.

"Yeah I can get weed right now, my roommate's got a shitload. I'll hook you up, but you gotta help me out first... It's up to you though. Maybe you can just get it somewhere else." We both knew I couldn't. I wouldn't be asking a stranger on the street, at two in the morning, if I could get it somewhere else. He kept going...

"Yo... you don't even have to do anything, but lay there. I'll take care of the rest. You get some good head, and then I'll take you to get your shit. I don't know. It sounds like a deal to me... up to you though." He was trying to act indifferent, but came off like a desperate car salesmen trying to close a deal. I told myself to walk away again, and then I ignored myself again. I didn't trust this guy at all, and started picturing different scenarios at high speed.

I figured there was about a one percent chance that this guy would come through with the grass, but I was desperate enough to be attracted to a one percent chance. I asked him where we would do it, hardly able to hear my own words with the all the screaming going on inside me.

"I know a good spot, not far... in the woods, by the train tracks. You changin' your mind?" He asked, practically frothing at the mouth.

So this strange guy, who I just met in downtown Providence in the middle of the night, wants to take me somewhere in the woods to give me a blowjob. Afterward... maybe, I would get some weed to smoke for my troubles. I started picturing more scenarios in my head.

Maybe when we get into the woods this guy pulls out a knife or gun to mug, rape, or kill me. Maybe he leads me out to the tracks where some of his buddies are waiting to sabotage me, and they *all* proceed to mug, rape, or kill me. Perhaps he was a psychopath, and wanted to lure me into dark solitude, to skin me alive and make a new lampshade out of me!

"I'll get the weed right away?" I asked him. My very soul was wailing like a banshee inside me, trying in vain to stop the whirling madness. A voice in my head pleaded with me to stop. I told it to shut the fuck up! I reminded myself that I wanted to die anyway, and that I truly had nothing left to lose, with the exception of my pathetic life. If this cocksucker wanted to take it... he could fucking have it. I figured it would save me the trouble of doing it myself. A strange calm washed over me as I felt myself accept the possibility I was about to die.

He assured me I would get what I wanted, if he got what he wanted. I told him I'd try, and we started walking toward the black silhouette of trees, on the edge of the sleeping city. I let my imagination run wild some more.

I hoped he wouldn't just try to kick my ass or rape me. I'd end up taking his life instead. I couldn't handle going to prison for murder, but then again, I thought there wouldn't be any way to connect me to this person. I was a transient... a bum. I would probably get away with it, but that's not what I wanted.

As we entered the woods, I was well aware that I was willingly risking my life and flirting with disaster. I was perfectly numb to any emotions or rational thoughts. Novocain seemed to travel my veins, where blood use to flow. I was a vacant machine, programmed to die.

I was expecting the thugs I imagined lying in wait to jump me at any second. I was waiting for my new friend to show his true colors and pull out his weapon, which I would be all to ready to receive. None of my suicidal fantasies came to fruition, however. There were no surprises waiting for me, but there was a large flat rock set a few feet back from the tracks in a pocket of blackness. The guy from the bench gestured toward it.

"We can do it right here. Just lie down and relax. I'll take it out for you." He beckoned.

Disappointed I was still alive so far, I sat down on the rock. It was cold like me... unfeeling like me. I laid back on the rough, grey surface of my emotional twin, and my eyes played incredible tricks. I remember the shadows most of all. The moonlight poured them through the trees, onto the ground, and they slithered toward me in charcoal streams. They seemed alive, and interested in my activities. The shadows congregated, en masse, around the altar where I was sacrificing my dignity to the gods of anguish.

They changed shape like glands of oil in a lava lamp, and I knew my sanity was broken. Were they the lost spirits of the suicidal... gathering to welcome me into their ranks? I thought about the movie *Ghost;* how the shadows would come to life and drag the wicked souls off to hell. I gave in to the dementia, and invited their embrace.

In the real world, my "date" reached into his jacket, and I clung to the hope that he would take my life with lead or steel. Instead, he pulled out some chap stick and applied it to his hungry lips.

"Yeah... just chill and look up at the stars." He said, undoing my pants with practiced grace and putting my limp dick in his mouth. I took his advice and looked up at the stars, but I knew there was no way I was going to get a boner. It was the opposite, as if my dick wanted to invert itself and hide in my stomach. That part of my body didn't appreciate me volunteering it for this, and it remained absent, while I weaved in and out of reality.

I tried thinking about scenes from porno movies to give myself an erection, but the trees were shaking their fists at me. I tried to shut my eyes and pretend Pamela Anderson was going down on me, but the shadows were rising and falling out of the earth.

I thought about my third grade teacher, childhood friend's moms, every girl I ever had a crush on... nothing worked. I couldn't fool myself. There was a man sucking on my withering penis in the woods. I hate admitting that I even tried to get it up, but I had gone this far already, and was desperate to get my pot or die trying. Unfortunately, I became convinced that my pride was the only thing that was going to be a victim of murder.

"You nervous? You comfortable? What's up with you?" He'd stopped, and all of a sudden, the shadows were just shadows again.

"I don't know man... I told you I wasn't into this shit. I can't relax. I need to be high." Maybe he would go get my weed now in hopes of a better performance. Then I could just take it and head for the hills. Fuck him!

"I'll try a little more. Just think about your girlfriend or something." He told me as he bent back down for my flaccid prick, ignoring my comment about needing to be high.

I stared up at the stars wondering if there could really be a heaven. I was wondering if my mom might be looking down on me... ashamed. Weeping for what had become of her little boy. I closed my eyes and pictured the ghost of my father standing in those woods with me, shaking his head in disgust and calling me a fag for old times' sake.

"Yo, this aint workin' out. Maybe another time, huh." He lit a cigarette and started to walk away while I slowly fastened my pants back up in a state of shock. I walked back to where I kept my car parked, and by the time I climbed into the backseat at four o' clock in the morning, my shock had transformed itself into sharp self-loathing, disgust, and anger. I had completely lost control of myself. I'd become possessed by a powerful force, and I witnessed its destructive path from a crevice in my soul.

I had a dark and disturbing secret to keep after that night, and I vowed to myself that I would never tell anybody. I met Paula a few months after this incident, and then a few years after that I broke my vow of silence and immediately regretted it.

We were watching a movie called *The Basketball Diaries*. It was a memoir about a high school basketball player. He became heavily addicted to drugs, was losing everything, and living on the streets. There was a scene where the main character lets an old man go down on him for cash to buy drugs. I hadn't thought about my secret in years, but the scene struck a nerve and I started to weep uncontrollably in spite of myself.

Of course, Paula wanted to know why it had such a dramatic effect on me, and overcome with emotions, I decided to share that dark piece of my past with her. It was a big mistake. She called me a "pathetic prostitute" and stormed out of our apartment, somehow making me feel lower than I already did. Paula had a natural talent for proving you wrong when you thought things couldn't get worse. Again, I decided never to speak of that night, and slowly vanquished it from my thoughts all together.

The memory has resurfaced now, and instead of turning away from it in disgust, I'm embracing it. I think it can teach me something about myself, and the pattern of behavior that enslaves me. The *Cycles* punch holes in my mind, creating places for me to hide when I charter a course towards self-destruction.

When I'm at the mercy of my disease, I start making decisions that could end my life immediately, or eventually. I invite danger, and create bad situations that make recuperation nearly impossible. On a sub-conscious level, I try to make my life suck as much as I can, eradicating any chance of maintaining my will to live. I look to justify my potential suicide by collecting as many excuses for it as possible.

When I hit rock bottom *this* time, I cheated on the love of my life and damaged my whole family. This is now the most ashamed I've ever been of myself! At least when I went off into the woods with that guy in Providence, I was only risking my own well-being. Everything is different now. I can't hurt myself anymore without affecting the people I love. I'm starting to see things clearly.

18.

JOURNAL ENTRY
(Relapse at the Circus)

02 / 04 / 12

There's nothing more frustrating than having a relapse! Thinking everything's fine one day, then waking up to a change in gravity and realizing you're on the dark side of the moon again. It happened to me today, or yesterday... I don't know. It's three-thirty in the morning, and I feel confused.

It has been months since I've had a debilitating episode. I've been living in the real world with the rest of my family, and nurturing my desire to overcome my illness. I've kept quiet, and refrained from exposing myself to more stimulation than I can handle. This may have given me a false sense of security. I've spent most of my time writing feverishly, and breaking through the very doors that, I myself, sealed shut. I can't deny feeling enlightened, yet I suppose, in many ways I remain baffled by my ever-changing mind.

I haven't cut myself in several weeks, and there have been no phantom visits from my late parents' ghosts. Stores have not transformed themselves into funhouses, and the outside world in general, has not stricken me as a nightmarish landscape of brewing hostility. In other words, I've made some undeniable improvements, though I still struggle with my diet and sleep.

I wasn't ready for the circus though...

I had Hailey get a ticket for me weeks ago, in foolish haste, succumbing to the illusion that all was well. Even as the date approached I remained convinced I could handle all the sights and sounds of the Greatest Show on Earth. I actually fell asleep the night before, looking forward to the event, and imagining it through my son's eyes.

I acknowledged the fact that, months ago, I would have panicked over the twelve-thousand people that would attend. I would imagine them standing elbow-to-elbow and bumping into me... invading my personal space. I would've stressed over the ever-changing lights, the pyrotechnics, and the crowded sounds of chaos...

But, I'm better now...

That's what I thought until I woke up twenty-two hours ago. I opened my eyes and could feel the weight of the universe, pressing me into the mattress, not wanting me to get up. My mind was boiling over with noisy thoughts that made me deaf, and dizzy. I realized I could feel the embrace of the fourth Cycle, again, holding me with renewed power. Hugging me like a friend who'd been away for a while. With this, came deep despair and hopelessness. I withdrew, and remained silent in bed, until it was nearly time to leave.

I remember getting into the van's passenger seat... and then I blacked out. I don't recall the drive to the arena at all. I remember blackness, and I remember counting, with my digits reaching one hundred... repeatedly, and with hypnotic redundancy.

I see myself in the parking garage... briefly.

Then I'm waiting in line with Chris on my shoulders. Hailey's talking to me, but I don't understand what she's saying, and I jump back into the blackness.

Now I'm in my seat, and a stranger is tapping me on the shoulder and speaking to me. I don't understand him either, and waive him away, annoyed. I bury my head in between my knees and hug myself... rocking. I'm in the "airplane crash position".

I can hear elephants, and they sound like they're pissed off at me. I think, "Fuck you, elephants! Just leave me alone!" My internal shout makes my ears pop, and I'm deaf.

The building appears to be on fire, and I can feel the intensity of its heat smothering me. It looks like the people in the front row are burning, but they're cheering for more, in muffled silence. I'm distraught, and look to my family. They're applauding silently, and then disappear in a pulse of darkness.

The next time I find my way back to the world, my eyes are following the broken lines on the highway. The sky is dark, and we're heading home.

Hailey went to bed shortly after we returned, and I could tell she was sharing my immense frustration. It breaks my heart, having her tethered to my madness, and along for this ride. While she was sleeping, I cut myself, just once, to make the shadows stop moving toward me.

Fucking shadows... my most consistent imaginary friends. Writing extensively about a forgotten night spent on a rock in the woods was a reminder of the first time I saw the shadows come creeping to life. To this day, when I'm nervous, lost, and alone, I can still see them slide across the walls and floors in unnatural motion.

Are they bodiless entities that can smell my misery and sense my loss of will? Sometimes it's hard to convince myself it isn't real. On nights like this, I still wonder if lost souls are

173

waiting for me to join them. Maybe they are real. Maybe they know something I don't.

I feel desperate, like I should pray for help, but I have no gods to believe in... There is only me.

19.

ANOTHER POEM

MY SHADOW

The pills hit my stomach... the bottle, the floor
I collapse, to exhausted, to lock my front door
There's no use fighting the Sandman's tight grip
So with my weary eyes shut, into slumber, I slip
Moonlight brings shadows through the glass in the wall
They're innocent shadows... until one starts to crawl
Menacing... Slithering, its way 'cross the floor
Its shadow black hand, then locks my front door
It scales up the bedside and circles the frame
A wet, raspy sound seems to whisper my name
Its long, forked tongue flicks away at my ear
Then its serpentine eyes see my last, lonely tear
The shadow knows, why it is that I weep
Perched on my chest, it watches me sleep
It scratches me next... it has something to prove
Its claws draw my blood... but I don't even move
It bites me. Shakes me. Scratches some more
It hisses at the bottle it sees on the floor
It torments my room, from the walls to the ceiling
Enraged that my body just lies there, unfeeling

My much-needed rest fills the shadow with sorrow
It knows if I sleep there will be no tomorrow
It's desperate to rouse me from the spot where I lay
And it's relentless 'till nighttime surrenders to day
With the morning, it leaves me, with its own tears to shed
It's summoned to hell, while its body lay dead
One thing is certain... I'm hard to wake when I rest
I tried to wake me all night, as I perched on my chest

20.

BEING A SATANIST

I tend to keep my beliefs to myself. For one thing, it would be against my religion to preach my philosophies. I guarantee a Satanist will never knock on your door, or hand you a pamphlet in a parking lot in an attempt to recruit you. I also want to avoid as many pointless conversations with close-minded people, as possible. I usually just tell people I'm not religious at all... or agnostic. It would be an incredible waste of time, to get everyone who asked, "What religion are you," to see my point of view.

I'm a Satanist, and it's impossible to tell people that without them instantly picturing you in a black robe, cutting the head of a goat, and chanting to invisible monsters. Maybe, kidnapping babies in the night, and murdering beautiful virgins. There's a lot of false stigma to work against, and the reality is always confusing to people, whose only knowledge comes from horror movies and heavy metal music.

I'm not an official member of the *Church of Satan.* I don't carry the membership card in my wallet, but I do wear their symbol in the middle of my chest, in the form of a bold tattoo. It's a black pendant hanging from a chain around my neck. *The Sigil of Baphomet,* it's a goat's head in the center of an inverted pentagram, surrounded by two circles that contain five Hebrew letters.

The goat is an Egyptian symbol that represents man in his most carnal form... an animal. The pentagram itself is a multicultural occult symbol, and the Hebrew letters start at the bottom of the two circles and read counter-clockwise. They spell "Leviathan," a sea creature from Judaic mythology that even Yahweh feared.

People always fear what they don't understand, and this recognized but misunderstood symbol definitely gives them the creeps. I can relate. A religious symbol makes me feel a little squeamish too. It's a man, nailed to a giant cross through his hands and feet, and dripping blood through his thorn-shredded forehead. To me, this is a little more visually disturbing than a goat, but no one bats an eye if you wear *that* macabre image around your neck.

I discovered Satanism accidently while I was researching evil for a book I planned on writing during my early twenties. I grew up with a strong curiosity towards all things occult related, combined with a passion for both reading and writing. It's always been a dream of mine to write the type of horror fiction that my mom and I loved so much.

I had come up with a story idea about a brutal serial killer, and I wanted to make him the most evil monster possible. I read dozens of true crime books and came up with the idea of making this killer a Satanist. I had a very limited and ignorant idea of what that actually meant, so I bought the *Satanic Bible* to study, and better understand the character I was creating.

I purchased the ominous, black book and started reading it right away. I read it cover to cover, and then I read it again. The pages contained common sense and a strong belief structure that also left room for personal interpretation. It was not the religion completely void of guilt, morals, or love, that I thought it was.

There was belief in rational guilt based on your own personal standards, not false guilt forced upon you by make-believe deities. This bible didn't preach hate and destruction as I expected it to, but instead accepted that *both* hate *and* love were equally important parts of a human being's nature.

I didn't find instructions for human sacrifice. Instead, I learned that *The Church of Satan* is one of the few churches in the world that has never spilled blood in its name to satisfy the invisible being it worships. I found that to be an amazing fact, considering the immeasurable amount spilled in the name of God, Allah, and all the other mainstream favorites.

I think the biggest reality slap I got as I poured over those pages, was learning that Satanists don't believe in the devil at all. It's just symbolism. I definitely believe that both good and evil exist in the world, but not in the form of mythological gods and devils.

The way I see it, one of the biggest forms of evil in our world are all the religions that raise people to believe they're being watched, judged, and ultimately punished or rewarded by a vengeful and wrathful god. These people live their lives looking over their shoulders worrying about judgment day and feeling guilty about their own human nature. I certainly don't condemn people for their faith; in fact, I appreciate genuine conviction. I just look at things a little differently.

In the "good book," the devil plays the role of god's greatest enemy. It's only fitting that the founder of the *Church of Satan* chose him as a symbol of opposition, boldly flying in the face of the more widely accepted, god-fearing paths.

I bought myself this book with the intention of learning the secrets of pure evil. In reality, I found a name for something I'd been all along, and just didn't realize it. I'm a Satanist. There's no god or devil in my world, other than me. I'm responsible for my own actions, joy, suffering, and ultimately my life. I will judge myself, and live my life according to my own free will.

Of course, it's not lost on me, that the bible-thumpers of the world would blame my pendulous insanity on my religious choice. They would preach to me about the path of the righteous, and promise salvation if I accept Jesus into my life. God will save me... if I just let him. Sending a check to the *Seven Hundred Club* won't hurt either.

If I suspend my belief that both Satan and God are no more than fictional characters, I would still be a Satanist. It would seem so unfair for God to create us, and instill all these desires and feelings in us, then punish us for pursuing them. It would be like sending a dog to the fiery pits of hell for not being able to abstain from chasing cats and licking his balls.

The god depicted in the bible wants us to transcend our very humanity and be god-like ourselves in order to join his side in Heaven. This is such an unreasonable expectation. We are not gods, we're people, and the only things we should be worshiping are our loved ones, our own human condition, and the beauty of the world around us.

The seven deadly sins are one of my biggest problems with the bible. They're no more than perfect examples of the natural traits we share as human beings. Not only should we feel no guilt over experiencing these "sins," we should indulge in them as often as we find both, healthy and gratifying.

Gluttony is simply consuming or indulging in more than one requires for sustaining life. This is something to think about next time you go to Ruby Tuesday's and order the appetizer, the salad bar, the entre' you know damn well you're never going to finish, and the three margaritas. Being a Satanist I feel no guilt over indulging in a great feast and going home with my pants unbuttoned to enjoy another wonderful sin... sloth.

Lust is one of my favorites. Hailey and I for example, are not married, but "living in sin." We have never professed our love for each other in a gilded temple, humbled before our god. We've only had sex once that resulted in procreation, but we've had sex thousands of times for fun. Expressing our most primal, carnal desires and celebrating each other's flesh. We have a healthy, animal lust for each other that we just can't deny. We're in love, and we want to make each other feel euphoric. Do we really deserve eternal punishment because we haven't tied the knot?

I masturbate too, so I'm really fucked!

It's normal for people to be attracted to each other, and it's natural and healthy to feel lust. Consenting adults should be able to enjoy acts of mutual pleasure without fear of judgment. Why would a god create such a blissful physical experience, and then have us live in guilt and fear for enjoying it. It's just plain mean. Like preparing the most delicious treats imaginable, laying them out in a glorious display for your children to gaze upon, and them telling them they'll face punishment if they eat any.

Pride and wrath are special sins, in the sense that they expose god's great hypocrisy. In the bible, he seemed to jump on any opportunity to exercise his wrath on the human race. Be it by flood, fire, or famine. That time he murdered the first born of every living creature to prove his point was classic "wrath of god."

As far as us humans go, we're supposed to turn the other cheek to get on our creator's good side. This places the burden on us to be better and more forgiving than god himself. As a Satanist, you can rest assured I don't believe in turning the other cheek. It's nothing short of demeaning, to allow people to walk all over you, treat you poorly, or take advantage of you.

Wrath, greed, lust, sloth, pride, envy, and gluttony are nothing more than raw human nature. I embrace them all without an ounce of guilt. I'm quite simply just being what I am.

This church has its own list of sins, but it's a little more reasonable and relevant to our current society. Things like stupidity, pretentiousness, and lack of perspective are examples of what we try to avoid as we live our lives on this planet. The punishment is more reasonable to. There's no eternal damnation, just a less fulfilling life with less fulfilling relationships and experiences.

I remember studying Greek mythology in school, and we all got a kick out of how ignorant those primitive people must have been to believe in such things as Zeus, Hercules, Mt. Olympus, and of course the underworld, Hades. The fables and legends were so far-fetched that it was hard to accept that people really believed that shit.

Harder to believe today, is the millions of civilized people who view the bible as fact rather than fiction. I read it, and was amazed at not only the endless contradictions and hypocrisies, but also the stories that were no more believable than the mythology we made fun of in school.

Noah's Arc is one of my favorite stories. My first problem is the reason behind it. God was upset so he decided to drown the entire human race, with the exception of Noah, his family, and two of each animal. I think he might have over-reacted a little. My next problem with this tale is the boat itself.

The story has this boat at sea, for forty days and forty nights. I can't even fathom the enormity of a vessel capable of housing that many living things. Not to mention, enough storage space to hold the wide variety of foods that would be necessary to keep all those creatures alive for such a length of time. One man, using the most primitive of tools, built this boat. It must have been a more remarkable sight than the Titanic itself.

The Noah's Arc story also leads to one of the many instances of incestuous sex in the bible, as Noah and his family must begin to repopulate the Earth when the great flood finally ends. Incest is an unholy act, as is made clear in the scriptures, yet it rears its ugly head time and time again.

I have some problems with Adam and Eve too... god's original children. Adam, created from the dust of the Earth, and then from his rib bone came Eve, for him to frolic with in the Garden of Eden. God being God puts a beautiful apple tree in the garden bearing the ripest, most delicious fruit you could behold... then forbids them to eat from it.

This is where you really have to be open-minded, because there's a talking snake in this part. The serpent convinces Eve to go against her creator and eat the forbidden fruit. Next thing you know God strips them of their innocence and casts them out of Eden. Thanks Eve, now babies have to go to Hell unless we sprinkle magic water on their foreheads, or dip them in the local pond.

Adam and Eve is also another troublesome story of incest. Allegedly, they were the first man and woman on the planet and were ultimately responsible for all forthcoming life. I find it difficult to accept that two people could ever successfully populate a planet. Wouldn't the offspring of this busy family be grossly mutated, and lack the ability to sustain new generations?

Doesn't it just seem more plausible that there was a slow evolution over the entire planet, where prehistoric ape-like creatures evolved into Cro-Magnon man, Neanderthal man, and eventually modern man? Is there not evidence of this very evolution to fly in the face of the Adam and Eve story?

My personal opinion is that it's all nonsense. Man created God, not the other way around, and the devil is just another character in this work of fiction. In the bible, Satan was "the accuser". He questioned God's plans for the human race and challenged his criteria for the human souls he would allow into heaven. God, not one for criticism banished Satan from Heaven and gave him Hell to rule.

God decided to allow only the righteous and worthy souls into Heaven, and the Devil would deal with the rest. As God's accuser, he's the most fitting symbol to represent *The Church of Satan's* opposition of the evil damage done to the human soul by "God fearing" religions.

The misconceptions that surround my religion are seemingly endless, the biggest one of course, being that Satanists worship the devil. I *do not* believe in, and therefore *do not* worship the Devil... period.

Another big misconception is ritualistic animal or human sacrifice, even the kidnapping and murder of children. This is one hundred percent bullshit. A true Satanist views both animals and babies as truly innocent and majestic creatures, held in the highest regard. Satanists don't condone or celebrate things like rape or murder, but in a situation where you or someone you care about is in danger, murder for defense would be justifiable. This is the only accurate definition of a "Satanic Murder."

Unfortunately, for the church, there are complete whack jobs out there that really do believe there's a horned beast in a fiery realm somewhere, and they call themselves devil-worshippers and Satanists. They run around wreaking havoc, and committing unspeakable acts to satisfy their imaginary masters. They draw their pentagrams and wait, in vain, for magical powers. These people aren't Satanists, they're delusional, dangerous, and the world would be a better place without them.

Another fallacy is that Satanists are hateful people. This is completely inaccurate. Like anybody else, we're capable of both love *and* hate, again, completely natural human traits. Those who have earned your hatred should be aware of it. Wasting false kindness on the unworthy could weaken the true kindness you have for the deserving people in your life.

Satanists are not evil; I navigate the world with a sensible set of rules. Don't give opinions unless asked, or tell your troubles to people unless they really want to hear them. Don't harm children, make unwarranted sexual advances, or complain about anything to which you needn't subject yourself. They're not even rules, so much as, the natural instincts responsible, rationale people already have. There's nothing *evil* about any of it. Animal sacrifice is considered an abomination, and so is being disrespectful to people that have done you no wrong. It's all just common sense.

Everything I have read has led me to believe god would be a monstrous and vengeful creature. He's a hypocrite who holds us to higher standards than he does himself, a spoiled brat who demolishes the game board when things aren't going his way. He teases us, tortures us, and burdens us with irrational guilt.

People don't worship God because he's a loving entity, and the embodiment of goodness, they worship him out of fear of what will happen if they don't. How can that feel right to anybody?

I hate what people say about having blind faith. "God has a plan for all of us" or "The lord does work in mysterious ways". Can somebody please tell me how giving little kids cancer, having natural disasters wipe out entire civilizations, and creating blood thirsty serial killers like Ted Bundy and Jeffrey Dahmer sounds like a good plan.

One of the more disturbing aspects to this religion is that a person like Ted Bundy would have a better chance of making it to Heaven than I would, because there's a loophole in the system. No matter how much evil you contribute to the world, if you repent in the end and accept God into your heart, you will have forgiveness... absolution.

Now, myself on the other hand...

I'm a respectful, loving, caring, and generous person, who certainly tries to do more good than harm in this world. I'm someone who loves my family with all my heart, appreciates and respects animals, the Earth, and all its gifts. I would never hurt anyone or anything unless provoked. I've always tried to be a decent person, but... I don't believe in god, so it will be eternal hellfire for me!

I won't be alone though. All the unbaptized babies get to go to hell too. All the homosexuals will be there, the atheists, agnostics, and people who chose other imaginary beings to pray to. Even the harmless, pacifist, hippies who worship nothing more than their mother Earth will earn eternal damnation in a lake of fire for their failure to bow down to Yahweh. It seems like a flawed system considering a "Supreme Being" designed it.

I do personally believe in the human soul and the potential for an afterlife, and I've developed my own theory on what happens to us. I have no faith or certainty in it, but enjoy pondering the possibilities.

I believe that human souls vary in a wide range of strength. I like to think that when a person with a very strong soul dies, once free of physical constraints, that soul truly becomes its own god. The now free and powerful entity can create anything, or anyplace it can imagine, just as tangible as molecular structures experienced during physical life. I also like to believe our souls can connect with each other, communicate, and share the worlds we create in the afterlife. I like the idea of families reunited to enjoy each other's eternal company in infinite magical realms. It's fun to imagine.

I think souls of average strength, or those who don't understand they're dead, become what we refer to as ghosts. I most certainly believe in ghosts, and have had a firsthand experience with at least one, but that's a story for later. I think countless spirits haunt our Earth in every corner of the globe, and I believe in time, one of two things happens. They get stronger and embrace their new existence... or weaker, and simply fizzle out, ceasing to exist all together.

I predict this fate for the truly weak souls. Nothingness... you just disappear. I think those who lack conscious have truly week souls, like pedophiles, blood-lust murderers, and serial rapists. Whoever can bring unjust suffering to another human being, and feel no remorse, barely has a soul at all, and is only human by physical standards. I think when these abominations die... they truly do die.

Really, I have no fucking idea what's going to happen after I take my last breath. These things are beyond my limited comprehension. I do believe a powerful force exists, that provides a balancing factor in the universe, but I believe it's benign and pointless to worship. It's not a thinking, feeling thing concerned with the living creatures scurrying about on endless planets.

It doesn't plot, judge, punish, or reward us. It's an unseen force, existing between science and magic, and will remain a mystery to us forever. As a Satanist... that's fine with me.

There are some aspects of my religion that I have no interest in, the black magic and dramatic rituals. You practice suspending reality, and attempt to summon raw energy from the universe. I do believe that the universe is full of energy. I also believe that with lifetime dedication, study, and practice, one might be able to somehow harness and channel some of that energy to varying degrees. The Chinese refer to it as *chi*, the new-age yuppies call it visualization or *The Secret*, and Satanists call it black magic.

Whatever you want to call it, the general idea feels like it could be in the realm of possibility. I've seen Shaolin monks do things that defy explanation, and heard compelling accounts of visualization bringing desires to fruition. I just don't have enough interest to explore these things with any real dedication, and it doesn't seem like something that would work if you were half-assed about it.

I'm not a Satanist because I want magic powers, orgies, or a black-hooded robe. I'm a Satanist because I believe in many of the same things that Anton Levay did... vital existence, wisdom, kindness, *and* vengeance. I appreciate indulgence instead of abstinence, and responsibility to the responsible without concern for the undeserving. I'm not a Satanist because I had a rough life and I'm mad at god. I don't believe in one.

I'm a Satanist because I think the god depicted in the Bible, as well as the worship of such a cruel master, are ridiculous and damaging. I want to make my life on this planet as pleasurable as possible. Live it with great passion, and without irrational guilt thrust upon me for being what I am... human.

These are my personal beliefs, and I would never push them upon anybody, or believe that they are indisputable truths. I have to acknowledge the possibility that I could be wrong, and will in fact, have to bow before a vengeful god at the end of my life... so be it.

The truth is... I respect every one's need to find something to believe in. If you have that, and it provides comfort and strength throughout your life, it doesn't really matter if it's all true or not. I respect people who have strength in their beliefs, whether I agree with them or not. If my own son wanted to don the white collar, and spend his life preaching the gospel, I would honestly have no problem with it. In fact, I would look forward to having long, open-minded, debates about our different beliefs, into the early hours of the morning.

To each... his own.

I'm suffering in my life right now, but I'm not going to pray for answers or salvation. I may not have the benefit of a higher power to help me in my time of need, but I also won't have the disappointment of waiting for salvation from a god that I don't think exists. I have inspiration and knowledge from others, the love and support of my family, and my own personal strength to rely on. That should be all I ever need.

21.

JOURNAL ENTRY
(Tired Ramblings)

02 / 29 / 12

I can't fucking sleep! It's almost painful. The dull, slow, ache of insomnia has inched its way into every joint and muscle in my body. I feel heavy, far beyond my weight in pounds. I'm not just physically tired, but I'm emotionally exhausted as well. Reliving a life filled with intense relationships and experiences, on a relentless mission of self-discovery, is draining me.

I won't allow myself to think about these things anymore, until I get some rest... but sleep eludes me, and my mind wanders to irrelevant things...

When, as a species, are we going to realize that burying our dead is a bad idea? Why does everybody need a polished oak casket, with silk lining to rot inside and litter the Earth? How much space on this planet is already a vast landscape of headstones and markers?

In congested areas, they've started burying people vertically, to make more room for the next generation. I think that's a step in the wrong direction. There are over seven billion people on this Earth right now. If we bury them all, there soon won't be room for anything but corpses. Let us be ash, and scattered to the winds.

The population is out of control and we have sacrificed quality for quantity as a race. If there were less of us, our resources would be plentiful, and poverty would practically cease to exist. The problem is the wrong people having as many babies as they want. The result is a world grossly over-populated, by people who take more from our society than they contribute.

I heard something in a movie once that has stuck with me my whole life, due to the simple and obvious truth behind it. I think it was Keanu Reeves in Parenthood, who said something along the lines of... "You need a license to drive a car, you even need a license to go fishing, but any asshole can be a father." It's true.

As a people, we have such strict rules and regulations for just about everything we do, but when it comes to the creation of our future generations, we just fly by the seat of our collective pants. Now it's out of hand.

Hailey had to go through the most rigorous screening I've ever seen to become a surrogate mother, everything from physical exams, to psychological testing. It lasted almost a month before they deemed her worthy to carry a child. I believe this same careful procedure should be applicable to anybody who wants to create a new life.

Yes, I'm saying you should have to apply for the right to parent children. We lose a freedom that we've clearly abused, but we would gain so much more in return. Imagine our world with only a fraction of the people inhabiting it, and those people, raised by nurturing responsible parents. Kindness, respect, and general caring would be in abundance, and our planet's resources would be plentiful.

Why do we design and build cars capable of exceeding our speed limits? It doesn't make any sense. Our civilian vehicles have high-performance engines that can do zero to sixty, in point four seconds, and reach speeds in excess of one hundred miles per hour. If the engine was more basic and could only reach sixty-five miles per hour, it would make for cheaper more fuel-efficient automobiles. There would be a massive reduction in injuries and deaths on the road too.

In a world with such financial problems, why do we pour such massive amounts of money into our entertainment industry? I respect the work of our entertainers as well as the joy they bring us. Nevertheless, aren't our priorities a little out of whack? Does Jim Carrey really need twenty million dollars per movie to make silly faces for us? That's just one person.

I can't even begin to fathom the collective wealth of every actor, musician, pro-athlete, comedian, etc. Pro athletes in every sport make millions of dollars to play a fucking game! I think entertainment is important, and the skills and talent that provide it are truly valuable, but can't we be a little more reasonable. Should these people really make more money than our doctors, teachers, and police officers? When did our court jesters become our kings and queens?

Why is alcohol legal, while weed is not? If you compare the two substances, it doesn't make any sense. Legalizing the use of marijuana would benefit our society on levels ranging from medicinal purposes, to new job creation. If you replaced booze with pot, it would eliminate a lot of domestic abuse, and parties that end in scenes of violence.

I find it strange that our society treats pornography as taboo, but horror films are a mainstream past time. I think most reasonable folks would agree that there's nothing wrong with consenting adults having mutually enjoyable sex. I'm also sure most would agree that torture, abuse, and murder are reprehensible acts that there's no room for amongst civilized people.

It just strikes me as weird that we look down on the porn industry as if it were a shameful, tasteless, thing. Yet we collectively wait on the edge of our seats for the next installment of Saw, or Friday the Thirteenth. If it's fine to enjoy the sights of people killing each other... destruction and dismemberment, why do we blush when we admit we like to see other people fucking?

Why don't we try to reduce death and crime by eliminating the sale of firearms to the public? Hunting isn't necessary for food anymore. Only those who dedicate their lives to public safety, and complete thorough screening, should have the right to bear arms.

It's disturbing that I could go into a store, and buy an Uzi, just because I have a clean record. Nobody needs a fucking Uzi, or a Glock Nine-Millimeter, so why are these items for sale on Main Street? Who can argue that most of the people that collect these weapons are exactly the kind of people that shouldn't have them?

I can't understand why so many white people in this country, so easily forget how we came to be here in the first place. The melting pot... remember? It's supposed to be a place where everyone in the world could seek, and find freedom, without discrimination or persecution.

Did our founding fathers not want that ideal world so bad that we used and abused the natives, ultimately bullying them out of their land, to get it? Now some people have the audacity to tell others, of different races, to... "Go back where they came from!" Yet, they're not buying plane tickets back to England, Ireland, Italy, or France. It's certainly not everyone, or even the majority, but a frightening amount all the same.

I know I'm far from perfect myself, and I don't have all the answers. Who would listen to me even if I did? I'm just a crazy guy in his basement, who cuts himself, and sees things. I'm suffering from extreme sleep deprivation, and rambling like a mad man. I should shut the fuck up.

I'm getting sick of myself.

I have to try to sleep.

22.

FAILING WITH PAULA

I can honestly say that the period of time I spent with my ex-wife, Paula Greene, was one of the darkest, most mind-altering decades of my life. I was scarred when I met her, and when we parted ways my collection had grown substantially.

When I think back on this time, a very ominous feeling comes with it. I can only imagine, but I liken it to serving a long stretch in a maximum-security prison, or being on a combat tour for the military during heavy wartime. She inflicted irreversible damage, and being with her changed me. For better or worse... in the end, I guess will be up to me.

My sister brought Paula into my life. I was trying to overcome our dark childhood, and spend some time with Michelle after the loss of our parents. I had absolutely no interest in seeking out any type of romantic relationship. I was suicidal, and at the peak of the first *Cycle*. A month before, I had let a man go down on me, in hope of death or drugs. I was homeless, dirty, and unhealthy, with nothing to offer anybody... and I knew it.

Paula worked at a convenience store next door to my sister's apartment in downtown, Providence. Michelle and I went there to buy some random groceries. I mentioned to my sister, that I thought the girl that worked there was pretty. I wasn't referring to Paula, but another cashier. The initial meeting of my future-wife was the result of mistaken identity.

The next time we were hanging out, Michelle went to that store and noticed Paula behind the counter. She told her that I thought she was cute, and invited her to come watch a movie with us. Even crazier than my sister initiating that contact was the fact that this girl accepted. Paula was interested, and agreed to come over after her shift. Michelle was quite proud of herself.

I was pissed!

I wanted to die! I felt disgusting in every possible way, and felt completely incapable of acting *normal*. There was a box-cutter in my back pocket, and I considered slitting my wrists with it and yelling at my sister... "See what you've done!" Instead, I locked myself in her bedroom, laid down and began to cry.

I was also making the false assumption that my sister had spoken to the right girl.

I laid there for hours, not knowing what to do. I laid there until the sun went down, and I continued laying there when I heard a knock at the door and a girl's voice breeze into the apartment. My sister knocked on the bedroom door, apologized again for traumatizing me, and let me know Paula was there. I didn't get up, at least not for quite some time, far more time than a gentleman should keep a lady waiting.

When I did rise from the dead, I went directly to the bathroom to shower and try making myself somewhat presentable. Things like being suicidal, and living in a car, don't promote the best personal hygiene. I felt like I was trying to gift wrap dog shit, and I felt bad for the stranger in the living room, waiting politely to meet me. A broken man already, at eighteen years old.

When I finally entered the living room to watch the movie, I saw... the wrong girl!

I wanted to ring my sister's neck, but at the same time, I felt a strange sense of relief, and was able to let my guard down a little.

Paula wasn't ugly... or pretty, but she seemed to have a friendly, child-like easiness about her that pulled me in. It was the opposite of how I felt, and I was fascinated with what it would be like to feel like this person. She was intelligent, but silly, and had an aura of innocence that I envied.

Her hair was a coppery color, long and straight, that framed a pale complexion hosting unremarkable features. Tall and thin, she favored a wardrobe of loose-fitting clothes that kept the landscape of her body hidden. She had black jeans and a white t-shirt, beneath a thick flannel jacket. The fact that this was the wrong girl, and neither one of us was much to look at, made me able to breathe a little easier.

I was surprised at how comfortable she made me feel as we talked throughout the night. I can recall thinking how cool it was, that this twenty-year-old "real person," didn't mind giving up a night of sleep to keep company with a hardcore insomniac like me.

That first night we spent getting to know each other, Paula wore a perfect mask of sanity. So well adjusted, and untouched by life's atrocities. Something bad did happen to her, in her teen years, and she shared this with me easily. I was inspired with how she'd come to terms so well with her own personal tragedy, and I wished I could let my past go as she had clearly done.

I told her some of my experiences. Opening up a little... then a lot, about just how fucked up I really was. Paula listened attentively, un-phased by the tales of my past. There was no judgment, or disgust... just soothing reassurance that everything was going to be all right. I felt safe, somehow.

Years of pain, confusion, and despair came out through words and tears. I'd never talked about all these things with anybody before, and this girl was hanging on my every word. I remember asking her at one point, "Is this what therapy is supposed to be like?"

"Pretty much," she smiled. "Don't worry, I won't charge you, even though *I did* study psychology in college."

Paula acted as if she had her shit together for the early months of our relationship. Working hard, and then spending all her free time with me. She loved music, and even played a little guitar. Like me, she loved books, kept journals, and wrote poetry. We smoked weed together, but she only did it in moderation and had absolutely no addictions whatsoever.

She might have a drink once in a while, and an occasional cigarette, but that was it. The best part about it was that in spite of the control she appeared to have over her own life, she never judged me for my self-destructive habits, and offered nothing but understanding and support. Without planning to do it, I gradually started to pull in the reins on my own bad habits. Smoking a lot less, and resisting my urge to cut my skin.

I have to give credit where it's due. I will forever be grateful for meeting Paula Greene. I can say with the greatest confidence and certainty, that meeting her put an end to the first *Cycle*, and ultimately saved my life. The fact that the inspiration would turn out to be bullshit is irrelevant. I estimate that I would've ended my life within a matter of weeks, if I hadn't met her when I did. I will remain aware of that forever.

I wanted to spend all my time with her, and became addicted to the way I felt around her. She saw something different than I did when she looked at me, and eventually that began to change my perspective on how I viewed myself. Paula thought I was strong for enduring the things I had, so I started to feel strong. She thought I was capable of having a real life, and worthy of having it, so I started to feel capable and worthy.

I started to feel like I could depend on this woman, and in turn, wanted her to be able to depend on me. I started to have hope for more than just survival, and found myself wondering more and more if I might be able to end up with a nice life after all. I began to feel reborn, and with renewed will, started to pick up the pieces of my shattered self.

Paula and her elderly parents graciously allowed me to move into their home, where she and I had a cramped existence in her tiny bedroom. After a while, the living arrangements were beginning to get a little uncomfortable. I found myself in the midst of another dysfunctional family. I got Paula a second job working with me at the printing press, and we started what she named, *"the get out of hell fund."* We started pooling our money together with plans of moving out into our first apartment.

It was real now. I decided I wanted to live my life, standing on my own two feet, with someone else counting on me as well. Things had definitely changed. I wrestled with an abundance of self-doubt, but at the same time, I was getting stronger every day. I was taking extra shifts at work, instead of blowing them off. I even joined a gym, started working out, and eating well again. I was beginning to look and feel like a healthy version of me.

Meanwhile, Paula seemed to be changing as well. She was letting her guard down and her mask of sanity was beginning to slip. Her parents were loud, and constantly fighting. Paula started injecting herself into these situations more and more, yelling and swearing at them to the point that it started to sound abusive and mean.

Sometimes her older siblings would stop by, and it would become a three-ring-circus. There would be ridiculous arguments that collided in the air, with thick French accents and broken English. I did my best to stay out of sight, and ignore the hostility I could see in my new girlfriend.

Paula called herself a "recovering Catholic," which I thought was funny. I had a strong distaste for religion long before I discovered Satanism. I considered myself agnostic back then, and felt out of place surrounded by rosaries, crosses, and statues of the Virgin Mary. This was clearly a very old school, religious family. I was the homeless, orphaned teenager, shacking up with these people's daughter under their own roof. I had to get us both out of there, and I felt focused and healthy.

The stronger I got, the weaker Paula seemed to become. I attributed it to having outgrown her parents dwelling, and feeling an impatient need for freedom. I had already accepted the fact that I owed this girl my life, and I made it my personal mission to put her above myself, and live a life designed to make her happy. I lied to myself, and then her, that I was in love. What else could be so powerful?

I hadn't heard of co-dependency yet.

I worked my ass off to rescue my love from her prison, burying all my own demons deep within myself, where they would lay dormant for years to come. Paula pulled her weight too, and I have to say she was always an industrious person, who held her own financially. We made a good team, and it didn't take long for us to save enough money to move out on our own. All the while I noticed more and more, a darker side to the woman I thought I knew.

By the time, we moved out together, I had become painfully aware that I might have bitten off more than I could chew. I had found that Paula could be downright hostile. The only thing that changed by removing her from her parents' dwelling, was me becoming the focal point of her increasing rage. It became routine for her to fly off the handle over trivial things, and verbally attack me until I'd break down and cry.

Playing video games, I'd be laughing and trying to have fun, but she'd get so frustrated and angry. If I didn't play well, she'd swear at me, call me names, and throw her controller on the floor in childish tantrums. If the cookies we baked burned, she'd smash them on the table with her fists, and cry for two hours. Once, she accused me of turning our pet cat against her, when she decided it spent more time in my lap than hers. It wasn't rational, but it was serious.

I was convinced that Paula was sick, and I'd only just begun to scratch the surface, but it didn't matter. I was committed to do whatever I could for her, because I felt so strongly that I owed her my life. I started to think that I might be able to save her, as she'd done for me, and I would do it or die trying. It was a powerful feeling of obligation that I mistook for love.

We had some good times mixed in of course, like going to the movies and the zoo, or staying up all night playing scrabble and sharing each other's horrible poetry. We explored our sexuality, for a little while anyway.

I had very limited experience when we met, having only been with one other girl, that I dated for almost a year when I was seventeen. Paula gave me my first blowjob, and seemed so sexually free and confident in the beginning. All of that changed too... drastically.

Sexually, we couldn't have been any more opposite. I grew up in an Atheist household, with a very open attitude and dialogue when it came to sex. I was young enough when Michelle molested me, that I was able to temporarily repress the memory most of the time, and not let it affect my attitude toward sex during my adolescence.

I was comfortable with masturbation. Viewed it as completely normal, and never saw a need to deny it. I had seen my share of porno movies, and of course had my subscription to Playboy magazine at the age of twelve. I didn't think there was anything taboo about healthy sex, and it was a beautiful and pleasurable thing for adults to experience.

With the openness and freedom came a very mature and respectful outlook. I didn't become a deviant or pervert, because my mom took guilt out of the equation as I raged through puberty. Instead, I was mature, and waited until I was sure I was ready before experiencing my first time.

Paula came from a god-fearing catholic environment, where her mother was constantly telling her she was possessed by the devil. You didn't so much as speak about your body in her house. Sex was a dirty and disgusting thing, endured for pro-creation alone. Masturbation was pure evil, and a one-way ticket to hell. You shouldn't even look at your body, never mind touch it. Believe me... I'm not exaggerating.

It was to the point of abuse, both mentally and physically, as her education involving her first period was not that much better than *Carrie's'*, from Stephen King's horror novel. Personal hygiene was too embarrassing a topic for discussion. I can't blame her for having issues, but she definitely kept them hidden from me until I was secure in her web. It wasn't fair how she lured me in.

Combined with growing up thinking God was looking over her shoulder and judging her at every turn, a traumatic event transpired when she was fifteen years old. It's not my story to tell, but she was open with me about its happening, yet not the depth of the damage left in its wake. Years later, as the self-help books and dark poetry kept piling up; there was no denying she was far from letting go of her own painful past.

I understand, and have put an immense amount of time putting myself in her shoes. I'm only stating for the record the contributing factors in our failure to be on the same page... sexually. Someone who seemed so free and confident in the beginning became cold and unapproachable. Eventually Paula would admit to me that she despised sex.

I developed a complex, and an inability to initiate lovemaking with any confidence or regularity. This problem would follow me into my future relationship with Hailey, and be difficult to overcome.

Paula was reading an article in *Cosmo* one day, about masturbation. Turning to me, she asked if I ever did that. I wasn't surprised it hadn't come up before; we just didn't talk about those things. I answered honestly of course, and the reaction I got was like nothing I could have predicted. She didn't talk to me for three days. I was perverted, she said, and had serious problems. I would find rude and nasty notes after she'd go to work in the morning.

"I don't even feel comfortable living under the same roof with someone like you anymore!" She'd scream at me, hurling a plate into the wall.

I was starting to get a better understanding of exactly how fucked up this young woman was, as she fluctuated between a wild-eyed mad woman and a lost little girl. I thought if I was patient, understanding, and kind, I could help her. I had to look beyond her problems... she'd done it for me.

We started working together again, this time at the beverage company. It was way too much time together as far as I'm concerned. It's so different with Hailey. We've never worked together, but there have been times when we're with each other twenty-four hours a day and we just never get sick of it. Having been with Paula makes me able to appreciate that fact even more.

Anyway, Paula and I are living together, working together, sexually incompatible and fighting more than we're getting along. Our roles had completely reversed. I was confident and sure of myself, passionate about bodybuilding again, and getting multiple promotions and raises at work. Meanwhile, my girlfriend was falling apart, and revealing more of her inner demon. She was an expert at hiding it from the rest of the world. The dark side of Paula was all for me.

In the middle of the night, she would slither quietly out of bed, ever so careful not to disturb my sleep. Then she would lay on the floor, cold and crying, until the sound woke me up. "Paula... What's wrong?" I asked the empty spot next to me. Taking a second to realize she was on the floor. "What are you doing down there?" It was kind of creepy the way she was laying there. Then she jumped up... furious with me! Hurt by me, and deeply offended by my lack of caring!

"I don't know how to handle the fact that I can get out of this bed in the middle of the night, and you don't even realize I'm gone!" She bellowed at me, hysterically. "You obviously don't love me anymore! Our relationship's a fucking joke!" She slammed our door on the way out of the room, leaving me stunned and wide-awake at two in the morning.

These events were always so, out-of-the-blue. I was always confused, and seldom knew how to respond. Mostly I just suffered in silence, waiting for the tide to recede.

After a while, I began to think I'd found myself entwined in a never-ending pattern of co-dependency with a woman who seemed more fucked up than I did. It still didn't matter. I still felt like I owed her my life, and I felt myself harden to the task. I would never leave her, so long as I felt she needed me. It was my penance for almost giving up my own life.

I toyed with the idea that fate kept me alive to help this troubled girl. There was an overwhelming sense of obligation to save her, at any cost. At the same time, I came to accept a pair of hard-to-admit facts. One, this was absolutely not love and two... I might never be able to leave her.

I tried to be understanding, but she was impossible to understand. She seemed to pluck her complaints and misery from the thin air. I tried not to judge her, but it was difficult. We both had issues, but handled them so differently. I internalized everything, punishing myself to avoid hurting the people around me. Paula externalized her demons, and her misdirected anger put me in the position of being her emotional punching bag.

Depression was eating away at her, and her sadness was enveloping me, as she talked about suicide on a regular basis. I begged her to stop speaking of such things, explaining to her how bad it would hurt me, and reminding her that I had been through enough already. My pleas fell on deaf ears.

This woman, who supposedly loved me, would be hateful, push me away, and then beat herself up about it. I would swallow my pride and comfort her. It was an unending routine with us. She would hurt my feelings, and if I couldn't hide it, she'd cry and punish herself. I'd rock her, like a baby, assuring her that it was fine she just emotionally ripped my guts out. I had to soothe the savage beast, and over time, my own feelings became numb and eventually lost altogether.

I did my best to keep up my charade of being a happy person, unbothered by my girlfriend's constant criticisms and harsh judgments.

"How can you be happy just being a warehouse guy?" She'd say with distaste.

"Don't you feel like a loser?" … with disgust.

"I feel like I'm going nowhere with you," with great disdain.

Reality became a blur. Was I incredibly weak, staying with an evil bitch out of fear that I wouldn't survive on my own? On the other hand, maybe I was strong; refusing to abandon the woman, I loved, while she battled mental illness? There was a long period, where I honestly didn't know the truth. The mental tug o' war was loosening the threads of sanity.

Paula became an expert at reading me, and manipulating my state of mind. If I were feeling confident and healthy, she would go on the attack. When I couldn't hide my depression and pain, she'd change, becoming attentive and affectionate. If my frustration started to show, she'd talk about how she knew she couldn't live without me, and would kill herself if I left her.

"Sometimes, I feel like you're thinking about leaving me." She'd cry into her pillow. "I know I'm mean, and I don't deserve you... I'm going to end up killing myself for sure!" Then her crying would escalate into screaming until I promised that everything would be fine... lying to both of us.

My hardened sole began to crack under the pressure, and I started to feel a familiar sense of dread stirring inside me. Feeling hopeless and empty, I started cutting myself again and wondering how long I could go on. I was losing myself in the situation. I felt trapped, and betrayed. Then my past, full of painful memories, began nipping at my heels like a pack of starving wolves.

In spite of everything that was going on behind closed doors, Paula and I projected an almost perfect image of a happy couple to our friends, her family, and our co-workers. As the years kept passing us by, the people in our lives started asking questions about when we were going to get married.

I did my best to ignore this for a couple of reasons. I knew that Paula and I would never survive a lifetime together, and I simply didn't believe in the institute of marriage. The thought of it never even crossed my mind. I'm all for spending the rest of your life with one person, and I definitely believe in soul mates or at least true love. I just never felt the need for the paperwork, ceremonies, or rings. Paula felt the opposite, but hid her feelings from me until she couldn't take it anymore.

We had been together for over five years when she finally confronted me on the issue of marriage, asking me if I ever intended to marry her, or if we were just going to be "roommates" for the rest of our lives. I had already begun to plummet down the rabbit hole in my mind, was lost somewhere within myself, and felt unprepared to answer her serious questions about our future.

I told her the truth about my views on marriage, and admitted I had never planned to propose to her. I could see the devastation in her eyes, and her face contorted from impatience to rage. I did my best to recover the situation, sensing catastrophe on the horizon. The two of us appeared to be on a collision course for dual mental breakdowns. I could feel myself... slipping.

I lied to her, and promised I intended to be with her forever. I apologized for my ignorance and lack of understanding toward her need for a more conventional relationship. I begged her to let us remain as we were, and not feel the burden of everyone's desire to pressure us into what society deemed the normal next step.

I was walking a fine line between adamantly not wanting to marry this woman, and wanting to fulfill my self-assigned duty to stay with her, protecting her from herself. The situation spun out of control and I withdrew deep within myself. I was numb and worsening at a rapid pace. I could no longer give Paula what she needed.

She snapped, and broke up with me. I was a loser, and I was holding her back from all her dreams she told me. I moved into the spare bedroom in our apartment, and Paula was reborn.

Her declaration of independence seemed to breathe new life into her, and she carried herself with an air of confidence and self-assurance that was baffling to me. She had an aura of insanity around her, which made it all seem false and unnatural. It was as if she just flipped a switch in herself and decided to be a strong, independent woman all of a sudden. As usual, we were on opposite pages, as the second *Cycle* was upon me.

I was lost and alone again. It was as if the last five years of my life never happened. I was right back to being a scared kid who just lost his parents, and didn't know how to function in the real world. Terrified by how unstable I felt, I quickly realized I was back on the road to self-destruction.

I stopped working out and taking care of myself. My insomnia was at its worst, allowing me only a couple hours of sleep every other night. I was smoking more weed and cigarettes than ever, becoming completely detached from reality, and developed a strange fascination with serial killers.

For a while, all I read were true crime novels, and all I watched were movies about infamous murderers. I couldn't relate to their blood lust, and I certainly didn't admire them, but they all described a feeling of emptiness and separation from normal society that I couldn't help identify with. I felt sociopathic, and I tortured myself like Albert Fish, burying sewing needles in my body. I started to wonder if I was just as insane as the monsters I read about... minus a collection of body parts in my fridge.

I knew I needed help if I was going to have any chance of surviving the feelings that dwelled within me. For the first time in my life, I sought out therapy and medication, having no idea how long and hard the road ahead would turn out to be.

Paula was spending all her time with a guy from work named Mike. I was spending all my time trying to figure out what the fuck was wrong with me. She was condescending and nasty toward me. Flagrantly, she rubbed my nose in her new relationship with this other guy. He would even spend the night under the same roof from time to time, and I'd endure the sight of them cuddled up together in the midst of the night when I would go to the bathroom.

I knew I wasn't in love with her, but it was all so painful. I felt like I needed someone in my life, and I had no chance of making it on my own even with the therapy and medications. Paula and the turmoil that came with her had somehow become my comfort zone, and for all the wrong reasons, I started to feel like I wanted her back. I was stuck between not wanting to live *or* die, and I was afraid to be alone.

It wasn't long before Mike proved to be a real ass-hole. He told everybody at work he was screwing my ex-girlfriend, and she was an easy lay. It fucked her up bad and she was more depressed and suicidal than ever. Her paper-thin disguise of a healthy woman was tattered and torn to shreds. Now Paula desperately needed someone too, and I was there to pick up the pieces and provide a shoulder for her to cry on.

We defined co-dependency.

Of course, her actions hurt me. She replaced my company so quickly, and showed such coldness towards me in my time of need. It just didn't matter though. I was in survival mode, so I swallowed my pride like a poisonous pill and dove back into my role as Paula's savior. It wasn't a conscious choice though. I was gone for the most part; the dark part of me that didn't want to survive was dictating my actions.

I knew Paula well enough to know that it would only be a matter of time before marriage became an issue between us again. The same part of me that laid down on a cold rock in the woods, the part of me that would someday break Hailey's heart, made plans to propose to a woman that made me miserable. Paula was just another razor I used to cut myself.

I bought an engagement ring and planned to propose on New Year's Eve 2000. I was proud of the ring, spending nearly three-thousand dollars on it. It was a simple design, one karat, and I put great effort into picking it out. Weeks before the proposal, it was my nightly routine to take the ring out of its hiding place in my sock drawer, and admire it in the light. I was programming myself for marriage, as I would someday program myself for starvation.

I threatened Mike's life, causing him to quit the beverage company and flee back to California, where he came from. I tried to forget he ever existed, and pretended I forgave Paula's betrayal. When the fateful night came, I threw my disbelief in marriage out the window along with a little more of my sanity, and got down on one knee.

Imagine my dismay when I put the ring on her finger and saw disappointment. I asked her if she liked it, she shrugged and said. "I guess it's adequate." Later she would take the thing to get it appraised. I couldn't believe it! As usual, I just absorbed the pain I felt from her harsh and shallow words, and bit my tongue instead of expressing myself.

I approached my marriage with the attitude that I was settling for the lesser of two evils. I knew how hurtful my future wife could be, but I was equally confident that I was incapable of making it on my own. I had mastered the art of faking my love and happiness... living a lie. The second *Cycle* had swallowed me whole, and left a sharp-dressed mannequin in my place to stand before the justice of the piece.

The honeymoon was an uncomfortable blur, and sometime during the ride home from the resort, I started to grasp what I'd done. I'd gone crazy and done something stupid. Now I needed to deal with it. Over the course of the next year, I would battle severe depression until the stubborn grip of my own mind finally released me. Eventually I found myself feeling mentally healthy again, but stuck in an unhealthy marriage.

I felt sane, but didn't trust it. I knew I was still fragile. Nothing else would make sense. One wrong move could have me cutting myself, and gambling with my life again. I steeled my nerves to the fact that there was a long road ahead of me, and I needed to travel with great care. It would be years before I reclaimed the strength I needed.

I accepted the fate of my false love and focused on having as normal a life as possible in every other aspect. It was a daunting and impossible task, as my new wife's depression, talk of ending it all, and mistreatment of my emotions started picking away at me all over again. Paula was only getting worse, and I felt like I was living with the little girl from *The Exorcist*. After a few years, even the rest of the world was starting to see her true colors.

My wife became obsessed with making friends. She would pick someone from work, a random person from her past, or one of my friend's girlfriends. She'd start buying them little gifts and cards, to the point that it made them uncomfortable. She'd spend weeks making these unsuspecting people quilts, or writing them poems.

If a few weeks went by without her "kindness" rewarded in some way, she would write long and irrational letters. Paula would declare these innocent people unworthy of her friendship, in a variety of insulting and offensive ways. It was becoming normal for people to offer me their sincere condolences for my marriage and wish me luck.

Controlling, abusive, judgmental, and mean, Paula alienated all of our friends to the point where we had none. Even her own therapist was blind to the depth of her problems; until he had us in a joint session and she let, her true colors come out. She exploded in a fit of rage and stormed out of the office. Her doctor looked at me with genuine confusion, having never seen that side of her.

All marriages have their ups and downs, but our *downs* were way the fuck down there and our *ups* were few and far between. I didn't understand her problems, and she didn't understand mine. Toward the end, we were in couple's therapy, and hadn't had sex in over a year. Even Paula couldn't deny the fact that we were doing irreversible damage to each other.

She finally ended things, and I'll never forget the night. There was a quiet intensity in the room as Paula broke the news to me that we'd be better off without each other. I was cautiously excited like a convict at a parole hearing. I knew if she set me free, I would somehow find the strength to make it on my own. I was scared, but I was ready.

Paula was erratic and never made a decision she didn't second-guess, or end up regretting. I was scared that she would dump me, only to change her mind and reel me back in. I knew myself well enough to know I wouldn't be able to reject her neediness if she were to crumble and fall like the last time she broke up with me. I had to be careful. I felt like my fate was in her hands.

That needed to change.

By the time the night was over, she remained adamant that our marriage had ended. I made her promise me that she wouldn't change her mind, and I warned her that future mind games would find no audience with me. She stayed firm in her decision, and set me free. I took my wedding ring off that night and went to bed, where I slept better than I had in years.

We continued living together, but had separate rooms, much like our previous break-up. Paula immediately had a new boyfriend, who she had been sleeping with all along. I honestly didn't care. The fact is I loved it because it made my freedom more real. Even Paula couldn't expect me to take her back if she changed her mind under these circumstances.

While she spent all her time with her new boyfriend, I began the process of starting a new life. I quit smoking marijuana, started working out again, focused on my new job, and let off steam with nightly journal entries. I was getting better, and I was doing it on my own. I was finally going to be a healthy, happy adult.

After over a decade it was over... well, almost. I was right to be concerned with her changing her mind, because she did. Her new boyfriend turned out to be a dick, and after he dumped her, she did make a futile attempt to sink her talons back into me. I was miraculously strong though, and able to resist her efforts. I resisted her attempts at ridiculous seduction, unwarranted guilt, and empty promises of a better future... "If we could just try... one more time."

Her tears and pleas had no effect on me. I'd grown calloused from being with a ruthless manipulator for so long. My ex-wife got the picture after a while and dove headfirst into another relationship, with a guy who would turn out to be her worst replacement for me yet. He was a single father, who liked to express his temper physically.

I tried my best to be a supportive friend as we continued living together for the next eight months. That's right about the time I met Hailey, and was wondering if love might still be a possibility for me. Paula's reaction to *me* meeting somebody was complete madness, and I found it shocking even for her... She was pissed!

213

She officially ended our marriage, and was in immediate pursuit of greener pastures. I passed no judgment on her and only wished her the best with the greatest sincerity. I remained single for eight months, happy to masturbate and be free of answering to a controlling partner. We came and went as we pleased, and split our financial obligations down the middle. I never so much as batted an eye when she would go out on her dates with different guys.

Paula was in between boyfriends and lonely when I met Hailey. She responded to my going out on a first date, as if we were a happily married couple, and I just blind-sided her with news of having an affair. It was beyond ridiculous, and I knew we had little hope of even remaining friends.

When I failed to come home one night, my ex packed all my stuff into boxes and put them on the porch. When I returned the next day, she acted as if I victimized her. Her brother even changed the locks on the door. I had to move out immediately, because she wasn't going to live under the same roof with somebody as vile as me. I hadn't even slept with Hailey at that point, but there was no arguing. Paula was beyond irrational and the blatant hypocrisy of the situation was completely lost on her.

I wasn't prepared to move out, but I didn't care. I knew I'd figure something out. Moreover, I didn't like the idea of dating someone new, but going home every night to a woman who was still technically my wife. I left Paula once and for all, and in a matter of weeks was living in my first apartment by myself.

We were both damaged goods when we met. Our issues proved to be incompatible and we slowly picked each other apart over the years. I seldom think of her at this point in my life, and I have never missed her at all. This is all the evidence I need that we were never in love. We did try to help each other through some tough times, and we did have a little fun, but the overall experience was a bad one.

I will never deny that Paula saved my life when I was a lost and lonely teenager, and I'll never cease to appreciate that. I tried to return the favor and be there for her, if only as a punching bag. I tried to help her, and save her as she'd done for me, but I failed.

I haven't spoken to my ex-wife in nearly seven years, and I wouldn't have it any other way. I've recovered from many of the unhealthy relationship habits that I developed with her, but I still have issues from our time together that may never completely go away. I don't ever want to see her again, but I do hope she's happy. I hold no grudge against her for any pain she caused me.

I was a willing victim.

23.

JOURNAL ENTRY
(Suffering the Aftermath)

03 / 28 / 12

My panic attacks are rare these days. It's been over a month since I've taken a razor blade to my flesh, but I still envision it more frequently than I'd care to. I haven't hallucinated since the night of the circus, and I haven't blacked out since then either. All of these positive changes have occurred, post-treatment and medication and I recognize the undeniable signs of getting better. Still, I'm more troubled than ever.

Hailey is working a lot lately and we miss each other. It's not a sad version of missing somebody, but more like a reminder of how connected and in love, we are. It fascinates me, that beneath the weathered scars of our long relationship, our love has somehow remained so pure and sweet.

More and more she's letting go of the past and starting to show the potential for true forgiveness. I wish for this so bad! Less and less, she's mentioning the mistake I made, and I'm carefully hopeful that I'll completely regain her trust someday. I feel like Hailey and I have a chance, not only to survive, but also to flourish... yet I'm still living in fear.

I have fully embraced the fact that I won't be returning to my old job. With Hailey working and the kids in school, Chris and I are growing closer than ever, and I know I could never abandon my little boy. With that in mind, it's only logical that my suicidal tendencies have ceased to pose a threat. So why do I still feel that grave danger is lurking around every corner? Why do I still cry more mornings than I don't?

Why do I still think, I'm going to die?

These Cycles that I go through are so frightening and traumatic, I have no doubt they've collectively taken years off my life. How could it not hack away at my mortal longevity? It was so bad this time that I really thought I couldn't possibly survive. I felt those familiar demons start pushing and shoving their way into my mind again. Breaking things, like inconsiderate houseguests.

It's hard to explain, but it's almost as if I triggered a self-destruct mechanism inside of me, as if my very soul was screaming out... "I CAN'T TAKE THIS FUCKING SHIT ANYMORE!"

I snapped and uploaded a computer program inside my mind to cease and desist from any efforts to sustain my life. Now I'm scared I can't shut it off.

As my problematic symptoms leave me one by one, I can't deny the evidence that it might be too late. I'm suffering in anguish and fear that I began this process and let it go beyond the point of no return. The thought that I'm going to die and be away from my family punches a hideous hole in my chest, and this is why I still cry more mornings than I don't.

I'm a train that has de-railed itself... now suddenly, desperately, wants to be back on its tracks again.

It's 1:30 in the morning and I'm in my basement smoking a joint. I just got naked and stepped on the scale... one hundred, fifty-five pounds. I've lost sixty-five pounds of fucking muscle tissue, and I can feel it. I've been starving myself for months, and I can't seem to turn that around.

The only time I eat is when Hailey starts getting scared and makes me. I hate myself for worrying her, and I honestly want to start taking care of myself again, but I just can't fucking do it! The textures and smells of food still bother me. The act of chewing still makes me sick. It's like the people that are hypnotized into believing their cigarettes literally taste like dog shit to help them quit smoking. My subconscious hypnotized me into hating food and the act of eating it, to help me quit living.

I feel week and disgusting.

My ribs feel sharp against my skin, my clothes fall off, and I feel the strangest sensations inside my body, as if it's eating itself. I'm suffering from dehydration... drinking coffee almost exclusively. I smoke weed and cigarettes, and can feel my weary lungs fighting for air during the most mundane activities, like getting dressed for example. I'm constantly coughing, hacking, wheezing, and occasionally make a strange whistling sound when I breathe.

I still can't shake the insomnia either. It's hard to fall asleep, and when I do, it's broken and not very restful.

I'm running on empty, and I feel like I'm on borrowed time. I get virtually no exercise, and the amount of smoke that passes through my lips far outweighs any nutrients. I'm in my mid-thirties, but I feel like a ninety-year-old man. Hailey must really love me to stand by my side when there is little reason to be attracted to me. How horrible, to have to watch someone you love wither away.

I hurt myself a lot this year, and my skin tells the tale in scar tissue. Remembering some of the things I've done gives me the chills. In the beginning of this nightmare, just over a year ago, I held a ten-pound barbell plate over my foot and then I let it go. I broke my big toe and fractured its two closest companions. I've put my body through hell in a wide variety of ways.

I hate to admit it, but I'm sure, when Hailey touches me now, she's disgusted. My clavicles and shinbones are jagged beneath my scarred flesh. My hipbones give her bruises, and my face is drawn. As if my emotional issues weren't enough, I now offer the physique of the living-dead. Hailey is the definition of a strong woman.

Why did I let it get this far?

What will happen if I die?

Will I simply fade to black and exist as no more than ash, transcend to something better, or will I remain anchored to the world of the living as a restless, wandering spirit.

24.

MY OWN PERSONAL GHOST STORY

I have one of *those* stories...

The kind of story that you feel like you just have to tell, even though you know damn well, nobody's going to believe a word of it. I hear similar stories myself and don't believe them. I certainly can't expect people to receive mine any better. Still, I'll tell my tale, because... it's true.

For a while, in my early twenties, I went through a phase where I read nothing but true crime stories. I was fascinated with the behavior of serial killers, and had an idea to write a novel about a female version of these brutal murderers. Of course, as I poured over unsolved mysteries, and encyclopedias of violent crimes, I came across the story of Lizzie Borden on more than one occasion.

Lizzie Borden took an axe,
and gave her father forty whacks...
When she saw what she had done,
she gave her mother forty-one!

The creepy little nursery rhyme usually seemed to accompany the story, which I believe is one of the most intriguing unsolved murders in American history. I'm not alone, there have been several movies and books based on the crime, and the scene where it took place. The Borden house appears on countless shows dealing with ghosts and hauntings.

Living in Rhode Island, the infamous home is right in my back yard. Periodically, throughout the decades, it has been open to the public as a bed and breakfast, as well as a macabre tourist attraction.

Paula made reservations for us as a surprise for my birthday years ago. She booked the room where Lizzie Borden allegedly took her own mother's life with an axe from the tool shed. It's debatable who actually committed the heinous act, and there have certainly been enough theories, but a bloody murder definitely took place in that room. I don't scary easily, but the prospect of sleeping there and perhaps waking up to a hovering specter and a chill in the air, definitely gave me the creeps.

It was a good gift.

When we arrived, I was slightly disappointed with the appearance of the house, even though I had seen pictures of the place in books. It just doesn't look special in any way, far from ominous, just an average looking house on an average looking street.

The way they ran the place at the time was by renting out all the bedrooms, as well as the space in the attic, to overnight guests. The couple that owned the house was there during the day, giving tours and telling the story of the Borden family. They didn't live on the premises, and would retire to their real home every evening, leaving a caretaker on site to be responsible for the property.

I liked the tour, and the woman pointed out interesting facts, like most of the furnishings being genuine leftovers from the Bordens. Even the doorknobs were original... the very same that Lizzie would have touched with her, possibly, murderous hands. Fucking spooky! They even had some of the old-style outfits they wore in that time on display throughout the house.

There were typical stories about strange occurrences, since her and her husband took ownership of it. Most of them didn't directly happen to her, and I was only half listening. I was busy trying to see if I could *feel* anything within the house. I didn't. There was no strange energy. There weren't any inexplicable drafts, but I don't deny feeling uneasy on some level the entire time I was there.

Our hostess did have one personal account to share, where she explained seeing, "Some kind of weird mist," out of the corner of her eye.

I remember, very specifically, thinking..."*Whatever, lady!*"

There was just something about the way she told it, that made it seem like bullshit to me. In retrospect, she'd probably told the same story a thousand times. Even the truth would lose its luster after a while. The atmosphere was still enthralling though, and I kept an open mind.

I was into it, and welcomed the eerie vibe that was undeniably in the air. I had Paula take my picture lying in the spots where they found the mother and father's bodies. I laid on the sofa, where Mr. Borden used to read the newspaper and take naps in the afternoon. Later in the evening, I would dress up in some old maids garb, and take a knife from the kitchen. I'd sneak upstairs to the attic, and scare the shit out of the girls that were staying up there.

I should probably point out that there were thirteen other guests staying there the same night we did. Fourteen freaked-out women... and me. I couldn't resist taking advantage of the setting and scaring them a couple times after we had a few drinks and become friends for the night.

In the evening, there were sandwiches for us, we had the run of the house, and were free to explore. The caretaker stayed out of sight, and we all made ourselves as comfortable as we could in what was widely recognized as a legitimate haunted house.

We drank some wine coolers, and ate our food. Then we spread out in the living room to watch *The Lizzie Borden Story*, starring Elizabeth Montgomery. Our hosts had mentioned this was a popular way to spend the evening.

After the movie, several guests, including a coven of Wiccans, retired to their rooms for the evening. Apparently, they'd gotten whatever they came for. The group of four girls that had rented the attic, decided to take a Ouija board upstairs to play with. I thought that was a little more like it, and commended them for getting into the spirit of things.

The Wiccan ladies were all freaked out at the mention of the Ouija board, and warned the girls to not to fuck around with forces they didn't understand. I thought it was comical how they acted, and was starting to feel like I was in a cheesy horror movie.

I loved it.

I'm not a skeptic when it comes to the occult or supernatural forces that we can't understand. In spite of this, I'm always skeptical about firsthand accounts, because I just think it's such a rarity for human beings to glimpse such wonders. I was extremely skeptical that anything otherworldly would ever happen in my presence.

I look at it kind of like the lottery. I know people win. There's no denying that, but it would be hard to believe it actually happened to anyone you know, never mind yourself. If someone told me, I had the winning numbers; I would probably check them in disbelief a hundred times before I could accept it as reality. It just comes down to, having to see something for yourself, in order to believe it.

After a while, I could hear the girls screaming upstairs, and I couldn't help laughing out loud, as I walked up to the attic to see what the hell they were doing. The four of them were sitting in a circle on the floor with the Ouija board in the middle. They were in hysterics and screaming that the thing was moving by itself. They were laughing too, and with the empty bottles strewn about, I didn't take it seriously for a second.

If there's one thing that's been my consistent experience with Ouija boards throughout my life it's this... every time you get some people together using one of these stupid things, there's always some jackass, who can't resist the urge to try moving it, undetected. It doesn't work. The second you try moving that thing, everybody knows that it's you, and you're an idiot.

I didn't think twice about the giggling claim of a supernatural event taking place, but instead saw it as a great time to dress up in the maid's costume I mentioned, and scare them with a big butcher knife. After I had my fun, I decided to hang out with them for a while and watch them make fools of themselves with Milton Bradley's portal to the land of the dead. I helped myself to a beer, and sat behind their little circle, so I could figure out which one of them was the ass-hole.

From a distance, it did kind of look like it was moving of its own accord.

Bewildered, I studied that placard as it moved around the board, responding to various questions. Nobody's fingertips were even making contact with the thing! The girls' fingertips hovered *above* the device, with space in between. I could not believe my eyes! The last time I experienced such a thing was at a David Copperfield show, but this was no staged illusion. Something was going on, and yes, the hair on the back of my neck was standing up.

I had to try it for myself.

As I said before, you know the second somebody starts fucking with the thing. Nobody was. Our fingertips were following *it*, not the other way around. It did seem to be trying to communicate with us, though the spelling was always off. Sometimes all it had to offer was complete gibberish.

We asked it if Lizzie Borden's spirit was in the house...

The placard shot to the "yes" space.

We asked... where?

It spelled out something that resembled the word, "kitchen."

We asked again... Where is Lizzie Borden?

H-E-L, it responded!

I'll never forget that one. I remember feeling as if I was in over my head, and just wanting to get in my car and go home. Of course, those thoughts were fleeting and I couldn't help being a typical human animal and flirting with disaster. For a few more minutes, we interrogated... something.

A couple of times the thing went off the board and stopped working. Repeated questions got contradictory or unintelligible responses. I was starting to analyze different possibilities in my mind, as I continued to stare in awe, at something that didn't make any rational sense. The girls were becoming less entertained and more terrified. All of a sudden, they wanted that thing as far away from them as possible. It didn't matter that it didn't always make sense when it responded, because... It responded!

That was enough.

I got the evil board game away from the damsels in distress, but I wasn't done. I got my wife, and pretty much demanded she try it with me, just the two of us. What could she say; this was my birthday present after all. At one point, the thing said Lizzie was in the kitchen, so I picked that as our spot to try it out. We sat, facing each other, and made sure our fingers hardly touched the plastic as we started asking questions. It worked in the sense that it continued moving, very much on its own, but nothing at all made sense.

After a short while, it stopped working all together and any hope for a conversation with the dead was gone. Disappointed in my lost connection, I retired to my room with my unimpressed wife.

I have to admit, I didn't sleep that night, thinking my original visions of spirits floating in the dark might be a real concern. I seriously didn't want to close my eyes, because I was convinced that when I opened them, I would be face to face with something horrid and nightmarish. Instead, I laid in the dark pondering the universe and the possibility of some kind of after-life. My wife slept fine, which is a little emasculating, but it's the truth. Paula was of the opinion, there was a perfectly logical explanation… she just didn't have one.

I found her indifference very annoying. Her attitude was like the nerdy girl from the Scooby-Doo cartoons. She might as well have said, "Jinkies Scoobs, there's no such thing as *real* ghosts."

Paula experienced that crazy shit first hand, and still couldn't let herself believe it. This also contributed to my sleeplessness, because I knew I was doomed with one of *those* stories. The kind you have to tell even though you know damn well no one is going to believe a word of it.

I have a very scientific mind myself, open, but scientific. Because of this, I'm only comfortable stating one thing from this story as an undeniable fact. An inanimate object moved several times with absolutely no physical persuasion. That is a fact that will never waver in my mind.

Now, as far as *what* was moving it? Of this, I can only speculate.

Theory one...

The house's rich and infamous history, combined with everyone's fear and nervous energy, created some kind of group-telekinesis. Everybody held intense focus on the same object, with similar expectations for it, in such a perfect environment. Perhaps it *was* us moving it with our collective energy.

That could possibly explain all the gibberish, and the occasional real word slipping out, if we all happened to have the same one in mind at the same time. If this is true, or even close, it's proof of a mental capacity that we're far from understanding.

Theory two...

It was a ghost, of course... or ghosts. How could I not view that as a real possibility? Someone that used to have a body or something that never did. Maybe it was a pathetic creature, trying desperately to reach out to us, or a bored entity that just felt our energy and sought to amuse itself. Perhaps it was honest and knew things about Lizzie Borden's spiritual whereabouts, or perhaps it would tell us whatever it thought we wanted to hear, just to hold our interest.

If it was a bodiless entity driving that placard around the board, this is proof that a physical form isn't necessary to exist. It's quite possibly proof of an after-life.

Either way... this experience changed my life and gave me something to think about when suicide tempts me with its cold embrace. It tells me that death might not be the end, and I have no way of knowing exactly what I would be getting myself into. That thought frightens me and gives me pause.

Until that night at the Borden house, I *believed* in the supernatural and the existence of things beyond our current scope of understanding. Now, however... *I know*!

PART THREE
GETTING MY LIFE BACK

25.

JOURNAL ENTRY
(Establishing a Plan)

04 / 16 / 12

I've been meditating... all I can find within myself is a dumb animal!

I don't want to smoke anything, anymore. I want to feed my body well, and become healthy again. I want to get some real sleep! I want to exercise, and reclaim some of my past athleticism. Most importantly, I want to be present, in my families' life. I really want these things.

But, I'm a dumb animal.

I still smoke weed, and too many cigarettes. I'm still not eating, nearly enough. I still stay awake until the early hours of the morning. With the exception of some minor physical activity that comes from daily housework and childcare, I'm completely sedentary, and feel like shit.

This is the dull backslide of the Cycle. All the intense debilitating symptoms have fizzled out and evaporated. Now I have a boatload of bad habits, created in the storm. This is a terrible feeling. I'm still living the lifestyle of the mentally ill, even though I'm feeling more like myself every day.

This was the longest, most taxing, Cycle I've ever been through. I thought it was bad when I went through it after

Hailey betrayed me years ago, but this time was so much worse. My hurting her was much harder on my mind and heart, than when she hurt me. When I was the victim, I put myself in her shoes and was able to be understanding.

My hurting her is beyond my capacity for understanding... or sympathy and I don't want to put myself in the shoes of the psychopath I was ever again. I haven't been myself in over a year, and now that I have once again risen from the ashes, I'm finding it more difficult than ever to pick up the pieces and recover.

I don't think it would be wise for me to try making drastic changes, or give up my habits, cold turkey. I don't want to set myself up for failure and possible relapse. Still, I need to start taking steps forward. I have to replace bad habits, with good ones.

I need a plan...

I'll give myself a low, daily allowance of marijuana and cigarettes for now. I'll force myself to start eating... little by little. I'll have three meals a day for a little while, then four, and then five. I'll take my time and put my weight back on, slow and steady.

I should start taking vitamins every day too, and drinking more water. Most importantly is getting some sleep. I need to establish a routine and be able to maintain it, so I have to be realistic and think things through.

When I do gain some of my musculature back, I'll feel comfortable undergoing some type of training program. For now, I should just go for walks, which is something my family can be involved with too. Even playtime at the park with Chris can be a great workout. I need my health back. I use to be an action hero! Now, I'm just a mess.

Deep breath...

I can get it all back if I want it bad enough!

I don't want to pursue bodybuilding anymore at the intense level I have over the past decades. It's too taxing on my body and stressful on my mind. I blame my Obsessive-Compulsive Disorder, for my all or nothing approach to working out. I've always been so anal about what time my next meal is. How many calories are in it, and what they consist of. What times of day to take the plethora of different supplements I'm on, so they work at maximum efficiency, etc.

It's maddening. That combined with the physical abuse I put myself through in the gym. It always becomes an obsession, and I always burn out in five or six months, with my body demanding a break. That one or two week break I plan on, tends to become months... months where I replace my healthy choices with bad habits, and lose half of what I'd gained during my training, which can be extremely depressing.

This is the yo-yo effect, and I don't want to play anymore

I think instead of trying to get as huge as possible for no justifiable reason; I'm going to adopt a fitness lifestyle that I can maintain for the rest of my life. I've been thinking about martial arts again lately, that could be exactly what I need in my life, or something like it. I've always wanted to run a marathon, and hike the Appalachian Trail too, but I'm getting a little ahead of myself.

One step at a time, I'll apply all these positive changes to my life, and feel myself grow stronger. I have a simple plan that I know I can stick with.

Hailey has my back, as she always does. Her and I are as in love as ever. Chris is quite a motivator too.

I've been beating myself up lately about not reading to him every night. Books, and good reading habits, are important to me and I want to pass that on to my son. This is something else to add to my list of positive and long overdue changes I need to make. I want a bedtime ritual for him too. I think that's important. We'll brush our teeth, read a book, and go to sleep. I know I can be a better father if I keep trying.

I'll get there.

One good thing I can say about myself lately is I never neglect my housework. Hailey doesn't have to lift her finger around here. I do all the laundry, and wash all the dishes. I feed and take care of the family pets. The house is always clean... well, almost always. I'm like Tony Danza in Who's the Boss... but stoned.

I'm turning over a new leaf.

I won't neglect my continued pursuit of self-discovery, through writing, either. It has proven to be the best form of therapy yet. Writing about my ex-wife gave me closure that I didn't even know I needed. Once I'd turned my back on that marriage, I never looked back. I should have though, if only to acknowledge that I did the best I could in a bad situation.

I wrote a lot about her, and reading back through it, it all seems kind of vague. I guess that's perfectly fitting. I could probably write hundreds of pages about her, and never have a clear grasp of our problems. Paula was just as complicated as I am, but in completely different ways.

One time, I returned home after being gone for a few hours... running errands and visiting with friends. When I got out of the car, I saw Paula hiding on the floor of the backseat. She'd been there the whole time! Wearing pajamas and a vacant stare, she was one of the most frightening sights I'd ever seen.

I had to help her into the apartment. She was incoherent and confused. This was after we'd ended our marriage. The guy she was dating blew her off that night, and this was her way of being close to me. I couldn't help but feel bad for her, but I'm an idiot.

The next day she turned on a dime again, wild-eyed and in the mood to break things. She spent the day hurling every insult in the book at me, and blaming me for things I couldn't rationally be held responsible for. I should have run away that day, but I was worried about her in spite of myself.

Everything is so different with Hailey. Now that I'm ready to move forward, out of the darkness. Her genuine need, to see me healthy again, is inspirational. My love for her is ever growing, irreversible, and perfectly mutual. We have been through so much together, and I know now, that we'll never grow apart.

26.

LOVING HAILEY

"No thanks Lori... My life is complicated enough as it is."
It was.

This was November of 2004, shortly after Paula and I ended our marriage. We were through, but still living together. I didn't view this as a point in my life where I should be starting a relationship. There would be way too much explaining to do on a first or second date with someone new.

Therefore, when my co-worker and friend, Lori Jenson, tried to fix me up with her daughter around Thanksgiving time I was truly all set, and that was my response.

Instead, I spent my holiday alone in a local bar getting drunk. I stumbled home to an empty apartment and watched a Cosby Show marathon. I was feeling the weight of my loneliness and the sappy holiday episodes made me weep in front of my cats.

In a parallel universe, a woman named Hailey Jenson wasn't doing much better. Her and her husband were going through a separation of their own, and much like I did, she drank and cried to celebrate the union of Pilgrims and Indians.

I don't believe in fate, but I can't deny that sometimes it does feel like things happen for a reason, that some things are inevitable. In spite of myself, I feel like Hailey and I were destiny. That nothing in the world could have kept us apart and our love will always survive any obstacle. The way we have come to love each other is so powerful it's almost as if we don't even have a choice in the matter... but I'm getting ahead of myself.

I was lonely, but unwilling to date until I could sever all ties with my ex-wife. Even if I were ready to go out with someone new, it wouldn't be Hailey Jenson!

Hailey wasn't only my friend Lori's daughter; she was also my boss's wife! Sure, their marriage was over too, and even a step ahead of my finished relationship, as he'd already moved out of their house. Still, in my mind it was a perfect recipe for disaster. They say that rebound romances never work out and I figured that was all we'd be to each other.

Then, there were the bonus problems that would be unique to us. I worked for her ex. Her mom worked for me. I had always dreamed of starting my own family, but Hailey already had two kids with someone else, and of course, the awkward fact that I still shared an apartment with my ex-wife.

I think it's safe to say the deck was stacked against us. So I said no, and Thanksgiving Day came and went. I continued in my increasingly hopeless and lonely state of being. Before I knew it Christmas was on the horizon, and I braced myself to experience some serious depression, as I faced the merriest of holidays... alone. Little did I know my life was about to be turned upside down and inside out.

Lori was inviting everyone in our department to her house for a Christmas party.

"Are there going to be any hot blondes at your party besides you?" I joked with her knowing I was still in no position to start dating.

"Well... my daughter's going to be there." She joked back, but I couldn't help notice a slight glimmer of hope in her eyes.

Here we go again, I thought with a mixture of annoyance and intrigue.

Party night came, and after getting slightly lost trying to find the house, I made my entrance. Within three seconds, I knew I was in trouble. I saw the most beautiful girl in the world, so of course it would turn out to be Hailey, my bosses *almost* ex-wife. How can I explain it without using every love-at-first-sight cliché in the book?

"My heart skipped a beat...

"Time seemed to stand still...

"I knew the minute I laid my eyes on her...

It would all be true. She was my own personal version of female perfection from her beautiful hair, eyes, and smile to her voluptuous body. I was immediately captivated, and I was immediately terrified. I wanted her, but I felt like she was out of my league. That, plus all the issues I already imagined we'd have.

It didn't take long for Lori to introduce us, and it seemed to flow from there. We talked and it was surprisingly comfortable. We drank and it was amazingly fun. The bathroom in the house was the smoking room for the night, and Hailey and I spent the majority of our time chain-smoking Newports in the tiny restroom. We were getting to know each other, and ignoring the rest of the party.

It was surreal to me, hitting it off with this hot blonde. I've never been smooth talking to girls, but this was coming easy. There was a natural connection between us. We appeared to have enough in common to be compatible, yet enough differences to keep it interesting. I was fascinated, and felt like I was under a dreamy spell.

We were both trying to recuperate from our wasted decades of staying with people we weren't in love with. Hailey was struggling with an addiction to alcohol and I could empathize, because of my experience self-medicating with pot. We both knew the utter despair that came from losing a loving parent. She had lost her dad, who was her best friend, just over a year before. We understood each other's problems and could easily relate, and sympathize.

As the night progressed, Hailey became too intoxicated to do much more than go home and pass out. So, that's what she did. Unfortunately, she did so before I had a chance to say goodbye, or get her phone number. This was a Friday night, and I spent the rest of the weekend fantasizing about what life might be like with this hypnotic woman. I couldn't wait to see Lori at work on Monday so I could find out if Hailey had been thinking about me too. I felt like I had to see her again... as soon as possible.

"I think I'm in love with your daughter!" I half-joked with Lori on Monday morning. Apparently, the feelings were mutual and my friend gave me her daughter's phone number and a look that said, *"I told you so."*

I was like an insecure teenager that night, pacing back and forth on my porch with my phone in one hand, and her number in the other. I was dialing half of it, and then hanging up. Planning on what to say, even though I knew the words would evaporate as soon as I heard her voice. I employed all your basic stall tactics before I finally located my balls and made my life-altering phone call. Once she picked up, it was easy, and our conversation eased into the night.

We continued talking on the phone and flirting with each other for a few days. I also went to visit her at her house a couple of times. It was intense, and then we were both teenagers again, sitting on her couch watching movies, holding hands, and falling in love.

The second time I went to visit her I was risking my life. It was the biggest snowstorm of the year. There was a state of emergency, and a warning for everyone to stay off the road. It was a thirty-minute drive to her house in good weather, never mind that shit, and my windshield wipers were broken too!

It took about two hours for me to complete my treacherous drive, looking through the one square inch of clear glass I had. I could tell when I got there; Hailey was touched that I made the journey just to spend a little time with her. She refused to let me go back out later that night and we shared her bed together for the first time as the snow silently gathered on the earth outside.

I hadn't had sex in over a year. I was obviously more than attracted to her, but I promised to be a gentleman, and I was. It wasn't easy and Hailey challenged my resolve by teasing me and flirting in the dark. I loved it, but as much as I wanted her, I wanted even more to show her a different kind of man. I was a man who thought with his heart and mind, not his penis. I believe I earned her respect and trust that night.

Soon, we had our first official date, and I get no points for originality. A movie and dinner at a restaurant she recommended. I drove around in nervous anticipation trying to keep the flowers I bought her from spilling out of my makeshift, *Aquafina,* water bottle vase.

Our date was comfortable and fun. I was falling hard for this woman, and we hadn't even kissed yet. The end of the night was pure torture as I went back to my ex-wife infested apartment, and Hailey went home to relieve her babysitter... her ex-husband. I was intoxicated from alcohol and emotion and I knew that my heart no longer belonged to me. It was hers already.

Soon, we celebrated New Year's Eve together, and our sexual tension laced the air. We had talked about it plenty, and both wanted our relationship to go there, but we really hadn't even touched each other yet.

All that changed, as midnight struck. Embraced by the New Year, our lips and tongues met for the first time, and I felt myself fall even deeper. In the early hours of 2005's first morning, Hailey became the third and last woman I would ever share my body with. Now, almost eight years later, the excitement I feel for her hasn't waned one bit. That's a rare phenomenon, and I cherish the fact that we share it.

I knew a few things at that point in time. I was in love for the first time in my life. I had to move out of my shared apartment, and I needed to let Hailey know the extent of my emotional baggage. I also knew that, even though she genuinely liked me, my heart had definitely won the race of love, and would now be waiting for hers at the finish line.

Hailey had warned me that she had confusing, mixed feelings about the end of her marriage. Having children makes it more difficult to make such a drastic change. I think Mothers in soured relationships must always fight the urge to *"stick it out for the kids."*

I decided to make a couple of bold moves to prove to Hailey how serious I was about her, and also to give her a chance to head for the hills before I became too emotionally invested. None of this came easy to me, and I feel like I should take a minute to reflect on why I was starting to get the sensation of jumping off a ledge over jagged rocks.

In my youth, I loved my sister, only to have her betray my young trust and obliterate my innocence. I loved my mom, only to have her swept away by the death coach far too soon, leaving me with a gaping crevice in my fragile heart. I loved my father, who had his own demons, preventing him from showing me any love in return.

As my family members were dropping like flies, I thought I was in love with a girl named Stephanie... I wasn't, but she knew better than I did, and abandoned me when the shit hit the fan. Then there was Paula, who I tried to force myself to be in love with... a ridiculous idea that proved to be impossible.

Then came Hailey, the woman of my dreams, and I felt a connection that I'd lost all hope of ever finding. Unfortunately, I had a tattered and torn heart that I knew couldn't withstand any more loss or abuse. I ignored that fact, held my breath, and jumped off the ledge... Fuck the rocks!

First, I asked Lori if I could move into her house immediately, while I looked for an apartment closer to Hailey. Then I opened myself up, as I never had before. Symbolically, I handed her my heart, in the form of my most recent journals. They were completely uncensored, and covered everything from my love-hate relationship with marijuana, to my strange habit of cutting myself. There was even an embarrassing story about me having sex with an inflatable doll I purchased at a porn shop on a particularly lonely night.

I wanted her to know me... the good, the bad, and the ugly. By letting her read those, I made myself completely vulnerable to her possible disgust, fear, or judgment. By letting her read those, I was letting her know me better than anyone ever had before. I know it was unusual to reveal so much that quickly, but I've had an unusual past, and I felt like I had a lot to lose.

After reading them, Hailey didn't judge me. There was no disgust, and she assured me she only felt stronger about me. Of course, she was a little fearful about the cutting and suicidal tendencies she read about, but not feeling that would be unreasonable, especially with her kids coming to accept me in their lives so quickly.

After she read them, I let go of my own fears and inhibitions and truly gave myself to her. Unfortunately, at that point she still hadn't quite caught up to me in the love department, and was still trying to let go of her past.

The past's name was Richard Perry, who was her ex-husband... and my boss.

Now I need to take a detour from my warm and fuzzy, fairytale romance. I have to explain the ugly love triangle that almost ended my life, and would be the nucleus of my third *Cycle*.

Hailey was clear from the beginning that despite the horrible experiences her marriage had brought her she still had confusing, lingering feelings for Richard. Of course, I found this frustrating and painful, but I was also very understanding of her feelings and appreciated her honesty. Sometimes, however, her honesty wasn't as timely as it could have been.

Whenever they were alone, if he was picking up the kids or what not, he would make persistent sexual advances toward her. Hailey always told me the things he would say and do. Of course, it worried me. In fact, worry is an understatement. The venting about her disgusting ex-husband, however, always came with the assurance that she resisted him with equal persistence.

I trusted her completely.

I was living with Lori, and Hailey's grandmother Glenda. It scared me how they would laugh at me for my trust in her. I thought I knew her better than they did. I'd asked Hailey many times, if I needed to be worried, or if I should back off so she could figure things out.

"You have nothing to worry about." She would always tell me.

There was a huge snowstorm one night, and the kids wanted their dad to sleep at their house for old times' sake, and to go sledding the next day. The idea of this guy staying overnight terrified me. I could picture him, relentlessly pushing himself on his estranged wife, all night long. I trusted her, but not him. For all I knew he would try to rape her. It wasn't an unreasonable concern after some of the stories she'd told me about their past sex life.

I expressed all my concerns thoroughly, and repeatedly, but she was adamant she could handle herself and I had no need to be concerned. I hated it, but there wasn't much I could do... his house, his kids... my fucking nightmare!

I didn't sleep a wink that night, and the clock was my enemy, stretching its minutes out to unreasonable lengths, just to mock me. An uneasy feeling made me cry in both short and long bursts. I was beginning to question my sanity for putting myself in such a potentially disastrous situation. Her possible betrayal could be the straw that broke the camel's back.

I was still wide-awake when Hailey came to me in the morning. I was beyond nervous when I heard her coming up the stairs to my bedroom. She looked deep into my eyes with her beautiful blue ones and told me that nothing happened. I was relieved, and stupidly felt ashamed of Lori and Glenda, for not having as much faith in Hailey as I did.

It was all a lie!

We had been dating seriously for approximately two months, when she dropped the bomb on me. It was confession time. Fueled by alcohol, and her therapist telling her she needed to be honest with me about cheating, she told me the truth.

Every time they were alone together, they were having sex! Every time I asked her if, anything happened I should know about... she lied. She looked deep into my trusting eyes, with her beautiful blue ones, and lied to my fucking face!

We broke up, and I was devastated! I felt the Earth shift beneath my feet! Something awful and all too familiar welled up inside me! Dizzy, I teetered on the edge of insanity!

Why does everyone betray me? Why does everyone abandon me? Why aren't I deserving of having love in my life, without having it crumble and slip through my fingertips? Questions with fists, bludgeoned my mind day and night!

I had moved out of Lori's house and into an apartment, where I would live alone, for the first time in my life. I was insecure already, and now my job was suffering too. Working with Richard, knowing he was always trying to fuck the love of my life, was bad enough. Working with him, knowing he *was* fucking the love of my life, would soon prove to be impossible.

I'd started cutting again and stopped sleeping, and eating too. The downward spiral had begun. I was having panic attacks, which were new and scary to me, and spending a shameful amount of time crying in the bathroom at work. It didn't help that the son-of a-bitch was walking around the workplace talking about how pathetic I was. I overheard him once in the break room telling one of his friends how I was a loser, and how he had it made...

"It's great! He buys flowers, pays for dinner, and then drops her off at home so I can get laid." He was laughing about it, referring to our first date. That night was special to me, and the revelation that she was fucking him while I was driving home, longing for her, broke my heart and stirred up a maelstrom of violent urges.

Meanwhile, after the break-up, Hailey was dealing with guilt and regret. I've always been fair in my assessment of her behavior in the beginning of our journey. She was genuinely conflicted, confused, and scared to change the lives of her children. I understand, but my understanding has never been able to dull the wicked pain.

I ignored her calls for a while, but it was a futile effort. I was in love with this woman, and enslaved by a need to be with her at all costs. We started talking, and eventually seeing each other again. I was scared, and tried to be careful with my heart, but it was a tricky situation.

We became a ridiculous on-and-off couple over the next few weeks. Breaking up and getting back together more times, than I can remember, as she tried to figure out what she really wanted, and I wrestled with my pride and dignity.

I would call everything off when the pain from what she did would become so bad I didn't think I'd ever be able to trust her again. I didn't know if I could forgive her for what she did to me, when she knew how vulnerable I was. Then, *she* would end things when she felt like I needed more than she had to offer in the way of commitment. That combined with her kids crying for their daddy, and his constant efforts to keep her emotionally enslaved, were too much for her to bear.

When we weren't together, I made a habit of driving by her house at all hours of the evening... torturing myself. I wanted to see if his vehicle was in the driveway, it usually was, and I would drive home trying to see the road through my tears. I felt like a pathetic stalker. Richard even saw me drive by once in the middle of the night, much to my dismay and humiliation.

It went on like this for a while, and then it got worse. We were together for a good month, and I was starting to drop my guard again. More and more, she started leaning on me, and admitting that her ex-husband would never be able to make her happy like I would. I was starting to let the love, which I'd never stopped feeling for her, fill my heart and nurture my hopes again.

We were happy, for a couple of weeks, and then Hailey started acting cold toward me.

"Richard and I are going to give things another chance." She told me, without even batting an eye.

My soul left my body to float in a dismal abyss, and I was a shell of a man. The third *Cycle* bit down hard, with finely sharpened fangs! I had a nervous breakdown at work, and could no longer function. I left, never to return. I sought therapy and medication, as a greasy, black cloud settled in over my life and started to pour its rain on me.

Hailey and Richard's reunion was short lived. All he wanted was a steady lay, and to crawl back out from his parent's basement where he'd been living. Moreover, she knew me now, and loved me no matter how much it scared or inconvenienced her. I think she loved me all along... truly loved me. It just took her a long time to find it, identify it, and figure out what to do with it.

After a lot of painful debating and careful apologies, I agreed to stay with her and work things out. It was better than trying to live without her, now that she finally knew what she wanted. In other words, I chose true love over foolish pride. Everyone thought I was making the biggest mistake of my life. Everyone's advice, including my shrink's, was to run and never look back. They were all wrong. I'm proud of my choice to be with Hailey after that rocky road. Love... if it's real, is much more important than pride.

It's too bad I had already slipped into a nightmarish state of mind. I tried to fight it and keep it at bay, as best I could, but there was no stopping the momentous collapse. Once the *Cycle* starts, it must run its course. I was dropping weight fast and hallucinating; visions of my mom, beckoning to me, while I played tic-tac-toe on my flesh with a razor. I tried to hide the horror show from my love, but it was impossible. We were intimate lovers, and my collection of scar tissue was growing at a rapid pace.

My confusion reached mind-toppling proportions, as my heart argued that I couldn't live without her, and my mind warned that she was the devil in disguise. Twice now, she'd betrayed me and I couldn't figure out if I was behaving like a man of conviction, or a complete fool.

Hailey tried hard to free me from the web of mental illness. The timing in the beginning of our relationship was never on our side. She finally figured out that she loved me and needed me, and it's as if I was gone. I was falling apart, and torturing her with the sight of it. I loved her too much to make her watch my self-destruction, so I pushed her away.

I broke up with her again, and set sail on my maiden voyage into Agoraphobia. I locked myself up in my apartment and stopped answering my phone. I stopped eating completely and prepared for the coming of inevitable death. I didn't realize I'd made another crucial error, while I was functioning in a fugue state of mind.

At some point during this turmoil, we found out, she was pregnant. I was so lost and fucked up in the head at the time that I honestly don't remember when it could have happened, but it was a disaster all the same. Ultimately, Hailey did the right thing and had an abortion. I wasn't even talking to her anymore and she was starting to fear the worst, as it pertained to my mortality.

I've never been mad at her for making the decision without me, because there was no me. I only feel sorry that she had to deal with it alone, without me by her side. She did what was necessary so that she could focus on one thing... the fact that I was going to die and I needed her.

It took her a while to find her love for me, but now that she had, she would never let go. Several times, she sent the police to my apartment to make sure I was all right, because I wouldn't answer her endless calls. I tried to ignore them, but cops can be persistent when they think there might be a body on the other side of the door. It became clear she wasn't giving up on me. I couldn't die in peace.

I had just enough clarity left to make a lifesaving decision. For the first time in my life, I realized I was completely incapable of caring for myself. I hadn't eaten in days, and I knew I had less than a week to live. I went to the emergency room and from there to a mental hospital, where I signed myself over to their care.

Hailey was there for every possible visitation, and called me every night. She was so supportive, caring, and loving. It was hard to accept at first, but once I did, I started to fight my way out of the pit for both of us. I wouldn't have tried without her, and I wouldn't have succeeded without her by my side.

When the hospital released me, I moved into Hailey's house so that I could continue my recovery with her nurturing support. I was getting healthier every day with her help. Eating good and working out again, so I quickly started putting weight back on. I stayed out of work for a while to avoid possible stress or relapse, and concentrated on building the relationship with my girlfriend, that I always felt we should have. I was sleeping better and my dark, self-abusive, compulsions dissipated into the great unknown.

This was our time! After a dramatic year of hell, there were no more obstacles in our way. We were finally free to explore the beauty of what we had. Hailey and I were in love, and I could see the third *Cycle* getting smaller in the rear view mirror of my mind.

I was... happy.

We were both happy.

We have learned the hard way that we can't be apart from each other. We thrive in each other's company, and feel a great absence when separated. There's a real gravitational pull between us. It's an irresistible force... frightening in its magnificence. Of course, we have our highs and lows, but I can honestly say I've never seen a love as strong as ours... not in real life.

We have the best sex life, and after almost eight years together, Hailey still turns me on as if it was New Year's Eve 2005 all over again. That's rare, and I appreciate it after so much celibacy in my last relationship. Even when I masturbate, it's thoughts of her that get me off. Hailey says the same things, and I know it's true. We're still that attracted to each other, and I have reason to believe that will never change.

We have the best communication, and don't waste each other's time playing stupid games, as we had to with other people. We couldn't, even if we wanted to, because we can feel each other's emotions. One of us always knows when something is bothering the other one, and we talk about.

If I pissed my ex-wife off, I might not find out about it for weeks or months. In a wild-eyed rage, she'd start going off on me for something I only vaguely remembered. If Hailey's mad, I know it right away, and vice-versa. We don't fight, but openly express our feelings. When an apology is due, it's given with wholeheartedness, and accepted with grace. At the worst we'll agree to disagree and move on, but we never fight... we discuss.

Our partnership is an amazing institution that I will never take for granted. What we have transcends everything I use to think love was. It's bigger than a marriage. It's bigger than anything I've ever known. I tattooed Hailey's name on my ring finger years ago, because I know she is my partner for life, and I want everyone else to know it too.

Hailey Ann Jenson is a truly great woman, a truly great person. By looking at her, you would swear she was the cheerleader in high school, but she was the athlete. She was one of the best softball pitchers in the state, and made her dad proud every time she stepped up to the pitcher's mound and lead her team to victories and championships.

There's a brain beneath that beautiful, blonde, mane of hers too. She's smart. I know she'd disagree, but I think she's smarter than I am. I might have a great capacity to memorize and absorb, but she's intelligent in much more useful ways. I might have the genius IQ, but I can't recall how many times I've wondered... *why I didn't think of that,* after she did something I found impressive. I'm lucky to know her, and her kids are lucky too.

Hailey is an awesome mother. Considering the relationship, I had with my own mom, that's important to me. I have high standards for motherhood, and I don't think every woman has it in her. I wanted a child my entire adult life, but would never have done it without the right partner. I have that in Hailey.

It's such a good feeling to watch her interact with Chris and know that my son is as well off in the mom department as I was. Hailey would do anything for her three wonderful children. She'd choose them over me if she had to, and I wouldn't have it any other way. Her dedication to her family is unparalleled, and she has always managed to hold down a job at the same time.

Her work ethic is awesome. I've known her nearly eight years and I think I could count the times she called out sick on my fingertips. She's definitely not afraid to get her hands dirty, either. There's something hot about a girl who does ninety percent of her own home repairs. I've seen her bring vacuums, washing machines, and furnaces all back from the dead. I would be just as likely to open the bathroom door and see her under the sink fixing a pipe, as I would to see her above it looking in the mirror.

Her strength is admirable... working, raising three kids, and maintaining a smooth-running household. She has overcome both alcoholism, as well as an addiction to pain killers. Then there's the roller coaster ride that I can be, not to mention an ever-present, annoying, and vengeful ex-husband. There's a lot on her plate, yet she's one of the most even-keeled people I know. I envy her consistent ability to handle the world, usually with a pretty smile on her face.

Hailey can be downright hilarious. It's always effortless, and I don't even think she realizes how funny the things she says are, until I bust out in boisterous, hard-to-stop laughter. I can't tell you how important that is to someone like me to have found someone to share such humor and light-hearted amusement. I need that in my life as crucially as oxygen. She gives me everything I need, and then some.

A genuinely caring person, who seems to want to help as many people as she possibly can. A shining example would be the plans she has if she were ever to win the lottery. Whenever we fantasize about that, I'm talking about buying pirate ships and robots, while she's talking about going on the news to invite everyone to write her if they're in need of help.

She talks about how awesome it would be to pour over the mail and help as many of them as she can. Letter's from strangers, asking for money, is most lottery winners' biggest complaint, and that would honestly be her favorite thing about it. In so many ways, I know she's a better person than I am... so incredibly generous.

A few years ago, Hailey decided to become a surrogate mother. She wanted to find a couple that couldn't have children of their own, and carry one for them. This was one of those times where we agreed to disagree. I was against it. I didn't like the idea of her taking on the health risks that came with pregnancy for complete strangers. Expressing my concerns, I told her I really didn't want her to do it, but it was up to her. If she went through with it, I promised I would support her and help in any possible way.

Hailey found a couple who needed help. She made the commitment and began the process. I was scared, but stayed behind her every step of the way. That's one of the best things about her and I. We support each other's endeavors whether we agree with them or not.

It did turn out to be a difficult pregnancy. For the first few months, she could hardly get up for more than a few minutes at a time. It was the same with the last few months too, all to be capped off by the excruciating pain of delivering someone else's baby. It didn't end with the birth though.

The day after she was released from the hospital her heart rate and blood pressure went through the roof. An ambulance rushed her to the emergency room, where they admitted her into the hospital. She was there for a week, with a diagnosis of preeclampsia. She could have died!

It was a living nightmare for the both of us. Hailey, pumped full of magnesium, wondered if she was going to survive the ordeal. I spent every day by her side, consoling her, and telling her that everything was going to be all right. At night, we'd struggle for sleep without each other, and our love grew even more.

All this because she knew she had a gift for healthy pregnancies, and wanted to share it. Hailey knows how important and special motherhood is. She sympathized with those who desperately wanted that magic in their life, but couldn't do it on their own.

Not once, during the entire process, did she complain or feel sorry for herself. This was proof-positive that she believed in what she was doing, and I have infinite respect for that. I have never witnessed such a selfless act of generosity or bravery.

I admire her as a human being for that immense sacrifice. To me she achieved a goddess-like stature by following her heart, and helping the less fortunate. I know there's a happy family out there that is finally complete. That wouldn't be the case without Hailey.

She's my best friend. We can have as much fun together in a grocery store or doctor's office as we could in an amusement park. We know each other as well as we know ourselves, perhaps even better.

Hailey would say similar things about me that I've said about her, and I would argue that she was exaggerating or blinded by love. In turn, she would be to humble to acknowledge the truth in the things I've written about her. That's us... our own worst critics, and each other's biggest fans. We give each other some much-needed balance.

The two of us have grown a lot over the years. We've grown as a couple. Hurt each other, and even put each other through hell at times. When the smoke clears, however, there we are... hand in hand. We brush each other off and get ready to take on the world again. All this from a couple that nobody thought stood a snowball's chance in hell of making it work.

My prediction for us is a long and happy relationship. We will raise wonderful children into amazing adults. We will have fun and enjoy life whenever we can, and help each other through the tough times when necessary. When we're old, we'll hold arthritic hands, and see a rich history of true love in each other's eyes.

27.

JOURNAL ENTRY
(New Beginnings)

05 / 08 / 12

Our family dynamic has changed drastically lately, as David has decided to leave our home, and move in with Richard. His motivation is to switch schools. Supposedly, the middle school near his dad's residence is far superior, I must admit, that seems to be the case.

Hailey is feeling his absence deeply, but handling it much better than I thought she would. Amy, I think, has never been happier, with less sibling rivalry now and more attention for her. Chris misses his big brother being around, but his young mind doesn't let him dwell on things like that for more than a few minutes at a time, a good thing of course.

I love David and I miss him a lot too. He was five years old when I first moved into this house, and he's been like a son to me all these years. I hope this is the best move for him. He's a good kid, but he does need more discipline than I'm comfortable giving him. Richard's motivation might be less than admirable but I think he'll be able to give his son what he needs for now.

He does seem happier since he moved in with his dad, and that makes me happy for him. He likes his new school, and says the kids there are friendly enough. I know how hard it is to be the new guy, especially at the end of a school year. I'm rooting for him. Every kid deserves to be happy and have a sense of stability.

I want to be happy too. In so many ways I am, I just need to keep moving forward. I need to achieve perpetual motion in my life.

Hailey and I seem to be in the best place we've ever been, as far as our relationship is concerned. We're a great support system for each other, and she has helped me so much over the past few months. Writing about our history together recently, was a wonderful reminder of the incredible love we share.

Our sex life is incredible, even after all these years... and problems. It's the only healthy sexual relationship I've ever had. My first time, excluding my sister of course, was with my girlfriend Sherry when I was seventeen. I remember how confused I was after this brief encounter, honestly not knowing if I was still a virgin or not.

I had slept over her house with some other friends while her parents were away. In the middle of the night, she pulled my dick out, straddled me, and slid herself up and down on it three or four times. That was it! She dismounted, rolled over, and went to sleep.

Just when I was thinking to myself... "Oh my god, I'm finally getting laid," she jumped ship. With a scorching case of blue balls, I stared at the ceiling wondering what the fuck just happened! I suffered in silence, never one to be pushy about sex, but I couldn't help being pissed off that she would purposely tease me like that. Eventually we had real sex, but it was sloppy, uncoordinated, teenage sex.

Paula was next, and admittedly hated intercourse. Sometimes she'd cry during the act, regardless of how tender and caring I was. I would always stop at the first sign of tears, even though she'd tell me not to. It made me feel like a rapist, and stripped me of my ability to approach her with my needs.

It's impossible to enjoy lovemaking when you're studying you're partners face for signs of suffering. After a while, I just tried to leave her alone in the bedroom. Paula being Paula, then complained that "real men" initiated sex occasionally. As usual, I couldn't win with her.

My lack of confidence in the bedroom followed me into me relationship with Hailey. My mind and body are so entwined, that I can't even get a hard on unless I feel like I'm making a real connection with my lover. I needed prescription meds to get a boner for six months after I found out she'd cheated on me.

It was worth it, and she was patient and understanding as I learned not to be so analytical when I'm naked between the sheets. Hailey has made every aspect of my life better than I thought possible.

We have a good, but temporary system in place right now. She's working a few days a week at a new restaurant, kicking ass, and bringing home the big tips. I'm collecting unemployment insurance while I raise our son full time, and maintain the household.

We're financially stable... for now, but I am preparing myself mentally, to return to the workforce as soon as possible. I get a little excited when I think about it. I've been searching the job market weekly, submitting applications, and exploring my options.

I did get an immediate callback from a decent-paying warehouse, but had to decline because the second shift hours won't work with Hailey's schedule. The interest was nice though, and I'm starting to feel confident I'll find something soon.

Hailey likes things just the way they are, and wants me to stay unemployed for as long as possible. That's cute, but I don't want to tempt fate like that and risk running out of time. Plus, I have a natural inclination to be a productive member of society.

I just don't think I ever want to be the boss again. Being responsible for me is all I can handle. I'd be happy just driving a forklift, stocking shelves, or picking orders. Assuming it will still allow me to provide well enough for my family.

I've been writing less in my journal, but more on the computer. Examining my life from every angle and writing, what I've been privately referring to as, the chapters of my life. The essays are about the people, places, and events that have shaped who I am today.

The therapy this has provided is priceless to me and I don't know why I never thought to do this before. It's allowing me to look at the things that have damaged me, and exercise them from my system through the written word. This is giving me a sense of closure on some issues that have haunted me for a lifetime. It's been emotionally draining, and I've cried through half of it, but the benefits of soldiering through to get to the other side could be life changing.

As well as writing, I've re-discovered my love for reading. It's a wonderful and harmless way to take a break from reality without slaughtering your brain cells. It's also one of my favorite things to do with my son, and I do believe I hear him calling me now, to do just that. His voice is adorable, floating down the stairwell to find me, and I have a genuine smile on my face. I love being a daddy.

28.

STEP-PARENTHOOD

I had a step-dad, and it's fair to say, I was less than fond of him. His name was Steve, and he somehow managed to sweep my mom off her feet and marry her. I didn't like him, but I loved my mom and was able to get along with the man for her sake. I'm sure it wasn't much different on his end.

I did call him Dad after a while. Not because I felt that he could be the daddy I never had, but because I knew it would make my mom happy. It sucked, and he must have had enough intuition to know my efforts to bond were never genuine. I always knew *he* was full of shit.

He was a strange guy who said he studied witchcraft, and called himself a "warlock". He refused to go into the ocean because he claimed it caused him to have "overwhelming visions," and he said he couldn't wear gold because it "burned." For all I know he just said all that crazy shit because he knew my mom was interested in all things supernatural. I lived with the guy for six years, and he mostly just sat at a table doing crossword puzzles, drinking blackberry brandy, and smoking menthol cigarettes.

Steve had no work ethic, especially when compared to my father. He mooched off my mom after she sold our house... not working for over two years. Later, he got temporary jobs, but never seemed to stay at one place for very long. This was the nineteen-eighties, and the economy was fine.

When my mom was receiving financial aid, after her diagnosis, he stopped working again and lived off that. Then, after she died, he was too distraught to work and fully injected himself into the welfare system. We parted ways after she was gone, and I have no idea where the man is today. I don't care.

I could deal with all that shit if I thought he really loved my mother, but I don't think he did. He made her feel so alone and unwanted at the most vulnerable stage of her life. It's true, I didn't like him from the start, but the way he emotionally abandoned her at the end of her life made my feelings intensify... I hated him!

When my mom was at her sickest, and knew that death might find her any day, she was more alone than she should have been. Steve never touched her anymore, showed no affection, and wouldn't even sleep in the same bed with her. He made her feel isolated, like a contaminated *thing*, and I use to hold her while she would cry about it. I find this unforgivable, and inhuman. Love never appeared to come naturally to this guy.

I had a stepsister too, but I don't know anything about her, and always found it odd that she wasn't part of our lives. Her name was Mandy Wilson, and she was the product of his first marriage. In the six years I knew Steve, he only saw his daughter a few times, and she only lived a couple towns away. He constantly bitched about paying child support, and I can remember the police coming to our house to arrest him for failing to pay on more than one occasion. He was not a good husband or father, and he was definitely not a good step-dad.

When I met Hailey at her mom's Christmas party, I met her kids too. There was David, who was quite shy... and Amy, who was not. That little four-year-old girl introduced herself to me by sneaking up from behind, and choking me with a plastic grocery bag. Later that night the two of them had fun shoving crushed up Doritos down the back of my pants.

It's hard to play it cool for the hot girl at the party when your underwear is full with one of America's favorite snacks... but I was cool. I thought they were funny, and was able to laugh at myself with them. I genuinely liked them right away. Both of them were adorable, and as they were pointing and laughing at the nacho cheese dust on my pants, Hailey asked me if I was "ready for this?"

Was I ready for it?

I loved it! Those kids were clearly part of her down to their every fiber. Seeing her interact with them, that night was one of the things that turned me on about her the most. She was a good mom. My love for Hailey was born on that night, and her kids were very much a part of it.

When I met them, they were four and five years old. Amy was just learning the alphabet, and poor David was crying himself to sleep every night, because he missed his dad. Now, nearly eight years later, neither one of them can even remember what life was like before me.

David is a handsome and intelligent kid. If he applies himself, I know he'll have the potential to do whatever he dreams. He's a soccer player, and I love how happy he makes his mom when she watches him play. I will always have a soft spot for any son's relationship with their mother. He has moved in with his dad for now and is searching for direction in his life. When he finds it, I know he'll do great things. I also suspect he'll be living with us again in the near future.

Amy has incredible self-discipline, and it's hard to believe she's only eleven. She's almost completely self-sufficient, and takes her education very seriously. She constantly impresses me. It's her dream to grace the silver screen as an award-winning actress someday, and I really think she can do it. She has an abundance of natural charisma.

I have a son of my own now, and David and Amy will always be his big brother and big sister. He loves them, and it makes his day when they take the time to play with him.

Having been both a parent as well as a stepparent, I can honestly say it's harder to be a stepparent, and I commend those who do it well. It's such an unfair situation. You share all the same responsibilities as the parents, but with the deck stacked against you. You are *not* the parent, and the children know it. You have to, very delicately, find a way to fit yourself into the family dynamic without crossing any lines.

It's no easy task.

At the same time, you're under constant scrutiny in your relationship with the kids, from your significant other, and even greater scrutiny from their exes. I've always had a recurring fear... one of the kids getting hurt on *my watch*! Thankfully, that's never happened. Every parent knows you can't watch your kids every second of every day, but that's an irrelevant fact when you're just the stepparent.

You live under a microscope when it comes to raising someone else's children. You play by a stricter set of rules, with less understanding, and harsher repercussions for any failure. It's a demanding position to be in that requires a lot of sacrifice, but it can be done, and it can be done well. Just not without real love.

Possibly the most unfair aspect of step-parenthood is the fact that the relationship you build with these children is attached to, and dependent on a relationship with your partner. I have lived with, and loved these kids for the better part of a decade. They are a massive part of my life. In the blink of an eye, they could become lost to me forever. If Hailey was to fall out of love with me, if something ever happened to her, they could be gone... just like that.

One of the only equal aspects between parents and stepparents is the reward. I've had a huge part in raising these two special kids, even more so than their father. They're good people, and I had a lot to do with that. I'm very proud of the role I've played in their lives so far. They love me... and nobody can ever take that away.

My specific situation is unique because of my history with David and Amy's dad. It's not typical, and adds a painful element to my relationship with these kids. I'm uncomfortable around their father, and have several serious problems with his existence in my life.

The fact that Hailey couldn't decide between him and I in the beginning of our romance, coupled with his disrespect during the entire experience, makes it impossible for me to be around him sometimes. It was one of the worst times in my life, and when I'm near him, I can still feel the pain. It makes me sick to my stomach.

I try my hardest to ignore my feelings, but in time, they always seem to get the better of me. Because of this, it's become routine for me to avoid situations where I know he'll be. When I can't avoid him, I become very withdrawn, from fear of starting a war with the children's daddy. I've missed too many things, because of this inner turmoil.

He knows I can't stand him, and I do wish I could hide it a little better. I blatantly ignore his attempts at small talk, never acknowledge his presence, and literally turn my back on him when he's around. I just can't fake it when it comes to this guy.

In spite of it all, I'm proud to say that I have *never* let my feelings for Richard interfere in my feelings toward his kids. I love them. Because of this, I have never spoken a bad word about the man to either one of them. Quite the contrary, I've always endorsed and supported his relationship with his kids, and even defended him on occasions when I thought one of them might be acting unfair toward him. It's important to me that they love their father, and not grow up with "daddy issues," like I did.

Richard has a different approach, and loves to say terrible things about both Hailey and I, directly to his kids. I think that's weak, and there's no excuse for it! We have no interest in anything he has to say about us. So all this does is confuse, and hurt his children. They're constantly telling me shit he said about me.

Amy cries sometimes, feeling like she's in the middle. I feel bad for them, that they have to deal with such immature nonsense. I always tell them to ignore it, and not worry about defending my honor. They shouldn't have to.

The truth is… Richard should be thanking me.

For the last seven years, he's lived the life of a guy without children whenever he felt like it. Hailey has always worked nights and weekends, creating countless opportunities over the years for Richard to have had his kids whenever he wanted them. For the most part, he has chosen to leave them with me.

He has used his free time for dating, hanging out with his friends, football games, and fishing trips. Meanwhile, I was reading the bedtime stories, wiping the runny noses, hosting the sleepovers, making the grilled cheese sandwiches, and tripping over neglected toys in the middle of the night.

He has taken advantage of me, used me as a built-in-babysitter, and taken for granted that I would take good care of what should be most precious to him. I can't relate to his indifference toward whether his kids are with him or me, and I will never understand it.

I have no illusions that he'll ever thank me for the dedication I've shown to the family he created, or the sacrifices

I've made for the sake of his kids, but at least he could stop talking shit about me.

I think I've been a good stepparent for the most part, though there's always room for improvement. If Steve was the benchmark then I've definitely gone above and beyond the call of duty. In many ways, I gave myself to those kids just as much as I did to Hailey.

I've been there for them as best I could, and done my best to be a positive influence in their young lives. I'm not perfect, but I love them, and that might be all you need. I'm proud to consider David and Amy my kids and I'm proud to have them be Chris's big brother and sister. Hailey and I have done a good job raising them, and it's obvious they are going to be fine adults.

In the blink of an eye, Amy went from carrying a *Disney Princess* backpack and reading *Green Eggs and Ham*, to sharing a wardrobe with Hailey and dreaming about falling in love. David was quiet and shy as a small boy, but now stands two inches taller than I do, and can be the life of the party with his sense of humor and silly brand of charm. It's been a great honor, being part of their lives, and watching them grow up.

I will continue to love them and do the best I can for them, for the rest of my days. They have made my life fuller, and more important, than it could have ever been without them. My family is everything to me, and I'm so glad that they're part of it.

29.

JOURNAL ENTRY
(I Want to Live)

06 / 21 / 12

I want to live!

It was nearly a year ago when I ventured into my basement in the middle of the night, picked up a pen and wrote the exact opposite.

I meant it!

Thinking back now, it gives me the chills. I can see myself in the basement that night... stoned, with a deep gash bleeding down my leg, and that pen in my trembling hand. I can remember how scared I felt, and how intensely close I was to death. In my mind's eye, I can see the grim reaper standing behind me, as I sat at my desk, thinking to himself... "He's really going to do it this time!"

I didn't, of course.

Instead, I wrote until I fell asleep, and then checked myself into the mental hospital the next day. It saved my life, in the sense that it gave me a place to hide from myself. I was in self-destruct mode, and losing touch with reality on a regular basis. I can't imagine what would have happened if I were left to my own devices that week.

I've come a long way in the last ten months.

Hailey and I recovered from the drama I brought into our lives last year. Somehow, she has found it in her heart to forgive me, and I feel like we're more in love now than we've ever been. I don't know any other couple who could have survived everything that her and I have, and still look at each other the way we do. Her happiness is everything to me, and I know that I'll never hurt her again.

The house we've been living in is going on the market this month. Everybody is struggling financially, and Hailey's ex-husband is in a rush to say good-bye to the mortgage payments. We're looking at this as a positive thing. The sale will alleviate the small debt we've accumulated through these tough times, and leave us with some money in the bank. I'm happy, because I've never enjoyed the fact that I live in another man's house. I can't wait to have a fresh start in a new place that Hailey and I pick out together.

The plan is to move into Lori's house for now, because she's having trouble keeping her head above water as well. I recall how well we all got along when we stayed there for a few weeks back in October. I think this is going to be good for everybody. Lori's lonely and needs help with her bills, and we need a place to recoup and figure out what comes next for us. Hailey wants to stay for a year, while she goes to nursing school. In the meantime, we'll be able to save money so we won't have to struggle so hard when we get our own place.

David and Amy are doing great. In their world, I seem to be the same man they've always known and loved. Thoughts about their stepdad's indiscretions and insanity are thankfully insignificant amidst Red Sox statistics and Hannah Montana lyrics. I'm grateful for their ability to forgive and forget.

David's doing well living at his dad's. I miss him a lot, but it's nice to see him happy when he visits us on the weekend. Amy is always doing fine, and keeps busy doing a million things... softball, acting classes, girl scouts, and she does it all while maintaining her good grades. I'm proud of both of them.

Last week I wrote about the relationship I share with my son, and how much it means to me. I cried the whole way through it. Not since I wrote about my mom have I shed so many tears. I had tears of joy, as I thought about the love that my little boy injected into my life. I had tears of sorrow, thinking about how far away I felt from that love this past year, and tears of guilt, when I thought about how close I was to ruining his life by ending mine.

I pictured him growing up just as lost and confused as I did and I'm still pissed off... but I don't hate myself anymore. I can't. I'll never be the man I need to be for my family, and myself, if I'm drowning in a sea of self-loathing. I see myself through the eyes of the people who love me now, and I can't help but love myself too.

I'm getting healthier on a physical level. I've always felt the need to be huge in the past, and would destroy myself in the gym to achieve that. Never was that need as strong, as when I would come out of a Cycle. I've always felt that my physical strength represented my emotional strength. My muscles were a symbol of how strong I was on the inside. Getting big and powerful was like a way to prove to myself that I was mentally healthy again.

For the first time in my adult life, I don't feel that need anymore. I don't have to prove to myself that I'm all right by inflating my biceps to nineteen inches. I don't need proof this time, because... I just know. This is a breakthrough for me.

I no longer have to protect my mom from my dad... my parents are gone. I'm the parent now, and I don't need to bench press four-hundred pounds to take care of my son. If I ever do pursue my efforts in the gym again, it will be for the simple reason that it feels good and I enjoy it.

For now, I have my sights set on the Kung-Fu school in town, for Chris and myself. I took him there to check it out, introduce him to Master Wu, and observe a class. He's into it, and excited to do this with his daddy. I'm not ready yet, but almost. I did a lot of damage to my body this year through starvation, sleep deprivation, emotional stress, and periods of chain smoking pot and cigarettes.

I'm still undoing the damage.

After writing hundreds of pages in my notebooks, and typing thousands of words into my computer, I feel that I've finally exorcised the demons of my past. That's a pretty big deal for me. The last three times I went through this, I definitely spent a lot of time thinking about my problems but I never really thought through them.

I'm sure this is what most people get from seeing therapists. Never before have I put myself under the microscope like this. I've had genuine revelations that I believe will help me live a happier, healthier life.

30.

CHRISTOPHER

The anticipation I felt for the arrival of my new baby boy was one of the most overwhelming forces I've ever had to endure, in a good way, of course! Sleep eluded me in the nights preceding his delivery, I was the poster-boy for nervous, expectant fathers... pacing and planning until the sun would come up. I was about to meet my son, and I had wanted this for so very long.

I was wise beyond my years, resisting my natural urge to start a family with my ex-wife. As far as I was concerned, it just wasn't an option. It was wise, as well, for Hailey to have an abortion while I was captive to the noose of the third *Cycle.* We waited until the time was right.

Hailey and I were in love, strong and united. I couldn't wait to be her partner for life, and raise this child we'd created... both of us happy and healthy forever. It's horrifying how close that vision almost came to ending, but amazing that the beautiful possibility of that fairy-tale ending remains.

The night before Chris was born I stayed awake, sitting on the patio in the backyard, chain smoking, and swearing to myself that I would quit really soon. I was happy, and I felt ready. I knew I would be a good dad. I even dared to think I might be a great one.

I couldn't wait to see what he'd look like, and feel his tiny little fingers wrap themselves around one of mine. I imagined holding him, feeling his weight in my arms. I wondered if I'd be good at changing his diapers. Would I be good at potty training? Would I be lucky enough to witness his very first steps? So many questions and random scenarios paraded their way through my mind.

At the hospital the next day, I never left Hailey's side. I held her hand, caressed her head, and did my best to advocate for her care and comfort. I tried to soothe her with my words and tender affection while the two of us waited for our son to make our family complete. This would be an irreplaceable memory. One of the most life-altering events two people can experience. Unbelievably, one of the nurses tried to get me to miss it!

"You should go get a sandwich or something."

"No thank you." I told the nurse. It was a ridiculous notion to me, that I could go eat a sandwich in the hospital cafeteria while Hailey was in stir-ups, about to give birth to our baby at any moment.

"You haven't eaten all day, and this could still be a while sweetie." She wore a well-crafted look of concern, as she wheeled a cart over to Hailey's bedside. "Go... you can get something quick."

"No... really. I think I'd kill myself if I missed anything." It was after five and my stomach was growling loud enough for the nurse to hear, but really. I'd been waiting for this moment for nine months, or my entire adult life, when you think about it. Finally, the nurse abandoned her efforts.

Nothing was going to get me out of that room!

If government officials burst through the door and told me that my mother didn't really die in 1993, that it was all just a big mistake and she was waiting in the lobby to talk to me.

Well, I'd be stupefied of course, but she'd still have to wait. I wanted to be present at every milestone in my son's life, and that began with his birth.

I focused my attention on Hailey and that's where it stayed... for three minutes.

Just like that, it was time! It went from, *"This could still be a while"* to *"The baby's coming,"* in the blink of an eye!

Imagine if I missed it all for a turkey club on stale wheat!

This was the first birth I'd ever witnessed. My only delivery room experience came from television and movies, so I expected a long, drawn out battle...

Pushing!

Breathing!

Swearing!

Hailey, perhaps, biting me or breaking my hand while she berated me for getting her pregnant. Fortunately, reality wasn't quite so hostile. Once the process began, it was over in two pushes. Being a man, I would never be stupid enough to say it was an easy delivery, but Hailey said it was the fastest one she'd ever experienced and I'll take her word for it.

Christopher was born, healthy and beautiful. I knew I was going to be emotional, and I was. I wept in jubilation as I cut the umbilical cord. My sobs came in emotional bursts of pure joy as I absorbed the moment. My eyes were on Hailey, who looked so beautiful, sweaty and spent. Then my eyes were on my son as he was carefully transported around the delivery room to various stations, being washed, weighed, and welcomed into his new world.

The proud mommy slept that night, exhausted from the emotional and physical demands of creating life, and a healthy dose of Tylenol with codeine. The proud daddy held his son until morning, staring in awe at new life, born from true love.

I felt complete.

It's only natural that I would reflect back on the relationship I had with my own father, as I held my son that night. I promised him softly, but with perfect conviction, that I was going to be a better daddy than the one I'd known. I put tiny kisses on his forehead and promised him that he would never have to be afraid of me. I rocked him gently, and told him he was safe and I would shield him from the horrors of the world for as long as I possibly could.

I loved him, as I do now, and I always will.

Chris would become almost a permanent fixture in my arms for the next couple of years. I would tirelessly carry him everywhere I went. Never feeling the weight of his body, but always feeling the weight of how much he meant to me. We were inseparable, and developed a bond that I like to imagine as unbreakable.

I had surgery on my leg shortly after he was born, which resulted in me being out of work for nearly two years. I used the time to better myself and explore different career options, but for the most part I focused on being the best "stay at home dad" I could be.

Hailey worked and eventually carried a child for someone else as a surrogate mother, while I absorbed most of the parenting duties with our new son. The diapers never grossed me out; neither did the spit-up, or urine. I became an expert and took real pride in my ability to change a diaper, not only fast, but in any surroundings and without waking him up if necessary.

I played with him, napped with him, and talked to him constantly as I pictured a day when the conversations wouldn't be so one-sided. I fed him, bathed him, and read books to him. I dedicated myself to raising this little boy, and never lost sight of how lucky I was to be able to spend so much quality time with him.

Inevitably, I had to return to the workforce, and Hailey gracefully and effortlessly took over the full time parenting. Still, I always made it a point to make sure we had a little special time together every day. Watching him get bigger and stronger over the years has been mesmerizing. It's amazing, the pride you feel as a parent over the simplest things... "Look honey! He just rolled over by himself!"

"He's crawling!"

"Honey... He pooped in his potty!"

"Oh my god... He just said Da Da!

It's powerful, molding and shaping his young life, and he's such a pleasure. Like most good parents, I think my son is cuter, smarter, and more special than everyone else's kids are. He is adorable, and seems to get special treatment wherever we go. I like to tell people that his good looks are his mom's fault. With his blonde hair, blue eyes, and warm smile there's no denying he'll get plenty of attention.

His intelligence is impressive, and I'm amazed at how different his generation is from mine. Cell phones are a good example. These devices, that are a hundred different things before you even get to the phone, can be confusing for adults. Chris, at four years old, is able to navigate through the various screens, download video games, and save or erase data as he sees fit.

It's amusing to watch him offer his grandmother instructions on how to use these complicated toys. When I was his age, I was trying to figure out why the star shaped block wouldn't fit through the triangular shaped hole in my plastic Playschool toy.

I'm back to full time parenting duties right now, and things are a little different. Gone, are the cribs, bottles, and high chairs. Now, my son happily provides real assistance with the daily chores. When I do the dishes, he tours the house looking for the ones that never found their way to the sink. He helps change trash bags, feeds his pets, and cleans his own room.

If I'm fixing something, or working on one project or another, he always wants to help me. I love that, and always do my best to find a way to make him feel involved. He's becoming mechanically inclined from being daddy's little assistant, and I'm proud of myself for making these kind of memories with him. I hope he always remembers the day he helped his dad build our patio table, fix the kitchen sink, or paint his bedroom.

I think one of his best attributes might be how affectionate he is towards those he loves. He's so thoughtful and caring. When he found out his cat was pregnant, he rushed around the house putting together a comfortable box with fluffy towels. He wanted her to have a warm, safe place to have her kittens. No one had suggested doing that. It was just his nurturing instinct, and I was touched.

Expressing his love comes naturally to him, and it reminds me of how verbal my mom and I were about our feelings. Chris tells us he loves us countless times a day, and the frequency always increases when he gets sleepy. It's cute. As he's drifting off, the *"I love yous"* to both his mom and I come by the dozens. They get quieter and quieter, until they turn into tiny snores. It's never too much as far as I'm concerned. Lately he's fond of asking us...

"Do you know what the most important thing is?"

"What?" We play along.

"I love you!" He tells us, and it warms my heart every time.

There is a bad side to being a parent though. I worry a lot... about everything, and my worries range from the perfectly reasonable to the irrational and paranoid. What would I ever do if he became ill, got hit by a car, kidnapped, or murdered? Just thinking about such abominable possibilities fills me with dread, and a hint of the pain I would feel reverberates through my core. How could I ever recover from such a cruel loss? I hate thinking about these things, but I can't help it.

One of the biggest challenges in parenting for me is having these concerns, and not falling into the trap of being an overprotective dad. Therefore, I hold my breath when he climbs a tree, but I let him climb. My heart rate quickens when I watch him cross the street to play with his friends, but I let him cross. I even let him eat now, without standing behind him waiting to apply the Heimlich maneuver at the slightest sign of choking.

It's not easy.

I spend some time worrying for him too... about me. I think about my own mortality quite a bit, and my heart breaks when I think about my son suffering the loss of one of his parents. I know the pain all too well. I wouldn't wish it on anyone, let alone my own child. Yet I smoke. I picture myself, on my deathbed with lung cancer, trying to explain to my little boy why he's going to have to miss his daddy for the rest of his life. It makes me feel sick, and I loathe myself for not being stronger and setting a better example.

I'm ashamed of myself, writing this now... ashamed that the thought of killing myself has gone through my mind. How could I hurt Christopher like that, abandon him, and fill his life with loss and confusion. I have to be honest, though. I thought about it a lot this last year. I know I owe my son an apology, weather he knows it or not. I'll put it in writing here.

I'm so sorry son.

I'm sorry for all my weakness and shortcomings, sorry I'm capable of thinking about ending my life and devastating yours. These are just thoughts though. Mostly I'm sorry that I affected you with my inner turmoil this year. I left our home and made you cry. I confused you, hurt you, and made you wonder why your daddy left.

I'm so sorry I left you!

I was doing so well. I *was* a good dad, maybe even great. I was the kind of dad who wanted to video tape all your birthdays, because they're special days that I don't ever want to forget. I ruined it though. I didn't live with you during your fourth birthday, and my guilt and anxiety kept me from even going to your party. I felt broken hearted for you, that you were stuck with me for a father.

I'm so sorry I missed your birthday party, buddy!

I can't take it back now, and none of my issues excuse it. All I can do is apologize... and do better. You're fifth birthday is right around the corner, and I promise that daddy will be there for this one and all that follow, so long as there's still life left in my body.

I love you.

I promise to be better. Not to punish myself for the mistakes I've made, but learn from them. I will become stronger, so that I can be present in your life, and help you become the best version of yourself possible.

Never before has my insanity done so much damage to people I love and care about. It's been an awakening. There's no more room in my life for selfish thinking. My death can no longer be an inviting, comforting option when I feel like I can't go on any more. I would rather suffer in silence for the rest of my life than hurt my family again.

I'm being honest when I promise that I'll never give in to that dark temptation. I will never burden my loved ones with that grief, so that I can have peace. There could be no act more selfish than that. Besides, I still have a lot of work to do.

I have taught my son a lot, but there's still so much more, like all the things that I had to learn on my own... how to swim, ride a bike, shave, and drive a car. I want to be there for everything, because he deserves that. I want to be there for him when some little girl breaks his heart, when he's trying to figure out what he wants to be when he grows up, and when he's holding his own child in his arms someday.

I want to be the kind of dad that my son can count on. I want him to trust me, and know that he can talk to me about anything at all. I don't want him to have to try figuring out how I felt about him, or if I loved him or not. I feel like I have the best son in the world, so it's only fair that I make the greatest effort I can to be the best dad.

I'm looking forward to watching him continue to grow. I love wondering what kind of man he'll be some day. I think he'll be a great one. I can picture him now... honest, hardworking, intelligent and kind. He'll probably be a handsome man with a good sense of humor, who helps far more people than he hurts, and leaves a positive mark on the world.

He's already so loving, caring, and affectionate.

I'll bet he'll be a great dad someday too.

31.

JOURNAL ENTRY
(What I've Learned)

07 / 13 / 12

A week away from my thirty-seventh birthday and almost a year since I began examining my life through extensive writing, this is probably my last journal entry for a while. The exhausting effort has served me well, and I've never felt so enlightened.

I've learned a lot.

I was born an extremely loving and affectionate person, with an immense need for the attention of my family, and their unconditional love. I longed for warm and healthy relationships with my father and my sister, but grew up wondering why they hated me instead. I always retained a little hope, however, that things might be different someday.

Everything changed in 1993, when I attended the back-to-back funerals of my parents, and attempted a doomed reunion with my sister. Before that, I was far from normal, and had already developed strange coping mechanisms, like cutting. I was already prone to feeling anxious in social situations. Not once, however, did I contemplate taking my own life until that fateful year.

The desire to commit suicide is the heart of the recurring battles I've been facing for the last twenty years. I've defined these Cycles, as times in my life interrupted by mental illness, rendering me incapable of functionality. This is true of course, but more to the point, the Cycles are the times in my life when I wanted to die.

When my mom passed away, I lost my best friend and biggest support system. My dad's death brought with it, the end of any hope for future reconciliation. I tried to bond with my sister, understand her side of things, and forgive her for her crimes against me. I did, but found a person I still didn't like, or respect. I realized the most important thing in the world to me... my family, was obviously lost to me forever. I was alone.

I wanted to die.

It would have happened in the early winter months of 1994, but I met Paula and became distracted from myself. I made her the focal point of my life, and soon felt the possibility of having a loving family after all. It felt like all my problems went away, and I flourished.

I didn't know it at the time, but everything I was experiencing before I met Paula, stayed very much with me. It hid, petrified, in the darkest recesses of my mind, patiently waiting to gain my attention again... someday.

In 1999, Paula betrayed me, and shattered the illusion that I had a family, in her. I'd felt like I had a second chance for that unconditional love I'd always craved, but it proved to be false. The suicidal tendencies I had developed over five years ago stirred, then shook violently awake. I was shocked when it happened, I believed I was all better, but that wasn't the case. I was lost again, detached from reality, and I made Paula my wife.

I wanted to die again.

Paula's own desire to end it all, and my unnecessary sense of obligation to her, eventually dulled the edge of the second Cycle. I had sought professional help that time, and when I started to feel like myself again, I remained naive to the developing pattern. In my mind I was reborn, became productive again, and patiently waited for my wife to dump me so I could search for true happiness.

I got my wish and later, in Hailey, found the happiness I was looking for. I was in love... really in love this time. Everything was perfect and a real family was finally within my reach. It was completely lost on me that I still hadn't dealt with any of my problems. They were all still there, lurking in the shadows of my past, and getting stronger.

Hailey broke my heart, in early 2005, and it was like waking a sleeping giant. This was the third time in my life I felt like a happy, healthy, loving family was forever out of my reach. Fate seemed to dangle my dreams in front of me, only to yank them away every time I got close. The state of mind I was in after my parents passed away, seemed to keep finding its way back to me, always with the gained momentum of another harsh experience.

I wanted to die more than ever.

Miraculously, Hailey stuck with me through what was undoubtedly the darkest time in my life. I hospitalized myself for the first time, and again traveled a long road filled with psychologists, doctors, and medication. Hailey's love helped me find refuge from myself again, and I started to feel better. I finally had the family that I'd always wanted, and made it complete with the addition of Chris.

This was the third, and final time, I would lie to myself, that everything was fine. I was genuinely happy, felt loved by my new family, and was finding success at work. I stopped going to therapy, weaned myself off my pills, and prepared to live happily ever after.

I was wrong again!

In the spring of 2011, I was blindsided, and knocked on my ass by a fourth Cycle of suicidal beckoning. It was different, in the sense that nothing triggered it. Nothing specific happened to bring on the madness. It's as if... it was just time.

The worst Cycle ever... and nothing caused it. This was an eye-opener to me. This fact is what caused me to really examine my own history, and finally recognize this life-threatening pattern. I noticed that I seem affected, approximately every five years. I believe this amount of time represents the limit of my capacity to repress my issues, and sustain my will to live.

A desire to kill myself was born when I buried my mom and dad. I never fixed that. I ignored it, hid from it, and buried it beneath an opposing need to survive. None of that worked, and I've learned that it will haunt me for the rest of my life if I don't face it once and for all.

It snuck up on me this time through panic attacks, flashbacks, and blossoming agoraphobia. I recognized the symptoms; they reminded me of the hell that Hailey and I went through the last time this happened. I was scared, and hid my growing problem from her, until I was convinced I was alone with it. I became terrified I was going to lose my family... again.

I made many mistakes in my confusion, and did a lot of damage to the people I love, in my sub-conscious attempts to make my life unbearable... unlivable. The guilt I felt from this appeared to be what I needed to finally justify throwing in the towel. The fourth Cycle opened its hungry mouth wide, and threatened to eat me alive with its jagged, rusty teeth.

I knew I was going to die!

So why am I still here?

The family that I've wanted to be a part of my whole life has helped to save me. Hailey just wouldn't give up on me, no matter what I threw at her. The kids didn't give up on me either, and somehow, still wanted me around during all my insanity. My son was still looking at me with unshakable love and admiration. Collectively, they convinced me that they'd stand by my side forever... if I would just let them.

I realized suicide wasn't an option anymore, but I also knew the insatiable tendency would return, if I didn't get my hands dirty and figure out exactly what was going on inside my mind. I had to do things differently, and take control of my problems. I started to write, and I started to heal.

Everything is different now, and I have an opportunity to make things right. I come from a long line of abuse, illness, and disorders. Each generation, seemingly more fucked up than the last. I can change it all. It can end with me. I want to be the one to finally stop, identify the problem, and start a new tradition of self-awareness and responsibility to my family.

I know if I take my own life now, I will be perpetuating the problem and passing it on to my son. Losing his father to suicide would fill his life with confusion, shatter his innocence, and forever taint the relationship we've shared. Chris has a chance to experience the family bonds and unconditional love that I yearned for my whole life. I have to do everything in my power to give him that.

After a lifetime of battles, I've finally won my war against suicide.

How can I be so sure?

For one thing, I have a much more realistic outlook on my situation. When I started this journey, my goal was to cure myself, expunge my issues completely, and never again suffer from mental illness. I realize that's not very realistic now. I'm a fucked up person, who's lived a fucked up life, and nurtured a plethora of self-destructive coping skills. I know it's going to take a long time to undo that damage, and re-learn how to deal with life's trials in a more healthy way.

I've accepted the fact that I'm a work in progress. I may suffer an urge to cut myself again someday, experience some panic attacks, or wrestle with insomnia. I'm all right with that knowledge, and I know I'll be able to handle these problems as they arise. I've grown wiser and stronger, while my demons have weakened and become transparent.

I have complete faith in my support system now. A healthy person would have realized this without requiring such drastic proof, but that wasn't the case with me. In the end, I have enough evidence to last a lifetime.

I will never again fool myself into believing that I'm alone, and can't talk to Hailey about anything that's troubling me. I will never again convince myself that my kids would be better off without me. If I ever start to feel like I'm slipping and falling again, I'm going to open my mouth, and my loved ones will catch me.

Finally, I've rediscovered my passion for writing. I've created a survival manual for myself, quite literally. It could very well come in handy someday if I need inspiration or a reminder of the things I've learned. When I was seventeen years old, I decided I wanted to die, and it has taken me twenty years to change my mind. Now that I've finally done it, there's no going back.

32.

SURVIVING THE FOURTH CYCLE

Everything was worse this time, which made recovering more challenging than ever. All my familiar symptoms catapulted to monstrous proportions. I've been cutting myself since my early teen years, and have always experienced an escalated need and frequency in the midst of the *Cycles.*

During the second, I became obsessed with routinely sticking my wife's sewing needles into my flesh. All the way in until the little, yellow ball on the end touched my skin. You know you have problems when an activity like this brings you peace of mind and clarity, if only for a moment.

During the third, the *amount* of cuts became the most worrisome aspect of my dysfunctional coping skill. I would fill my torso with long, dripping, lacerations by the dozens. Often, I'd do this while watching the disturbing reflection in my bathroom mirror. I remember Hailey sliding her hand up the front of my shirt one night; only to gasp... shut her eyes... and whisper

"What did you do?"

On that particular occasion, I had cut myself twenty-eight times. Twice across the throat, and I was aware of myself doing it, even if it was a *distant* awareness. That became the biggest difference in my cutting activities as I crawled my way through this fourth *Cycle*. I became less and less aware, or... mentally present, when I would go looking for a razor.

I was completely blacking out, and finding dizzying evidence of the psychotic acts later, in blood stained clothes and untreated wounds. I was afraid of myself, and thought I might slit my throat or wrists while I was psychologically unconscious. Bleed to death in the middle of the night, with no one the wiser. It was a legitimate concern. I developed Autophobia... fear of oneself.

Now I have to live with the reminders. Deep scars riddle my legs, and impossible to deny gashes will spell out cryptic messages in my flesh for the rest of my life. I do my best to hide my wounds, but I fear a day will come when I have to explain to one of my kids why my leg has words etched into it. I'm strongly considering covering the telltale scar tissue with tattoos. It wouldn't be the first time. I boiled a pot of water once and poured it on my left forearm. Two years ago, I put my son's name in bold, black lettering across the damaged terrain. It's a good cover up.

Cutting, of course, wasn't my only form of self-abusive behavior. I was also maintaining a constant state of starvation. Over a decade ago, I told a psychiatrist that I was going to kill myself by that very means... just go out into the woods somewhere, embrace the pain, and wait for nature to take its course. I don't know why I've always pictured doing it that way as opposed to a bullet, some pills, or a noose, but I have.

Again, this escalated to a completely new level, and I'm still retraining myself to eat and enjoy food on a regular and healthy basis. I literally reprogrammed my mind to hate everything about eating. The tastes and textures of food made me sick for the longest time. Even the smells and sounds were nauseating. It was a strong form of self-hypnosis, as I've stated before.

I no longer have trouble being out in public, as my agoraphobia has receded back into whatever circle of hell it comes from. It was amidst the third *Cycle* that this, most horrid affliction, introduced itself to me. Back when I re-arranged my living room furniture so my door was completely impenetrable and my phone was always off.

It was a little different this time, with a family and all the social obligations that come with having one. Repeatedly, I made the effort to go out and behave as normally as possible, sometimes with earplugs and sunglasses, usually with a hood.

When it's at its worst, everything you hear is a threat and everything you see is an abomination. I remember monsters at wedding parties, melting walls, slithering shadows, and threatening whispers. I remember getting lost in my head... counting... tapping... hiding from the world. Now, the irrational fears have left me, and I'm myself again.

I had a much different approach to my therapy this time, and it was born out of necessity. I tried the hospital, and though it did provide me with twenty-four hour supervision, it did little on a therapeutic level. They recommended I seek a good psychiatrist when released, but they warned me that the wait could be long, and this proved to be true. Almost all the shrinks we contacted had a waiting list to be seen that stretched months into the future.

I needed immediate help.

The only option for me at the time was to see one of the hospital's interns, once a week, for a twenty-dollar flat fee. Unfortunately, after a month of treatment, she told me that my case was beyond her, and she didn't think she'd be capable of helping me. Talk therapy was getting me nowhere fast. She gave me a number to call for intensive full time therapy, where you spend hours a day learning healthy coping skills.

I tried that too.

The problem was I'm agoraphobic, so whenever I was in these environments I was extremely symptomatic... but I always tried. I showed up, in my hood. I filled out all the paperwork, and had the ninety-minute consultation, where I answered questions to the floor while I stared at my feet. I answered too loudly sometimes, trying to speak over the buzzing noise that my interviewer didn't hear.

Three hours later, we got to the bottom line. It would be the perfect treatment plan for me, and it would only cost two hundred dollars a day... for three weeks! There was no way around the fee, and they too, apologized for not being able to help me.

Meanwhile, after losing my job, my insurance expired and I was at the end of my rope. My temporary disability insurance ran out, and I had to begin collecting unemployment benefits. I was in a tough position. I couldn't afford the help I needed, and what I could afford didn't help.

I weaned myself off the many prescription drugs I was taking, knowing I would no longer be able to get them refilled. It didn't matter, and I noticed no difference in my mentality whether I was on them or not. All I ever accomplished by taking those pills, was eliminating my libido.

I found salvation in my journals. Just thinking about all the things that had been affecting me my whole life wouldn't do. I wanted to feel them, learn from them, and find strength and understanding where there had always been weakness and confusion. I wanted to relive my hard life again, extracting from it what I could use to move forward and purging from it all that was holding me back.

In my dark and dingy basement, I wrote about my family.

My mother, whom I looked upon as a saint and held on a pedestal my entire life, was only human. She made mistakes, and I don't think I could have ever admitted that before writing over a hundred pages about her. I had too much information about the dark side of my parent's relationship when I was a little boy.

My mom told me things that she should have been shielding me from, and as a result filled my head with worries and fears that were beyond my ability to cope. She seasoned this stew with graphic horror movies, starting when I was as young as five. Later, she would put the weight of life changing decisions on my shoulders, on multiple occasions. The truth is… it's just as much my mom's fault, as it was my dad's, that I was pounding Maalox to treat my stress-induced ulcer in the second grade.

I'm not mad at her, but I feel like I understand her better than I ever have, decades after her death. During the seventeen years I shared with my mom, she never had a job or one single friend beyond her sister and I. For the last decade of her life, she stopped driving and always ended her day with a couple of drinks.

It has become clear to me now that she had serious issues of her own, and no one to help her. I'm sure it seemed that way anyway, and I can relate. I wonder if she had panic attacks, or bouts of agoraphobia. Did she see things that weren't there and do her best to ignore it, while we walked around town seeing movies or dining out?

I'll never know for sure, but my memory of her behavior is eerily similar to my own at times, and it's shocking to me that it has taken this long to have such a revelation. Two things are certain however, she loved me beyond measure, and she did the best she was capable of doing. I forgive her for any damage she might have caused me, and now that I'm looking at things more honestly, I feel happy that I might have helped her get through some scary times of her own, by being the one person she had in this world to talk too.

I'm proud of myself that I was able to be there for her in that capacity, and shoulder the burden at such a young age. I'm proud of my mom too because her life, from beginning to end, was filled with more turmoil than mine ever was but she never gave up. She's an inspiration, and I love her more honestly than ever.

I had equally powerful revelations when writing about my dad. I had an image of a monster burned into my mind, and it's been that way my whole life... until now. It's true he was a scary guy, who instilled fear in the people around him, and I'm sure it's true that he had real psychotic episodes. He never laid a hand on *me* though.

He never laid a violent hand on his son, but my fear of him and his potential violence steered me down a path of physical training that made a very tough person out of me. I like that about myself. I like that I'm tough and have a better than average ability to protect my loved ones and myself. I have to acknowledge that this aspect of who I am is a gift from my father, in a rather sick way... of course.

He was mean to me and definitely abusive in the verbal and emotional sense, and there's no excuse for that. I know he loved me though. I can *feel* that I'm right about that, but he sucked at it. I think he realized both those things himself eventually, and I also think we would have been able to make amends in time. Tragically, that possibility vanished when he choked to death in his friend's apartment, and I feel the loss of what might have been for the both of us. It's hard, and I thank him for making me tough enough to handle it.

I will never understand my dad to the degree I do my mom, but I understand enough to know that he was just a man, not a monster. He was a man with problems not unlike myself, and later in life, he struggled to be a better person for his estranged family. In his own way, he taught me a lot about being a man, even if half of it came from "what not to do" experiences.

I have undeniable respect for so many aspects of who he was. I forgive his ignorance in how he spoke to me in my youth, and appreciate that his harsh words never turned into harsh fists. I have spent most of my life denying it, but I love my dad very much, and I miss him!

When it comes to my sister, she might as well be dead to me too. I know how horrible that sounds, but it's real and it's honest. My thoughts and feelings toward my big sister have varied over the years, from hating her guts for what she did to me, to an over-inflated sense of understanding and forgiveness. I have avoided her and ignored her existence throughout my entire adult life. I've convinced myself that she's a powerful emotional trigger that I steer clear from as a means to self-preservation.

For the longest time I harbored an incredible and venomous hatred toward her. At times, I held her childhood atrocities toward me, almost solely responsible for my difficulties in life. I haven't been fair. I never made myself acknowledge the fact that she was still a little kid too, older than me, but a child none-the-less. There's no way she could have comprehended the gravity of her crimes, or their inevitable repercussions. I'm sure in many ways she was just as confused about what she was doing to me as I was. After all, she was a victim herself. So I do understand, and I do forgive.

I shut my eyes and think of her, paying close attention to what I feel. There's nothing there. I don't feel any hatred toward her, or any love. I don't wonder where she is or what she's doing. I don't feel loose ends or a need for closure. I feel nothing.

Why?

It's because she was never really my sister anyway, not in the important ways. She was cruel and indifferent to me as a child, she abused me, and then she was gone. I got to know her again after our parents died, and I didn't like anything about her. I thought she was a terrible mother, and an ignorant person. Being around her made me feel uncomfortable because she had such a negative and draining personality.

One of the things I learned this year is the fact that she molested me is completely irrelevant to my lack of feelings for her. I'm over that, and what's left is a person related to me by blood alone. I honestly just don't want anything to do with her. I don't like who she is, and don't want to expose my family to her delinquencies.

This is a cold, but important realization because I'm not playing the victim card anymore. I'm just a guy who has turned his back on his sister because I don't feel like dealing with the drama I feel she would bring into my life. I forgive her, and now I just want to forget her too. I know it's not admirable, but it is a fact, and I stand by it.

Examining these relationships so thoroughly has helped me find an important truth. Reality is just a matter of perception. I perceived my mom to be a saint who could do no wrong, and my dad to be a monster that did nothing right. The truth is they were just my parents. I created these images of them after they died and held fast to them over the years. It kept me from truly knowing them, learning everything I could from them, and loving them as completely as I do now.

I perceived myself to be a victim of child molestation my whole life, so that's what I was, but no more. The reality is... I was only my sister's victim during the acts themselves. During my *Cycles*, I've victimized *myself*, using the images and memories to inflict emotional pain and drive myself deeper into despair.

Wielding a warped image of my past as a weapon against myself was just another form of self-abuse like cutting and starvation. It's all been part of my recurring self-destructive tendencies, and my sister is not responsible for that.

Writing through these relationships has given me a much more honest view of my life. Being truthful with myself, however painful, has dulled the serrated edges of my past and made it a far less foreboding instrument to use against myself. At the same time, I've become wiser, and gained a lot of strength through the hours I spent hunched over my desk with a pen in my cramped hand.

My ex-wife taught me that it's all right to fail sometimes. I've always had a problem admitting it to myself when I'm incapable of something. I know at least half of me stayed with her for as long as I did for the simple and shallow reason that I didn't want to admit I failed.

In my eyes, I failed to save her and fulfill my self-appointed obligations. I failed at making her happy and ultimately at loving her. The truth is I just wasn't the right person for the job, and the fact that I felt like a job should have been a big clue. I just chose to ignore such obvious facts for an incredibly long time. The big lesson I learned is that, trying to succeed at something you don't believe in makes you a failure right from the start.

I've had success in my life too. I forced myself to admit I'm not the weak, lowly creature that I sometimes feel like. I've spent so much time in the past thinking and writing about all the negative aspects of my life, but it's not healthy to be so one-sided. To achieve a sense of balance, and possibly salvation, I had to see everything there was to see about myself, even if it didn't come naturally to me.

During the times in my life when I've felt vibrant and alive... the four to six year spans between *Cycles*, I've done some impressive things. I've rapidly moved up the ranks in every major job I've ever held, sometimes moving from entry level to management positions in less than a year. In between jobs, I've gone to great lengths to make myself more employable, and have an incredible knack for learning new things quickly and completely.

I studied the art of tattooing to capitalize on my uncanny ability to draw, and became proficient at it immediately. I still get a kick out of knowing there are a hundred or so people out there with my permanent artwork on their bodies. I also studied my ass off to become a certified personal trainer. and went to school full time to get my tractor-trailer license.

I did these things to better myself when I was out of work. I've always made a strong effort to take full advantage of my spare time by learning new things. I like this about myself. I'm industrious and seldom lay stagnate for long.

I've been able to speak at seminars, and do quite well at it. I've conducted meetings for large groups of employees. I even jumped into a WWF ring in front of a hostile New York City crowd, tore my shirt off, and grabbed a microphone... making an attempt at realizing a life-long dream. When I'm feeling the weight of social anxiety and agoraphobia, it's important for me to realize that I'm capable of these things. There are times in my life when I'm not afraid of anything and I feel that I can accomplish any goal I set.

I think about the countless times I embarked on intense training regimens to achieve certain bodybuilding goals. During these times, that would go on for months, I had an iron will and never faltered from the stringent rules I would apply to myself. No alcohol, cigarettes, weed, or caffeine. Six perfectly balanced meals a day at two to three hour intervals, supplements taken at very specific times, and water being the only liquid to cross my lips.

There are no exceptions or "cheat days" during these times, and I always make impressive gains that have people thinking... *he's on steroids*. It is a fair assumption when somebody adds thirty pounds of muscle to their frame in two months, but I've always done it naturally, with food science and will power. I have to admit... and remember, that my self-discipline is one of my most impressive and useful traits.

These are the things you lose sight of when you find yourself in the blackness. Keeping my journals and writing extensively about my entire life shed light on that darkness. I've remembered and realized things that will make it nearly impossible for me to use my memories to hurt myself again in the future. I feel like this is groundbreaking... as if I've taken away my enemies most powerful weapons. While at the same time, my own arsenal grows ever stronger.

I know the cross bearers would scoff, but I've gained strength from my religious beliefs. Writing about being a Satanist reminded me that, ultimately, I'm the only person responsible for my happiness, health, and success. I don't have a higher power to turn my fate over to. I don't have a personal savior or invisible man to pray to. Ironically, I don't even have the benefit of a devil to blame my many shortcomings on. There's only me, and with the love and support of my family, that's all I'll ever need.

I will never take my own life, and knowing that... really *knowing* that it's the truth, has even further deflated the intensity of any possible psychological attacks in the future. To hurt my family like that would be an act of pure evil. I glimpsed the devastation when I walked out on them last year, and the after-shocks from the most crushing guilt I've ever felt still reverberate through my soul. Enduring a lifetime of hell on earth would be worth not hurting them like that ever again, so I'm here to stay.

I'm not convinced suicide would even bring the peace I'd be seeking. Writing about the Ouija board incident, at the very least, gave me food for thought. It's very possible I wouldn't be putting an end to anything, but perhaps opening a door to a much more nightmarish existence. Who knows for sure?

I imagine myself as a horrible ghost, fueled for eternity by the rancid guilt and sorrow I'd feel after seeing Hailey and the kids weep and scream for me at my own funeral. I shudder and have to shake these images off. It's just my imagination, but knowing there could be an element of truth to it, is enough to scare the shit out of me.

I had one of those "AH-HAA!" moments when I wrote about a lost night by the railroad tracks. This was a truly repressed memory, gone from my thoughts for more than ten years. When I discovered it in the catacombs of my mind, it was proof that I was repeating the same self-destructive pattern since the time of my parents' death. I recognized the out-of-control feeling I had that night, and realized it was a recurring theme throughout my *Cycles*.

Picture driving a big city bus and you're in the driver's seat... in control. You can see clearly through the windshield, and all the commotion made by your passengers is behind you, and does not disturb your focus. This is a metaphor for my *healthy* mind functioning in the world around me.

At the peak of the *Cycles*, my perception changes drastically.

Now I'm driving the same bus... but, from the *back seat!* I can barely see the windshield anymore, never mind the world beyond it. At the same time, I notice that all my rowdy passengers are the ghosts of my past. They obstruct my view and demand my full attention. If you picture driving the bus like this, it really captures the way it feels for me to navigate through my life when I'm at my worst.

It's time like this when I've been capable of extremely uncharacteristic behavior. It's times like this when I go into the woods with a man whom I hope might take my life, or propose to a woman that I know I'm not in love with! I might impregnate someone who I don't trust, or kiss a desperate old woman at work, who chooses to ignore the vacant, hollow look in my eyes.

Now that I've woken up to this fact, and recognized a dangerous pattern that keeps disrupting my life, I feel like I have the power to eradicate the bulk of the madness. It has taken me half my life to figure this much out, and it has been a taxing journey.

I've spent most of the year crying and reliving painful memories. I forced myself to be honest about everything I thought or felt, and write it down. Learn from it. Use it to help me protect myself... from myself. In the past, my journal entries were just detailed complaints about all the shitty things that had happened to me. I used them to vent, not to discover. I've done myself a great service this time.

I have survived the fourth *Cycle*, but it's much more than that. I survived the first three too, only to have the pendulum swing back with greater intensity each time. That's over though, and I know I've changed my future for the better.

I've taken control of my life and more importantly perhaps, how I perceive it. When it would rain before, I would *make* it pour. The snowball effect would take place and I'd bury myself in a distorted avalanche of every negative thing that has ever happened to me. Now that I can see this clearly, I can limit its devastation in the future.

I always became extremely introverted, and stubbornly tried to deal with things by myself. I didn't want to burden the people that care about me with my suffering. I can see how naive that logic was and how foolish I've been. I convinced myself I was alone in my struggle, but it was just another self-destructive lie. I have a family who loves me, and I never have to feel alone again.

I expect to go through another *Cycle* again someday... maybe a little further down the road than usual, but I also know I'll be better equipped to deal with it than ever before. It will be much weaker and less interruptive; now that I've exposed the man behind the curtain... there is no great and powerful Oz!

I will handle things differently from now on. Perhaps I'll take a little vacation, change jobs, or find a new hobby. I'll write, of course, from that honest place in my heart that I've finally found, and I'll learn even more about myself. I *won't* be all better, as I've lied to myself in the past, but I *will* be better. Shedding my suicidal tendencies, once and for all, has liberated me and rendered me incapable of ending my own existence. Everything else is manageable now. Surviving the fourth *Cycle* opened my eyes to that, and I'm ready to live my life.

CPSIA information can be obtained at www.ICGtesting.com
Printed in the USA
LVOW06s2009131113

361176LV00032B/2047/P